PIER GIORGIO FRASSATI
LETTERS TO HIS FRIENDS AND FAMILY

Portrait of Pier Giorgio Frassati by Alberto Falchetti

PIER GIORGIO FRASSATI

Letters to His Friends and Family

Preface by Bishop J. Peter Sartain

Translated by Fr. Timothy E. Deeter

Edited by Fr. Timothy E. Deeter and Christine M. Wohar

First published in Italy in 1950 by Studium, Roma under the title *Pier Giorgio Frassati: Lettere*. The Letters found here were selected from the original volume edited by Pier Giorgio's sister Luciana Frassati.

All photographs in this book are from the archives of Blessed Pier Giorgio Frassati's family, and the rights belong to the family.

Library of Congress Cataloging-in-Publication Data

Frassati, Pier Giorgio, 1901-1925.
 [Lettere, 1905-1925. English]
 Letters to his friends and family / Pier Giorgio Frassati; translated by Timothy E. Deeter; edited by Timothy E. Deeter and Christine M. Wohar.
   p. cm.
 Includes bibliographical references and index.
 ISBN-13: 978-0-8189-1305-1
 ISBN-10: 0-8189-1305-3
 1. Frassati, Pier Giorgio, 1901-1925—Correspondence. 2. Catholics—Italy—Correspondence. I. Deeter, Timothy E. II. Wohar, Christine M. III. Title.
 BX4705.F735A4 2009
 282.092—dc22
                                  2009013680

Visit our web site at www.albahouse.org (for orders www.stpauls.us) or call 1-800-343-2522 (ALBA) and request current catalog.

Produced and designed in the United States of America by the Fathers and Brothers of the Society of St. Paul, 2187 Victory Boulevard, Staten Island, New York 10314-6603 as part of their communications apostolate.

ISBN 10: 0-8189-1305-3
ISBN-13: 978-0-8189-1305-1

© Copyright 2009 by Wanda Gawronska

Printing Information:

Current Printing - first digit   1   2   3   4   5   6   7   8   9   10

Year of Current Printing - first year shown

2009   2010   2011   2012   2013   2014   2015   2016   2017   2018

"I hope with the Grace of God to continue along the path of Catholic Ideals and to be able one day, in whatever state God wills, to defend and propagate these rare and true things."

Pier Giorgio, December 16, 1924

G. BATTISTA MONTINI
CITTÀ DEL VATICANO

25. 7. 1950

Gent.ma Signora,

Avrò molto caro – per la dedica gentile, per il contenuto, per la cura pia e saggia con cui queste pagine sono state raccolte – il bel volume ch'Ella mi manda con le Lettere di Pier Giorgio. Torna così a noi la Sua voce, la Sua presenza; si riaccende il desiderio dell'imitazione, dell'emulazione; si conforta la certezza che una giovinezza forte e limpida è possibile e vicina; si sente l'interiore anelito verso una bontà superiore crescere nel cuore; e si pensa

To: Luciana Frassati Gawronska

I will treasure the fine volume of Letters of Pier Giorgio that you sent me, both for its kind dedication and for the devoted and wise care with which these pages have been compiled.

And so his voice and his presence return to us. The desire to imitate and follow him is rekindled, and the certainty that a strong and sincere young adulthood is possible and attainable comforts us. One feels an interior longing for a higher good growing in the heart, and one thinks that all this is good and is also because of these pages that we are brought into Pier Giorgio's confidence and, in a way, led into conversation with him.

May God bless you for this good work; and together with your own children, may many other people draw from this belated yet still fresh testimony new advice and encouragement for living a noble Christian life.

With my kindest regards, G.B. Montini

NB: Giovanni Battista Montini became Pope Paul VI

CONTENTS

Letter from Pope Paul VI to Luciana Frassati Gawronska / vi

Editor's Note / xi

Preface by Bishop J. Peter Sartain / xiii

Pier Giorgio's World:
Church and State in Early 20th Century Italy / xxiii

1906 – 1916 / 1

1917 / 16

1918 / 20

1919 / 24

1920 / 27

1921 / 32

1922 / 75

1923 / 110

1924 / 148

1925 / 193

Notes for a Speech about Charity / 239

Appendix: Homily on Blessed Pier Giorgio Frassati, World Youth Day 2008 / 243

Index of Names and Abbreviations / 253

EDITOR'S NOTE

Since they were first published in Italian in 1950, *The Letters of Pier Giorgio Frassati* have long been awaited by English-speaking readers. At last, we have the opportunity to get to know more personally the Man of the Beatitudes, the concerns of his heart, the passions of his soul. Until now, we have only heard what others had to say about him; now we can hear from him directly.

The reader should note that not all of his letters are reproduced here. Following Pier Giorgio's death, many of his letters could not be retrieved. Of those originally published in the Italian text, approximately 123 letters written between 1921 and 1925 have been omitted from this edition because of duplication of content.

Some revisions to punctuation and grammar have been made but only where confusion would have otherwise resulted on the part of the reader. Most of the capitalization, or lack of it, is as it was in the original format. The Italian version edited by Pier Giorgio's sister Luciana Frassati includes many footnotes of historical significance to Italy in the early 1900s. Wherever possible, Luciana Frassati's original footnotes were utilized; others have been revised to be more pertinent to the reader in the U.S. Additional footnote material was contributed by Fr. Deeter, Wanda Gawronska and myself. Also, I am grateful to Claudia Giliberti Ziu who helped complete the translation.

May the Man of the Beatitudes inspire you to follow him on the path of holiness. Verso l'alto!

Christine M. Wohar
Executive Director, FrassatiUSA

PREFACE

I met Pier Giorgio Frassati quite by accident. As a seminarian in Rome in the mid-1970's, I frequently passed the 12th century Church of San Lorenzo in Piscibus on the Via Pfeiffer, but much to my chagrin it was always locked. One afternoon I happened by and noticed a steady stream of young adults coming and going through a rear door. Taking my cue from them, I entered. Though the ancient interior of the church caught my attention, I was immediately drawn to an exhibit on the life of a young Italian who had died in 1925 at about my age. There were photographs and other memorabilia of an avid outdoorsman and athlete, Catholic youth activist, lover of the poor, and man of prayer. The young people streaming in and out of San Lorenzo that day had come to learn about an extraordinary life, and like them I was drawn to learn more. I went straight to the closest bookstore and bought everything I could find about the young man featured in the exhibit.

Pier Giorgio Frassati was born in the northern Italian city of Turin on April 6, 1901, son of a prominent journalist, Alfredo Frassati, and his wife, Adelaide Ametis, a painter. Alfredo was the founder of *La Stampa*, a daily newspaper still published in Turin. He served as senator in the Italian parliament and later as Italian ambassador to Germany. Their second child, Luciana, was a year younger than Pier Giorgio, and the two were always extremely close. It was particularly difficult for Pier Giorgio when Luciana, newly married, moved to the Netherlands with her husband in early 1925. She died in 2007 at the age of 105.

The Frassati children were reared in a cultured, upper-class home, and Pier Giorgio developed a lifelong appreciation for literature and the arts. Recognized in his teenage years as a leader of uncommon charisma, faith, humor and drive, he loved to ski and hike the mountains. Such outings were opportunities for both solitude and recreation with his circle of cherished friends. Friendship was always important to Pier Giorgio. Just two months before his death, he wrote to his friend Marco Beltramo:

> *In this earthly life after the affection for parents and sisters, one of the most beautiful affections is that of friendship; and every day I ought to thank God because he has given me men and lady friends of such goodness who form for me a precious guide for my whole life.*

In the last year of his life, Pier Giorgio formed the Tipi Loschi Society ("Shady Characters Society") with seven of his closest friends. The goal was to keep their friendship alive, even when their circumstances would inevitably change as they moved through life. As the members of the society socialized, skied and climbed mountains together, their relationships were marked by good humor, puns and practical jokes. For Pier Giorgio, the ultimate purpose of the Society was to be united in prayer, which he understood as the highest form of solidarity.

Although he was devoted to his studies, Pier Giorgio's grades were often average and below, and his interests did not seem to lie in making a fortune or a name for himself as had his father before him. Eventually he entered the Royal Polytechnic University at Turin to study mining. His goal, he told his friends, was to "serve Christ better among the miners," a group known to suffer oppressive work and living conditions.

To understand Pier Giorgio Frassati is to understand Christ at work in him. One must consider his spontaneous and profound love for God, his total immersion in the Catholic faith, his unfailing dedication to prayer, his heartfelt devotion to family and friends, and his untiring commitment to active Christian love. In addition to his involvement in studies, Catholic youth groups, politics and social issues, Frassati gave his time to the Lord Jesus and to the poor. The connection between the two was obvious to him, and he once said, "Jesus visits me each morning in Holy Communion, and I repay him in my very small way by visiting him in the poor." To a friend who had asked how he could stomach the filthy environments he often visited he replied, "Remember always that it is to Jesus that you go: I see a special light that we do not have around the sick, the poor, the unfortunate." He would often have to run home for dinner, having given his tram fare to the poor he had visited in the afternoon. It was because of such seeming irresponsibility that some thought he frittered time away, considering him a disappointment to his parents.

The avid skier and mountain climber once told a friend that he had left his heart on a mountaintop and looked forward to retrieving it on a climb to the summit of Mont Blanc. Since prayer and the Eucharist were the integrating factors of the many spheres of activity in his busy life, it was his custom to make a visit to the Blessed Sacrament after each climb.

Frassati climbed his last mountain on June 7, 1925, less than a month before his death on July 4. He died only six days after the onset of acute polio, which doctors later surmised he had contracted from one of the poor he had been visiting. A photograph taken of him the day of his final climb bears his own handwritten caption, "Verso l'alto" – "Toward the heights," a phrase that would become a posthumous emblem of his brief life. In the short span of twenty-four years, Pier Giorgio Frassati had indeed climbed the summit of Christian discipleship – through prayer, the Eucharist, and active love for family, friends, and the poor.

Pier Giorgio's death came only three days after the death of his beloved grandmother. Preoccupied with her final days, his parents had failed to realize the severity of the medical condition of their typically robust son. At his funeral, his doubly grief-stricken family expected to see their colleagues and friends. They were astounded, however, to find the streets of Turin lined with thousands of the poor, who knew Pier Giorgio as the young man who had always been there to help them. It was only after his death that the Frassati family learned the full extent of his impact. In fact, it was the poor of Turin who asked their archbishop to open Frassati's cause for canonization.

In his homily during Frassati's beatification liturgy on May 20, 1990, Pope John Paul II said,

> *Faith and charity, the true driving forces of his existence, made him active and diligent in the milieu in which he*

lived, in his family and school, in the university and society; they transformed him into a joyful, enthusiastic apostle of Christ, a passionate follower of his message and charity...

Entirely immersed in the mystery of God and totally dedicated to the constant service of his neighbor; thus we can sum up his earthly life!

He fulfilled his vocation as a lay Christian in many associative and political involvements in a society in ferment, a society which was indifferent and sometimes even hostile to the Church. In this spirit, Pier Giorgio succeeded in giving new impulse to various Catholic movements, which he enthusiastically joined...

I am struck by the ironic relationship between Frassati's "Verso l'alto" and Pope John Paul II's favorite reference to the Latin translation of Luke 5:4, "Duc in altum." Jesus commands Peter the fisherman to "put out into deep water." Peter had caught nothing all night but at Jesus' command casts his net one more time and pulls in a great catch of fish.

"Verso l'alto" – "Duc in altum." "Toward the heights" – "Put out into the deep." Those two phrases encompass the scope of our calling as Christians. We are to reach for the heights and plumb the depths of faith. That was the life of Pier Giorgio Frassati.

Every mountain climber needs a guide, and Pier Giorgio found his in St. Paul. In *La Fede*, a collection of personal testimonies about his faith from those who knew him well, his sister Luciana wrote, "Pier Giorgio always carried St. Paul with him in a pocket-sized book; it was St. Paul whom Pier Giorgio quoted non-stop, whom he recited in the street, or read in his friends' rooms, whom he recommended with enthusiasm to everyone as the surest rule for Christian living."

St. Paul had contemplated with wonder his ground-breaking vocation to preach "the inscrutable riches of Christ" to the Gentiles. He longed to delve more deeply into Christ. From prison, he wrote to the Ephesians:

I bow my knees before the Father... I pray that, according to the riches of his glory, he may grant that you may be strengthened in your inner being with power through his

Spirit, and that Christ may dwell in your hearts through faith, as you are being rooted and grounded in love. I pray that you may have the power to comprehend what is the breadth and length and height and depth, and to know the love of Christ that surpasses knowledge, so that you may be filled with all the fullness of God. (Ephesians 3:14-19)

God's plan of salvation affects the universe in all its dimensions – "toward the heights" and "into the deep." St. Paul hungered for all to be "filled with all the fullness of God." He knew that no Christian would reach that fullness if he or she stood still. The Christian life is about growth in Christ. But first we must *want* to grow.

One of my Roman seminary professors once warned us that the temptation to mediocrity is great. It is tempting to settle into comfortable and ordered, but mediocre and unfruitful, lives of faith. Baptism has opened for us the inexhaustible riches of Christ, and we will spend our lives climbing his heights and plumbing his depths. If we do not seek to grow in faith, we risk stagnation – or worse, we risk letting go of Christ altogether. If we are not striving forward – hiking, climbing upward – we are being lulled backward. Mediocrity is not the path to spiritual fulfillment. As Pier Giorgio wrote to friend Isidoro Bonini,

> *…every day I understand better what a Grace it is to be Catholics. Poor unlucky those who don't have a Faith: to live without a Faith, without a patrimony to defend, without a steady struggle for the Truth, is not living but is just getting along. We must never just get along but live, because even through every disappointment we should remember that we are the only ones who possess the Truth, we have a Faith to sustain, a Hope to attain: our Homeland.*

It was about the time my professor offered his wise counsel that I came to know Pier Giorgio. Extraordinarily bold and passionate, deeply prayerful and humble, he was anything but mediocre. He immersed himself in the Lord Jesus in a lifelong act of joy-filled surrender and self-sacrifice. He climbed to the top in every sense because he treasured above everything the presence of the Lord deep within. His words and his life echoed St. Paul's personal reflection to the Philippians:

> *Yet whatever gains I had, these I have come to regard as loss because of Christ. More than that, I regard everything as loss because of the surpassing value of knowing Christ Jesus my Lord. For his sake I have suffered the loss of all things, and I regard them as rubbish, in order that I may gain Christ and be found in him, not having a righteousness of my own that comes from the law, but one that comes through faith in Christ, the righteousness from God based on faith. I want to know Christ and the power of his resurrection and the sharing of his sufferings by becoming like him in his death, if somehow I may attain the resurrection from the dead.*
>
> *Not that I have already obtained this or have already reached the goal; but I press on to make it my own, because Christ Jesus has made me his own. Beloved, I do not consider that I have made it my own; but this one thing I do: forgetting what lies behind, and straining forward to what lies ahead, I press on towards the goal for the prize of the heavenly call of God in Christ Jesus. (Philippians 3:7-14)*

The letters in this beautiful collection are an intimate part of Pier Giorgio Frassati's legacy. Not only do they offer an unselfconscious glimpse into his daily life; they provide, more importantly, a privileged insight into his very heart and soul. Some of these letters could have been written by any of us, from the childlike scrawls of the kind our own parents preserved in scrapbooks, to the intense reflections of a maturing young adult. There are letters of affection and postcards from vacation, letters filled with the mischief of a young man who laughed often and with infectious joy. There are letters of heart-felt and hard-fought conviction, letters of intense passion for the well-being of his beloved Italy. And there are letters of simple yet uncompromising love for God and his poor, letters of a faith that was at once profoundly childlike and profoundly mature.

In a 1923 letter to his friend Antonio Severi, Pier Giorgio commented on the tragic death of a lawyer who had died climbing a glacier. His words reveal both the influence of his high ideals – and his preoccupation with the stack of books awaiting his attention:

> *This is what will happen to me in a few years' time and so the moral is: when one goes to the mountains one should*

sort out one's conscience first, because one never knows if one will return. But despite all this I'm not afraid and on the contrary I want to climb the mountains more than ever, to conquer the most daring peaks; to feel that pure joy, which one can only have in the mountains.

My studying is going along fairly well, Hydraulics doesn't seem too hard, but on the other hand Chemical Metallurgy is very boring and difficult.

Writing to Marco Beltramo at about the same time, he said:

Do you still intend to climb to the top of the Rognosa by the crest this spring, if God gives us life? I'm always ready because every day I fall in love with the mountains more and more and, if my studies would allow me to do it, I would spend entire days on the mountains contemplating in that pure air the Greatness of the Creator.

Pier Giorgio's contemplation of the "pure air" of God bore fruit in down-to-earth wisdom. In an open letter "To the Catholic Men and Women Students of Bonn" published in a German newspaper in 1923, he wrote:

Modern society is drowning in the sorrows of human passions and it is distancing itself from every ideal of love and peace. Catholics, we and you, must bring the breath of goodness that can only spring from faith in Christ.

Pier Giorgio's love for the Eucharist was zealous and unfailing, and he urged his fellow youth "to approach the Eucharistic Table as often as possible." In a 1923 speech to the members of "Catholic Youth" of Pollone, he explained that every apostolate finds its source and strength in the "Bread of Angels." To be "consumed by this Eucharistic Fire" fills us with strength, gratitude and peace. "We must sacrifice everything for everything: our ambitions, indeed our entire selves, for the cause of faith."

☦

The 12th century church that was the scene of my first encounter with Pier Giorgio now forms part of the San Lorenzo International Youth Center inaugurated by Pope John Paul II on March 13, 1983. On that occasion, the Holy Father said

> *Together with the memory of the ancient cross of San Damiano and the example of St. Francis, I want to recall to you as an incentive for striving toward high ideas also the figure of a young man who lived in our era, Pier Giorgio Frassati. He was a "modern" youth open to the problems of culture, sports, to social questions, to the true values of life, and at the same time a profoundly believing man, nourished by the Gospel message, deeply interested in serving his brothers and sisters and consumed in an ardour of charity that drew him close to the poor and the sick. He lived the Gospel Beatitudes.*

Every day youth from around the world gather at the San Lorenzo International Youth Center, a place of welcome, prayer, formation and friendship. It is also the site where the World Youth Day Pilgrim Cross is kept when not traveling the world. The church is open daily for prayer, and when I visit Rome I never fail to make a visit – and I never fail to think of my first visit. Through World Youth Day celebrations, another inspiration of Pope John Paul II, Pier Giorgio is now known to millions, who recognize him as a patron of youth.

"Verso l'alto!" "Duc in altum!" We climb to the Summit and plunge into the deep Fullness who made us. The fulfillment that awaits us is greater than we can possibly imagine, because the mystery of God is inexhaustible. Pier Giorgio Frassati surrendered his life so completely to God and those he loved – a true sacrifice of charity – that he remains a sure guide to all who seek to climb the heights and plumb the depths of God.

Writing to Marco Beltramo about the importance of friendship, he mentioned the names of several mutual friends who were inspirations to him. In describing them, he was unwittingly describing himself:

Surely Divine Providence in His Marvelous Plans sometimes uses us miserable little twigs to do Good and we sometimes not only don't want to know God but instead dare to deny His existence; but we who, by the Grace of God, have the Faith, when we find ourselves in the presence of such beautiful souls, surely nourished by Faith, we cannot but discover in them an obvious sign of the Existence of God, because one cannot have such a Goodness without the Grace of God.

Blessed Pier Giorgio, pray for us! May we be a breath of goodness springing from faith in Christ, like you.

    Most Rev. J. Peter Sartain
    Bishop of Joliet, Illinois (USA)
    April 6, 2009
    108th anniversary of Blessed Pier Giorgio's birth

PIER GIORGIO'S WORLD:
CHURCH AND STATE IN EARLY 20TH CENTURY ITALY

The period in Italy following the First World War was marked by serious social upheavals, the birth of Communism and the rise of Fascism, along with a strained relationship between church and state resulting from the reunification of Italy in 1870 at the cost of the Pontifical States. This political landscape served as the background to Pier Giorgio's social and political activity and was often referenced in his letters to his friends and family. The following brief historical survey will assist in placing his letters in the proper context.

The rise and fall of the Pontifical States

The collapse of the Western Roman Empire in the 5th century created a political vacuum in Italy. So, the bishops of Rome took on the role of political governors and the Pontifical States came into existence comprising a large central portion of the Italian peninsula. Soon this became one of the most influential and prestigious political entities in Europe.

This situation lasted until the 19th century when the spirit of nationalism swept like a tidal wave over Europe. Italians wanted to unite their peninsula that for centuries had been composed of rival city-states. In 1861, the northern part of Italy, ruled by the House of Savoy with its capital in Turin, successfully united with the southern kingdom.

Pope Pius IX, however, refused to cede the territory of the Pontifical States, thus standing in the way of the formation of a united Kingdom of Italy that would have Rome as its capital. The nationalists, led by Giuseppe Garibaldi, with the royal army of King Victor Emmanuel II of Savoy, finally entered Rome on September 20, 1870, and claimed the territory by force – putting an end to the Pontifical States, and with it more than 1000 years of papal temporal power.

The stand-off between Church and State

Pius IX sequestered himself in the Vatican and the king took residence at the pope's Quirinale Palace. Pius IX maintained that the new government was illegitimate and excommunicated the king. In 1874, he promulgated a decree *"Non expedit"* forbidding Italian Catholics to vote in parliamentary elections, take part in Italian politics or hold any government positions. His successor, Leo XIII, author of the famous encyclical *Rerum Novarum,* supported this position.

It seemed Italians had to make a choice: either be good Catholics or good Italians. Thus, they became very private about their religious practice. Those who were loyal to "the Pope-King" (as the pope was sometimes called) were ignored, ridiculed, or even assaulted during events like processions or other public manifestations of the Faith. Those who supported the government and wanted to see Italy take its place among the nations of Europe felt that they had to keep their distance from the Church. Many practically abandoned churchgoing, while maintaining – especially on their deathbeds– their belief in God.

Moreover, the country was strongly divided over World War I with tension brewing between those who supported involvement and those who wanted Italy to remain neutral. Alfredo Frassati, Pier Giorgio's father, through his influential "La Stampa," the second most important newspaper in Italy, strongly opposed Italy's involvement (a position that later proved to be correct) while the rival paper "Corriere della Sera" supported Italy's entering the war (which happened in 1915).

Few events in Italian history had such a traumatic effect as did the First World War. In its aftermath, the already-divided nation endured a period of violent conflicts on both the social and political levels. Into those turbulent times, came Luigi Sturzo, a Sicilian priest, who formed the *Partito Popolare Italiano – PPI* (Italian People's Party) in January 1919, immediately following the lifting of the *Non expedit* by Pope Benedict XV. The PPI was based on Catholic social teaching, namely *Rerum Novarum*, but operated independent of the Church hierarchy. Strongly advocating peace among nations, the PPI also rode on the wave of enthusiasm that swept Turin and all of Italy when U.S. President Woodrow Wilson toured the country in January 1919 to promote the League of Nations. In its first foray into national elections in September of that same year, the PPI sent 100 members to Parliament, signalling the complete re-entry of Catholics into Italy's political life. Their enthusiasm was riding high.

But a social and economic crisis was hitting the country. Factories were occupied by striking workers; the struggle for their rights resonated throughout northern Italy. Turin became "the Red City," the focus of Italy's own Bolshevik movement inspired by the Russian Revolution, with violent confrontations between workers and their employers, between Red (Communist) and White (Catholic) trade unions. Violence was on the increase, dividing city and country dwellers, industrialists and farmers, upper and lower classes, and the Church was a frequent target of the Bolsheviks.

Students at the University of Turin became inflamed with the revolutionary spirit that was spreading throughout Italy. Turin was also the city of lay activism. Soon, religious movements like Catholic Action, the St. Vincent de Paul Society, and FUCI (Federation of Italian Catholic University Students) became very popular, inviting a new generation of the laity to find ways in which they could put their faith into action and become a leaven in secular society.

In the midst of this turmoil, violence and rioting, the government appeared weak. The upper classes and the industrialists began to look with interest upon the formation of the Fascist movement led by Benito Mussolini (derived from the Socialist Party which recently split giving birth to an Italian Communist Party). The Fascists opted to give the Bolsheviks a taste of their own medicine, using violent tactics to bring order back to Italy. But this violence was also used against those Catholics who defended their trade unions, those who condemned that movement. However, many Italians welcomed

Fascism because order was restored, strikes ceased, and Bolshevik violence was put down.

As the Fascists grew in strength, Mussolini rose to become prime minister in 1922 and, eventually, dictator of Italy. Initially, some PPI members of Parliament supported Mussolini and even became part of his government (something that upset Pier Giorgio very much because he recognized immediately that Fascist policies were undermining Catholic principles). The honeymoon was short-lived, however, and the PPI became the object of intimidation and violent attacks which climaxed with the assassination of a priest, Fr. Giovanni Minzoni, who was clubbed to death in 1924.

Meanwhile, Germany was not faring much better. The Treaty of Versailles had obliged the German Weimar Republic to pay war reparations after its defeat in World War I, but the country was unable to meet its obligations. Therefore, French and Belgian troops took occupation of the Ruhr Valley, Germany's rich mining zone, in 1923. (It is noteworthy that while Italy was experiencing the rise of Mussolini in 1922, Alfredo Frassati, who at the time was the Italian Ambassador in Berlin, almost prophetically advised his government that the humiliation of Germany following World War I was setting the stage for the rise of National Socialism and World War II.)

In 1926, the Fascist government declared the PPI to be illegal and the march toward dictatorship was accomplished. Pier Giorgio's death in July of 1925 spared him from witnessing this turn of events, from witnessing his father's great grief of being compelled by Mussolini in 1926 to give away his antifascist newspaper "La Stampa." Oddly enough, it was Mussolini who, in 1929, finally ended the long dispute (known as the "Roman Question") between Italy and the Pope by signing the Lateran Treaty with Pius XI.

Pier Giorgio's response to his times

Pier Giorgio was at the forefront of political and religious events. If physical violence erupted, he tried to bring the voice of reason to the situation. When this failed, he was never afraid to break up groups that interfered with processions or to protect a priest from being pushed around by royal guards during a demonstration.

He quietly entered a factory yard to speak to workers seething with Bolshevik anger, spoke up forcefully during arguments with fascists in the classroom or in group meetings, and chased down anti-cleric types who were vandalizing posters for Catholic events.

He fervently encouraged his generation to be loyal to the Pope, but he also led them in passionate loyalty to the nation, fighting for justice at a time of political upheaval.

His way of understanding religious commitment and the role of the laity anticipated Vatican Council II by forty years. In discussing his heroic virtues in 1987, the Congregation for the Causes of Saints stated, "We are not accustomed to that kind of sanctity.... Pier Giorgio Frassati opens new perspectives for understanding the concept of sanctity as it is lived by the laity in a lay environment, dealing with issues that teachers of spirituality would do well to reflect upon."

Pier Giorgio's death in 1925 "shook all of Catholic Italy and left a decisive mark on the history of the religious revival that took place between the two world wars" (1919-1939). Many PPI members and Catholic Action youth who were infused and forever changed by Pier Giorgio's example went on to become high-ranking members of the Christian Democratic Party and the government of Italy in the years following World War II. Pier Giorgio's influence was felt so far and wide that his beatification in May 1990 was officially attended by the President of Italy and the entire Italian Government and was considered "the most eagerly awaited religious event in Italy."

"To live without a Faith, without a patrimony to defend, without a steady struggle for the Truth, is not living but existing." – Pier Giorgio (from a letter to I. Bonini, February 27, 1925)

Professor Francesco Malgeri

Pier Giorgio with his beloved grandmother Linda Ametis in 1907. They died within three days of each other in July 1925.

1906 – 1916

To His Father

1906[1]

Dear wonderful daddy,

I love you so much so that you will be happy I will not hit Luciana any more. Happy feastday[2] I will pray to Baby Jesus for you. He kisses you your

Dodo[3]

[1] This date is not exactly certain.
[2] Throughout his life, Pier Giorgio remembered the feastdays of the members of his family.
[3] Pier Giorgio gave himself the nickname Dodo as a child.

NOTE: *On the same page is added:* My wonderful daddy, best wishes, I promise you that I will not tell any more lies. A nice kiss from Luciana.

August 14, 1907

Dear Daddy,

On this your birthday I am writing to send you lots of good wishes for your good health. I will pray to Jesus for you and I promise to be good and to study to make up to you for all your work and the sacrifices you are making for me. Happy birthday and lots of good wishes from your

Pier Giorgio

To His Mother

Pollone, November 7, 1907

Dearest mama,

I love you very much I will be good with Luciana. Are you having a good time in Venice? We are sending you two little kisses. Greet aunt[1] for us.

Yesterday I went to Burcina[2] and with the help of the sisters I did this little work which I am sending to you.

I wrote a postcard to daddy today we will do the dictation. We are all fine the cat and Jor[3] too; I am sending you the numbers.

Greetings from everyone.

Pier Giorgio

[1] Aunt Elena Ametis, the sister of Pier Giorgio's mother Adelaide, is frequently mentioned in Pier Giorgio's letters. She lived with the family.
[2] Burcina is a park in Pollone.
[3] Jor was the family dog.

December 19, 1907

Dear Mama,

I love you and I am very pleased to write you this letter to send you my good wishes for your feastday. Here is a present for you of a basket made by Luciana and me. Yours

Pier Giorgio

To His Parents

1908

Dear parents,

The other day we went to Grandmother Frassati's and she gave us some pretty roses. The weather is nice in Pollone and how is it in Turin? How is Delfina? How is Frau Dagnele? How is mama? and papa?

The red cat is going into grandmother's bedroom to see if the gray cat is there. All these days that it's been nice outside we have gone to the garden.

Come to Pollone soon. There are some beautiful roses, and also some poppies, and some geraniums, and some vanilla. Grandfather is fine and grandmother too and aunt too. In the evenings I go to the garden with grandmother and then at nine I go to bed. Today I woke up at eight-thirty, and I ate which was at nine-thirty Luciana woke up at eight. Many little kisses to mama and to papa from your dear

Pier Giorgio

To His Father

Alassio, August 1908

Dear papa,

We are swimming a lot and we are also playing (with) Emilio, Monday we will have a boat, Emilio and I are going fishing. Yesterday Mrs. Garbasso left. The weather is nice here, the sea is a magnificent blue; the sand burns but there is a nice wind.

There are some mosquitos in my bed. Say hello to Anna Maria and Camillo and ask them what's new. Greetings to Papa Falchetti and tell Bertino[1] that we are already totally black. Come for sure on the 10th. Many kisses from your

Pier Giorgio

[1] Papa Falchetti was an accomplished painter. Bertino was the nickname for his son, Alberto, also a painter. Alberto was a great friend of the family. After Pier Giorgio's death, he painted most of the portraits of Pier Giorgio which have often been reproduced in books or on prayer cards.

To His Parents

1908

Dear daddy and dear mama,

Today I was bad I made my mama and my daddy cry, who love me so much. I did two very bad things today, so I was told by the teacher, and her stern and sad face told me that she is not happy with me.

I hurt everyone and I am upset, I did wrong, but I beg you to forgive me. I really repent and I promise you that I will become good to make you forget how much you have suffered today.

Forgive me.

Pier Giorgio

To His Grandmother Linda Ametis

Turin, December 1908

Dear grandmother,

How are you? I am fine; I am going to gymnastics: and also to dance lessons.[1] Is the weather nice in Pollone? Come at Christmas and spend nice Christmas holidays with us. Yesterday the weather was bad in Turin and today it is fine. The cat is sick.²

Many little kisses to you and grandfather; and from mama and papa and aunt and from your dear

Pier Giorgio

¹ Pier Giorgio was enrolled in a school of dance for a short time but tired of it right away.
² A blond Angora cat, Scimbo, who was very intelligent and perhaps the children's closest friend at that time. Pier Giorgio writes about him in many letters.

At home, May 15, 1909

Dear Grandmother,

The weather is nice in Turin. How are the three cats and Ior?¹ Today is the opening of the Flower show in Turin. How are you?

One day we and the Marchisio girls went to Cumiana. Papa rode the horse, we ate and mama painted. One day Mrs. Marchisio invited us to dine in the evening.

Many greetings from everyone and a kiss from your loving

Pier Giorgio Frassati

¹ Ior is the name of the family dog which Pier Giorgio also spelled Jor.

To His Mother

At home, October 22, 1909

Dear Mommy,

I am very sorry that you are away from Pollone. Yesterday I picked up the fruit that had fallen on the ground. Today we are taking exams with the teacher. The other day I got an eight-plus for my homework and a ten for my lessons.

Every day I go to watch the cows drink. Yesterday I helped to round them up.

Lots of little kisses and a greeting from your most loving

Pier Giorgio

October 26, 1909

Dear Mama,

    The other day I helped carry the flowerpots. Yesterday there was a terrible wind. Today we are taking the Language exam tomorrow Arithmetic.

    Today I telephoned papa who said that if he doesn't phone it is a sign that he is coming on the last train.

    Many greetings and many kisses from your Little Boy

Pier Giorgio

Pier Giorgio and his sister Luciana in Pollone with one of the family dogs.

At home, December 19, 1909

Dear mama,

My heart is very heavy to see you so sick. Get well dear and good mama. Tomorrow is your feastday, your feastday will not be happy as it was last year because you are suffering in bed. My heart will be happy when you get well but until then it is saddened. Mommy I wish you a speedy recovery.

I will pray to God so that he will make you better and God will hear my prayers.

Receive very loving best wishes and kisses from your most loving

Pier Giorgio

February 17, 1910

Dear mama,

I am very sorry that you are sick in bed for your birthday. I always pray to God to make you well. I promise you that I will be a very good boy and very obedient and very studious. I will keep this promise. I have a heavy heart seeing you suffering in bed.

Get well soon dear and good mommy. I wish you a good recovery dear mama. Best wishes and many kisses from your most loving

Pier Giorgio

April[1] 1910

Dear mama,

I received your postcard and it pleased me a lot. Papa always corrects our homework and makes us recite our lessons and the teacher is a little happier. Yesterday I got a 9 and a 10 on my lessons and a 7 for homework and a 7 for the dictation. It is hot here in Turin.

The other day I went all the way to Santena[2] with Mrs. Banzatti and the two children and with grandmother and papa. Papa went to the woods with a man to see how the plants and poplar trees were doing[3] and we went to visit the tomb of Camillo Benso di Cavour and the great dining room. Thank you for the postcard.

Many greetings from papa and from grandmother and a kiss from your most loving

Pier Giorgio

[1] The exact month is uncertain.
[2] Residence of Camillo Benso, count of Cavour, one of the leaders of the movement to unify Italy in the 19th century. The group toured the Cavour home and burial place.
[3] Agriculture, with entire mornings spent among the plants, nurseries, and cows in the Biellese farmsteads, was Mr. Frassati's greatest pleasure.

Turin, December 20, 1910

Dearest mommy,

I am writing this letter to wish you a happy feastday and I tell you that we have written a pretty poem in German which will please you. With this letter I offer you a beautiful bouquet of flowers.[1] I will try to do everything possible to pass the exams to please you.[2] And I promise to be good.

I have prayed for this and I always ask the good God that he will always make you happy and keep my dearest papa in good health along with you.

Best wishes also on behalf of the Salesian priest[3] and lots of kisses from your most loving

Pier Giorgio

The Frassati family in Pollone 1910.

¹ Flowers were one of Pier Giorgio's great loves. From his childhood, he followed his grandmother step by step when she went down to the garden. He was interested in growing things and happy that he was able to pick them.
² From the earliest years of his life, Pier Giorgio considered school to be an absolute duty. Study was his principal family obligation, until the day of his death.
³ Pier Giorgio took exams at the Salesian Institute "Collegio Don Bosco" in Alassio in preparation for enrollment in the middle school "Massimo D'Azeglio" in Turin.

February 17, 1911

My dear Mother,

Today is your birthday, good Mother, and I am very happy to offer you my best wishes and blessings, and I will make this even nicer for you because I am writing in German.¹ I promise to always study harder and to always be good.

Many kisses from your son

Georg²

¹ Pier Giorgio was studying German and wrote this letter in German as a great gift for his mother on her birthday.
² Pier Giorgio signed this letter with the German name "Georg." When Pier Giorgio was born, his father wanted to name him after his own father, Pietro (Peter); but his mother didn't like the name. She finally agreed to link the name with Giorgio (George) as Pier Giorgio. The family sometimes called him Giorgio or the diminutive Giorgetto (Georgie), but never simply Pier.

December 19, 1911

Dear mama,

Tomorrow morning is your feastday and I am writing this letter to you.

I will ask the Lord to keep you with us for many years.

Then to make you happy I will be better. I will not hit my sister anymore. I will study more to pass the exams.

In the meantime we hope that you have a good day.

Best wishes and a greeting and a kiss from your most loving

Pier Giorgio

I hope that you are happy with this letter which is a bit short because I did not know what else to say.

To His Aunt Elena Ametis

April 1912

Dear aunt,

Is mama's painting[1] in a well-lit place? It must have been beautiful to see the historic parade passing by during the opening of the Exhibition as mama had already told me and also the inauguration of the bell tower of San Marco.[2]

I would like to be with you there to see mama's painting. I hope the King congratulated mama when he saw the exhibit.[3]

Grandmother sends you lots of kisses and greetings and all of us say hello.

Receive a kiss. Your most loving nephew.

Pier Giorgio

Excuse me for writing poorly.

[1] Mrs. Frassati enjoyed painting under the guidance of Alberto Falchetti, and she frequently exhibited her works in local and national shows. Her accomplishments brought great joy to Pier Giorgio and Luciana.

[2] The famous belltower of the Basilica of St. Mark in Venice collapsed and was partially destroyed in 1902. It was rebuilt over the next 10 years and dedicated in the presence of King Victor Emmanuel III on April 25, 1912.

[3] King Victor Emmanuel III had acquired one of Mrs. Frassati's paintings on the occasion of a Biennial Exhibition in Venice and this fact became one of the family's great memories.

To His Mother

April 1912

Dear mama,

I am always waiting for you because I can't wait to see you. How beautiful Venice must be. I received your postcard this morning and I am very happy that you have had a good trip and that you have a good room and are having beautiful weather. School is going well and I study all day long.

Papa says that today Mr. Balzano came to La Stampa from Il Corriere[1] and this man said to papa that the seashore at Marina di Massa where you want to go on Sunday is crowded and you don't feel comfortable there and they turn the beach into a pigsty. That man and papa advise against going; you do as you want and give me an answer.

Excuse me for writing poorly.

Many greetings and many kisses from everyone. Everyone is fine.

I send a greeting from me and from grandmother; a kiss from your most loving

Pier Giorgio

[1] This is short for *Il Corriere della Sera*. *Il Corriere della Sera* ("The Evening Courier"), and *La Stampa* were the two most important papers in Italy at that time and are still very well read today. *La Stampa* ("The Press") was the newspaper founded and published by Pier Giorgio's father, Alfredo Frassati. In 1926, Mussolini's Fascist regime compelled him to sell the newspaper for a paltry sum.

To His Father

August 14, 1913[1]

Dear papa,

I am very sorry that I cannot come to Turin to celebrate your feastday with you. I couldn't come because I cannot skip my lessons.

I promise to keep your promise.[2]

I wish you a happy feastday and a hundred years of good health. I hope to see you again soon. Best wishes and many greetings; a kiss from your

Pier Giorgio

[1] The year of this letter is uncertain.
[2] "Your promise" is the promise Pier Giorgio made to his father that he would study.

To His Mother

Pollone, September 20, 1913

Dear mama,

It snowed a bit on Mucrone and on Mombarone.[1] Yesterday and today it was good weather; otherwise it has always been raining.

I am very sorry that you left but I hope to see you again soon in Turin. Every day I do an assignment and practice the piano, I read and I also do a little gymnastics.

I am picking fruit, and today I weeded the rows of my vegetable garden, which was full of weeds.[2]

Many greetings and many kisses from your

Pier Giorgio

[1] These are two mountains near Pollone.
[2] Pier Giorgio had a small piece of land not far from the house for his own little garden. He worked in it with great seriousness and enthusiasm.

Pollone, September 25, 1913

Dear mama,

Thank you for your letter, I have not been able to write back right away, but today because I have had less to do and because I had a half-hour free in the morning I thought I would write to you. These days are taking forever to go by and it seems like it's been a year since I've seen you. The professor made me take a math exam and he told me that I can be promoted. I will take my exams in geometry and Italian very soon.

Yesterday it was cloudy and today it is a bit nicer.

Thousands, thousands and thousands of kisses from your

Giorgio

Pollone, September 1913

Dear Mama,

Today is the last day that I'll be in Pollone. It has been raining constantly the past two days. I am very happy that I'll see you again in two days. I will bring some flowers to Turin, some gladiolas and those blue flowers you like so much. There are still some gladiolas and also some roses. The Chrysanthemums are starting to bloom. It's very cold here; it seems like All Saints' Day.

Thank you for your letter. Lots of kisses, lots of kisses, and lots of kisses from

Giorgio

To His Father

Pollone, October 1913

Dearest papa,

I hope that school will start soon so that I can come down, or I hope that you can come to see us.

Mama is sending you a bill along so you do with it what you want.

Right now it is raining hard.

This morning I helped the gardener carry the flowerpots. The upper garden is all spaded, if it stops raining I will spread the manure.

Mama has gone to see Felicina[1] and her baby, who is fine. She promised to pay for Paolino's schooling so they decided to enroll him.

Please, if you can, find out when school starts.

See you soon, many greetings and kisses from your

Pier Giorgio

[1] Felicina was a member of a family of farmers who worked for the Frassati family.

Pollone, October 1913

Dear papa,

I am confused and miserable and I don't even know how to write to you; I saw how upset Mama was and I thought about you, so much that I don't know how to ask for a word of forgiveness. I am also sorry that I have to stay behind and I am ashamed in front of my classmates and my sister who have gone ahead of me.[1] I hope you will once again believe in the sincerity of my resolve to study this year and try to make up for everything as much as possible.

I received your letter: I already wrote you back. I stayed even more miserable when I read the letter of the professor to whom I am writing a couple of lines on mama's advice.

You will see that I'll try to prove my love for you with facts.

A kiss from your

Pier Giorgio

[1] Pier Giorgio was ashamed that he had failed Latin at the end of his second year at Massimo D'Azeglio state high school (middle or junior high school) in

Turin and would have to repeat the whole year. Instead, he was sent to a private school (the Social Institute of Turin) run by the Jesuit Fathers, where he could still advance to the next level and, at the same time, make up the work he had previously failed. Thus, he would not fall behind a whole year and could rejoin his classmates after successfully completing his studies at the private school.

To His Grandmother Linda Ametis

Turin, March 16, 1914

Dear grandmother,

I am very happy that the days are going by and that it won't be too long until I see you again. These months passed by slowly without you. I hope that you are well? Papa brought me some violets grown in the yard in Pollone which have a sweet scent.

Lots of kisses from everyone; greetings to aunt; your most loving

Pier Giorgio

Alassio, August 2, 1914

Dear grandmother,

We've had the most wonderful trip. I'm very sorry that you couldn't also be here with us. The sun is hot and so is the water. Greetings to Sister Angelica.[1] Many greetings and kisses from your

Pier Giorgio

[1] Sr. Angelica Barcellona was hired to help Mrs. Ametis in her later years. Many of Pier Giorgio's letters include a thoughtful greeting to her.

To His Aunt Elena Ametis

Alassio, August 3, 1914

Dear aunt,

I'm so very sorry that you also were not able to be with us to go swimming. Today the 3rd there's a good wind for sailing.[1] I might take a sailboat trip to the island of Gallinaria. Kiss grandmother for me. Write to me all of your news. The weather is beautiful. Many greetings from mama and Luciana; yours

Pier Giorgio

[1] Pier Giorgio's aunt had a great passion for sailboats.

To His Father

Rome, October 10, 1915

Dear papa,
   I received your telegram which pleased me very much, but aunt's letter has taken away every bit of hope.[1]
   Yesterday morning we visited the Roman Forum and those ruins made a huge impression on me. Afterwards we went to see the Coliseum, which I liked very much. Then we took a carriage to have lunch at the castle of Constantine, where we enjoyed a stupendous view. After lunch we visited the stupendous baths of Caracalla and I was impressed by the mosaic floors by the columns and by the baths and especially by the furnaces which had two clay pipes which sent the hot air into a room, where the Romans took the so-called Turkish baths. You can still see small pieces of marble of various kinds decorating the walls just as they were at one time. Today we went to the Vatican museums of sculpture and painting. We saw among other things a round basin made of porphyry, moved from the baths of Caracalla. We saw other notable things which I am not mentioning here. We stayed in the Vatican museums from 10 a.m. until 1:30. Leaving the Vatican we went to eat at Scarpone's outside the Porta San Pancrazio near Vascello and the Villa Glori. After we ate we went to visit St. Paul Outside the Walls.[2] And now I greet you and I am sending you a kiss. Your most loving

Pier Giorgio

[1] His aunt's letter dashed his hopes about his father's arrival in Rome to join the group.
[2] Pier Giorgio had boundless energy for this kind of touring. On one occasion, the group arrived back at the hotel very tired from the events of the day. His mother and sister were ready to go to bed. Pier Giorgio, however, right after supper, stood in front of them completely dressed, crying and asking: "And what am I supposed to do now?" So his mother sent him down to the corner stand to buy postage stamps, postcards, etc.

To His Aunt Elena Ametis

Alassio, August 16, 1916

Dear aunt,
   I hope that these congratulations of mine arrive in time for your feastday. Yesterday papa ate lunch at the Salesians and after lunch the others went to see the Bees and Father Besnate, who is the beekeeper,

had us taste the best honey. Papa left yesterday at four. Today the sea is a bit rough and the weather is not like it was at first now that we are in the last two weeks of August; the weather is becoming more cloudy. I go swimming with Axerio and some evenings after supper he invites us to his home or other places.

Two or three days ago I went sailing in Mascardi's Jole; it was fun speeding along except that it took on a lot of water. Who knows how happy you would have been if you had been here!

Wednesday the 23rd I will be back in Pollone and I'll see you and grandmother. Greet grandmother and give her a kiss for me and I wish you many best wishes and a happy feastday. I kiss you your

Pier Giorgio

To Carlo Bellingeri

Pollone, September 23, 1916

Dearest Carlo,

Thanks for the kind postcard, which gave me a lot of pleasure.

I'm studying a lot because the blessed exams are coming up soon!

I'll be in Turin on the 1st and I'll stay there until the 9th.

I hope that while you are coming to take French lessons, you will stop by to pay me a visit.

You would be doing me a real favor if you would tell me which professor will give us the French exam.

Give my regards to your mother greetings to Nanni and Alberto and receive a handshake and a greeting from

Pier Giorgio

Pollone, October 15, 1916

Dearest Bellingeri,

I'm delighted that I can give you the great news that I passed and so I'm in senior high school.

I hope that you will be promoted too. Write me as soon as you know anything.

Affectionate greetings and a handshake.

Pier Giorgio

1917

To Carlo Bellingeri

Pollone, March 31, 1917

Dear Carlo,

Excellent outing.[1] The weather here varies a lot. As for the excursion to Peveragno I thought that it was too long, because Peveragno is situated on the other side of Cuneo.

Greet our friends for me, give my regards to your family, a hug from your friend

Pier Giorgio

[1] It was a bicycle excursion.

Pollone, April 6, 1917

Dearest Carlo,

The weather varies a lot. We are coming to Turin on Wednesday and maybe I will come on my bicycle. I would be glad if you could come to meet me on the road near Chivasso, if your parents will let you. As soon as I have decided the time of my departure.[1]

Best wishes also from my Mama to all of your family and to you a hug from

Pier Giorgio

[1] This corresponds to the original. Pier Giorgio forgot to write the rest of the sentence.

To Alberto Falchetti

Pollone, April 6, 1917[1]

Thanks for the postcard and for the beautiful crystals[2] which I like very much. Today is a splendid day.

Best wishes for a happy feastday and for a happy Easter and greetings from

Pier Giorgio

[1] This was Pier Giorgio's 16th birthday.
[2] The crystals went to enrich his mineral collection. On a previous occasion, Falchetti had given him a little mineral with a trace of gold in it. This inspired him to display his collection in a glass-window showcase in his study under lock and key. Many times, as reported by his friends, Pier Giorgio came back from outings to the mountains loaded down with rocks, and was never tired after having used his mineralogist hammer all day long. This was even before he began his degree in mining engineering.

To Carlo Bellingeri

Pollone, August 15, 1917

Dearest Carlo,

I received your postcard and I thank you for the kind remembrance.

I am translating from Latin a bit of Quintilian, a little of the Tusculanae, and Horace's satires. It's not wasted effort because they are all books which we'll translate next year. Then from Italian (into Latin) some excerpts from the Decio Fantoni; but this book has a drawback, it's not annotated; so I asked my professor which book of exercises he advised me to get. He showed me books by Casagrande and Boralevi, both annotated. But the difference between Casagrande and Boralevi is that the excerpts in the former are easier. Do as you think best.

I still think about the beautiful hours spent at the Bonafous[1] with you and the beautiful walks I took with you and Camillo. By the way they still haven't sent me the diploma from Bonafous. Now I'm going to write a letter to the principal.

I am here by myself, so I rarely take walks; only the Marchisios are here, with whom I play billiards some evenings.

I've already picked the potatoes; I've picked a lot of fairly big ones, but the mole cricket nibbled at some.

Today I took a stupendous walk. I left this morning at six: the sky was clear, though tonight it's raining. Together with my father, Luciana, and the Marchisios I went to Favaro to take the tram to Oropa.

After we attended Holy Mass, said at the main altar of the Madonna, we went from Oropa to Sette Fontane, a farmhouse situated in the Elvo valley at the foot of Mucrone. It was eleven when we arrived; we ate a good plate of polenta concia.[2] A cool breeze was blowing overhead, and the sun was hot. Mucrone was beautiful up close and it made me wish that I could climb it from the steep side. But then came the fog, which covered everything; but once in a while the outline reappeared. Around two o'clock we went down to Pollone. During the return trip the weather changed at each instant, and now a storm is breaking.

You've seen that they've changed the headmaster; who knows whether the new one will be any better? Let's hope so.

Unfortunately I must now leave you because it's time to go to sleep.

Regards to your family, greetings from my sister, a hug from
Pier Giorgio

[1] An agricultural institute located in the suburbs of Turin. Pier Giorgio took an agricultural course so that he could be of help while the gardener was doing military service.

[2] This is a local specialty consisting of polenta (corn meal mush) drenched in butter and fontina cheese.

Pollone, September 19, 1917

Dear Carlo,

Tuesday the 11th I went to the lake La Vecchia,[1] in the Andorno valley, where I stayed two days. The weather has always been lousy almost as if on purpose and so I've hardly seen the lake except for a moment.

I'm studying a lot more now, because in two weeks we may come to Turin. And what are you doing? Write to me about what's new and you'll make me happy. Franco Fassò is here. Regards to your family, a greeting and a hug from
Pier Giorgio

[1] Pier Giorgio had gone to La Vecchia loaded down with fruit to pay a visit to Alberto Falchetti who was there painting.

Pollone, October 26, 1917

Dearest Carlo,

Maybe you already know that I failed. I really didn't think about flunking Latin, instead I was worried about composition and instead the opposite happened.[1] I will go to the Sociale, where I'll attend second year classes in hopes of taking the first year exams in February.[2]

And how have your exams gone? Write to me about something. Greetings from your friend

Pier Giorgio

[1] Both Pier Giorgio and Luciana had failed Latin that year!
[2] For the second time, Pier Giorgio transferred from the state high school "Massimo D'Azeglio" to the Social Institute of Turin, run by the Jesuit Fathers, so that he could make up the school year.

1918

To Carlo Bellingeri

Pollone, August 4, 1918

Dear friend,
    Unfortunately I have begun to study; I've spent the last two weeks of July working in the garden and helping the gardener, who happened to be on leave.[1]
    And what are you up to?
    I've sent you the literature book by Rossi; I don't know when you'll get it because the postal service between Santhià and Biella is really terrible.
    Franco Fassò and Anna Maria have arrived here in Pollone. Vittorio's sister wrote to my sister saying that Vittorio has been sent to distribute membership cards in the Ovada township. Greetings to everyone and to you a thousand kisses and greetings.
                                                        P. Giorgio

[1] The gardener was on leave from military service.

Pollone, August 19, 1918

Dear friend,
    Forgive me, Carlo, I haven't written to you for a long time, but it's not entirely my fault because I have a lot to study and in the evening I have to water the flowers. I've written back right away in response to your last postcard in which you told me about the birth of your little sister.
    Many days ago I went on my bicycle with Franco all the way to Viverone and on the way back to Cavaglià, while we stopped there to adjust the valves of Franco's tires we ran into your cousin. Two days ago I went to the top of Croce della Barma at Oropa, 2384 meters high, with Franco, Papa, Luciana, and Anna Maria, who suffered a

bit of dizziness on the way back, and we enjoyed a magnificent view; in fact, we saw all of Monte Rosa, Monte Cervino, Mont Blanc, Gran Paradiso, etc. It was a very wonderful and comfortable trip, it took 3 and a half hours from Oropa. On our way we met some women loaded down with cherries, wild but very good; we stuffed ourselves.

Anna Maria is leaving for Turin this morning and then she is continuing on to the sea at Recco.

Camillo hasn't written to me up to now, poor guy, he's very busy; he has to write every day to his girlfriend Miss Sapienza, who is now here in Pollone. He doesn't even respond to the numerous postcards which my sister, who is too good, sends to him.

Now, Carlo, may I ask you, if by chance you had written down on some paper a copy of the translation of Paradox, send it to me; because time is running out and I already have so many things to do. Without noticing it we switched the bells on our bikes and now I'm sending you yours and I ask you to send me mine.

Lately Vittorio, among other things he wrote about to me, asked me for your address, and I sent it to him right away.

Write soon and you'll make me happy.

Regards to your family, a kiss from your

Pier Giorgio

P.S. A big apology if this is a bit dirty.[1]

[1] In those days, letters were written with fountain pens and the ink could often smear. It was a bit much for Pier Giorgio to recopy or rewrite, but he never forgot to excuse himself for a messy letter.

Pollone, September 16, 1918

Dear Carlo,

I haven't received any more news about you; I hope that my letter reached you. Where are you with your studies? I've already finished the program in Latin, but I have yet to finish Greek and Italian. How is your new little sister?

Greet your parents on behalf of mine and a kiss from

Pier Giorgio

Pollone, September 28, 1918

Dear Carlo,
    Thanks for your nice postcard and excuse me for being so late to reply to you.
    Friday October 4th I'm coming to Turin, because my exams are from the 11th to the 15th. And when will you be going to Alba?
    Write to me about whatever and you'll make me happy. Vittorio will be having his ten days' furlough, but he doesn't know whether he will come to Turin or to Brunate.
    Cordial greetings.

Pier Giorgio

Pollone, Monday, October 21, 1918

Dear Carlo,
    I haven't heard from you for a long time, every time the mail arrives I search anxiously for a letter from you that will let me know that you are fine and if you've taken your exams and how they went. Not knowing your address in Alba, while you are there I've sent two postcards to your villa in Cascina Vica; I don't know if you've received them. Bersezio has written to me and he sends you a big hello. Imagine, the poor guy, they've even made him do guard duty at the prisons in Alessandria! Luckily he doesn't have any more military service in the territories now, because he's taking part in a pre-academic course studying topography, firearms, explosives, supplies, defenses and bookkeeping.
    The sun is shining while I'm writing to you, let's hope that it lasts because until now we've had a very lousy October.
    Do you know that Camillo wound up in bed in the Cernaia barracks because a large box fell on his big toe?
    I'm still studying and in a few days I'll have finished the Latin textbooks, then I'll review my Greek about which I know nothing and then I hope to come to Turin to take those blessed exams. Convey my regards to your parents greetings and kisses from

Pier Giorgio

Pollone, November 4, 1918

Happy that your feastday[1] coincides with the most beautiful day of our Country,[2] I greet you affectionately.

Pier Giorgio

[1] Feast of St. Charles Borromeo, November 4, patron saint of his friend Carlo.
[2] He is referring to the victorious end of the First World War.

Pier Giorgio saved his money a long time to buy his bicycle. When it was later stolen, he said that the thief "must have been someone who needed it more than me."

1919

To Carlo Bellingeri

Francavilla a Mare, August 5, 1919

Dear Carlo,

We've travelled a lot these days. Among the cities and villages we visited, I liked Aquila and Scanno most of all.

Aquila is surrounded by the mountains; the countryside which lies around it is completely green and every tiniest patch is farmed because there's an abundance of water for irrigation.

The grapevine grows only 20 centimeters high and is very well tended.

Francavilla is very beautiful, the sea is stupendous and I've already gone swimming 8 times.

Regards to your folks and kisses from

Pier Giorgio

To His Grandmother Linda Ametis

Francavilla, August 5, 1919

Dear Grandmother,

The beach is very beautiful, the sea is stupendous; it only lacks warmth and so my swims have to be very short. I'm already deep red.

Lots of greetings and kisses to Mama, greetings to Sister, to my brother,[1] to the rabbits, to Parsifal[2] and to you thousands of kisses from

Pier Giorgio

---

[1] Pier Giorgio and Luciana had playfully chosen the cat Nani to be their brother.

[2] Parsifal was Senator Frassati's horse, a stupendous Irish steed who was difficult to ride due to his indomitable character. As was the case with Mime and Wotan, the choice of his name was a tribute to the German composer Richard Wagner.

To His Father

Assisi, September 4, 1919

Dearest Papa,

Thanks for your nice letter. I've been here for two days; it's a real wonder, too bad I have to leave already. Tomorrow we're going to Perugia greetings and kisses

Pier Giorgio

Perugia, September 6, 1919

I've visited more or less thoroughly the school of Agriculture; it's very fine, it has a very wonderful agricultural museum;[1] then within 23 km of Perugia you are at a convent where one does the fourth year of studies. One must stay in college a solar year. Greetings and kisses.

Pier Giorgio

[1] Pier Giorgio told about his own journeys in very different ways: he viewed the paintings and monuments for his mother's benefit, while he visited agricultural museums for his father's sake, seeking to bring to each the news which would most interest him or her.

To Alberto Falchetti

Milan, September 11, 1919

Gigin de Cagian is coming to Milan for the second time.[1]

[1] He is referring to the Piedmontese saying: "Gigin de Cagian is going to Milan for the first time." The first time that Pier Giorgio went to Milan he had been accompanied by Falchetti.

To Carlo Bellingeri

Pollone, September 29, 1919

Dear Carlo,

Finally after a long silence I've heard from you. I was upset when I read that perhaps you were not going to take the exams. What will you do? Repeat the year or enroll in Agricultural school? I advise you to go to Perugia; one could find few cities so beautiful, you eat very well there and cheaply enough. If you want, I have the programs from the royal university printed in 1919, which I could send to you if they would be helpful. Greetings to all of your family from all of us and a hug from

Pier Giorgio

Turin, 1920. Pier Giorgio posed for this picture when he was a student at the Polytechnic University where he was majoring in Mining Engineering. He died two exams short of completing his degree. It was awarded to him posthumously in 2001, on the 100th anniversary of his birth.

1920

To His Father

Limone, February 17, 1920

Up until now the weather has been nice enough, but now it's snowing a lot. I ski all day long and I am practicing the telemark.[1]
Greetings and kisses to you and to mama and to everyone from

Pier Giorgio

[1] A turning movement in skiing.

To Luciana

Turin, May 19, 1920

Dearest Luciana,

I'm all alone these days because papa has gone to Rome; he'll probably return tomorrow. Yesterday evening I went to lunch at the Banzatti's, all of whom asked me to tell you hello.

Tell mama that the painting arrived today from Venice. We don't know if we should open the crate or have it brought to Via Cristoforo Colombo.[1]

Have you received my two telegrams? Thanks for the postcards.

We're all fine. Greet the Marchisios, kisses to you and Mama and to aunt from

Pier Giorgio

Mime sends a pawshake.[2]

Greetings from grandmother, who has gone out to visit her brother, from Sister Angelica, Carolina and Maria.

[1] This was the location of the studio of Alberto Falchetti and Mrs. Frassati.
[2] Mime was a magnificent Irish wolfhound given to Luciana by Francesco Pastonchi, a well-known Italian poet.

To His Father

S. Dalmazio di Tenda, July 20, 1920

Dearest papa,

Great trip, a bit too much sun on the plain. We found a delightful mountain breeze on the hills of Tenda. Greetings and kisses from

Pier Giorgio

To Luciana

S. Dalmazio di Tenda, July 20, 1920

Dearest Luciana,

A good trip with some little incident at the start. The road on the plain was very sunny, and we broke up the journey with six stops for meals.

We went on foot by the light of the stars from Limone to the tunnel, then we traveled with lanterns along the splendid curves of the road and the steep descent.

Now we're going up to Mesce where we'll visit the mines. Kisses to you, greetings and kisses to aunt, grandmother, Mama, greetings to Sister Angelica and to everyone; a kiss to Wotan, Mime, Uadi.[1]

Pier Giorgio

[1] Wotan, Mime and Uadi were the family dogs.

Albissola Marina, July 27, 1920

Dearest Luciana,

I made the return trip together with Carlo and Farina all the way to Albenga then I went to Savona and now I'm here in the Gambettas'[1] house. I saw Anna Maria who gave me news about you. I hope to be in Turin on Tuesday or Wednesday and to be in Pollone the 29th at the latest. Greetings to everyone, to Wotan Mime Uadi, and to you a kiss from

Pier Giorgio

Greetings from Laura Clelia and Mario Marina and Andrès.

[1] The Gambettas were cousins of the Frassatis. Pier Giorgio spent many happy hours visiting them.

To His Mother

Albissola Marina, July 27, 1920

Dearest mama,
    I'm here at Albisolla; I arrived in a pitiful condition, dirty as a pig. Now I am very well and I've already been swimming four times in the sea. Laura and Maria insist that I stay for a few days but time is passing and the hour to get back to my studies is approaching.
    Greetings and kisses from

                                    Pier Giorgio

Greetings from Laura Marina and Andrès Clelia and Mario.

To His Father

Albissolla, July 27, 1920

Dearest papa,
    I'm here at the Gambettas; I've already been swimming four or five times in the sea. Tomorrow I'll leave for Turin and the day after tomorrow I hope to be in Pollone. Greetings from everyone and a kiss from

                                    Pier Giorgio

Greetings from Clelia Laura and Mario Marina and Andrès.

To Carlo Bellingeri

Albissola Marina, July 28, 1920

Dearest Carlo,
    Right after we parted I began to have accidents on the trip. At Ceriana right after Albengo I had to fix the inner tube which went flat and so I wasted time until three. I was able to get to Savona from here in two hours, but right after Spotorno, a long way from town, my tire blew out again; so after failed attempts to repair it, I decided to take the bus to Vado. From there, having fixed the tire, I arrived in Albissola Superiore at 8:30.
    And how did your trip go? Write me.
    Hoping to see you soon, greetings to everyone and special greetings to you from

                                    Pier Giorgio

Oropa, August 18, 1920

Dearest Carlo,

And how is the promotion of Oropa[1] coming along?

Hoping to see you soon, greetings from

Pier Giorgio

[1] Oropa is the location of a famous shrine, situated in the Biellese mountains about a two-hour walk from Pollone, where the statue of the Brown Madonna is venerated and where Pier Giorgio often went to attend Mass and to pray.

Pollone, September 16, 1920

Dearest Carlo,

Yesterday I went atop Mount Mucrone where Holy Mass was being celebrated: unfortunately the fog prevented us from admiring the magnificent panorama which can be enjoyed up there.

On the first of October I'll be in Turin to study with a few of my friends and I hope to see you.

The 22nd of September I'm going to Biella for the military medical exam.

The 11th of September I went to lunch with the recruits from Pollone; we ate rather late, 3 p.m., which is an hour when I've never before eaten lunch.

I saw that there was a convention of the left wing of the People's Party in Turin; did you participate?[1]

Write something to me.

Regards to your parents greetings to your sister and a handshake and a kiss to you from

Pier Giorgio

[1] Pier Giorgio was very politically active and interested in news of this nature. He particularly supported efforts to raise an ever-greater consciousness on the part of Catholics with regard to the problems and needs of the masses.

Pollone, September 22, 1920

Dearest Carlo,

Yesterday I was with Anna Maria and my sister in Cavaglià at the Rondolino's house to watch the Moor of Venice. Rinaldo had the part of Othello; your cousin De Marchi was Desdemona; Iago and Cassius the two Olivieris and the other characters were played by the townspeople. I had a really fine evening and I regretted your absence. I knew through my mother that you were in Bra at a convention of the Italian People's Party.

Write to me about your impressions.

Regards to your parents, greetings to your sister and a kiss and a handshake to you.

Pier Giorgio

N.B. I passed my physical.

Pier Giorgio's father Alfredo Frassati, Italian Ambassador to Germany, 1921-22.

1921

To Alberto Falchetti

Sestrières, February 16, 1921

Magnificent weather, this evening there was a splendid sunset, the mountains and the sky were various shades of color.

Too bad you're not here to paint it.

Pier Giorgio

To His Grandmother Giuseppina Frassati

Berlin, March 7, 1921

A really fine, beautiful and enormous city! Today I had a nice ride on horseback with papa. A thousand regards and kisses.

Pier Giorgio

Berlin, March 17, 1921

Although I've seen little of Berlin, I know that it's a beautiful city.

Nearly every day I ride a horse in the Tiergarten, a very beautiful park near us, or else, only once in a while during the week, I ride with papa in Grunewald an enormous forest. I've already visited some museums, where one finds a number of beautiful things. Maybe in a week I'll go to Oppeln in Silesia as the guest of a family so that I can visit the mines.

Soon I hope to get acquainted with the situation for Catholic students and workers here and thus I'll keep to the same habits that I have in Turin.

Again a thousand best wishes and kisses from

Pier Giorgio

To Antonio Villani

Berlin, March 17, 1921

Dearest Villani,

Just today I met Dr. Sonnenschein, a likeable priest, who speaks Italian well enough and who also takes care of the Italians living in Berlin. He told me about the Catholic student movement and I learned that about one-tenth of the students in Berlin profess the same religion as we do.[1]

But Dr. Sonnenschein's work, which for 15 years has been aimed at preparing young students for a life of social consciousness, today, because of the misery evident in this class, has had to be somewhat carried out by protecting them, by looking for jobs for them, so that they can manage the high cost of living.

The organization is just like ours, independent of other Catholic organizations; but there are also Clubs made up of university students and workers.

Dr. Sonnenschein kindly invited me to the meetings that these mixed clubs will be having and so I'll be able to get to know the two environments.[2]

Write soon telling me your impressions about the convention in Rome of the youth from Emilia: also give me our Club's news. Have you organized something for that society of help among friends?[3] Greetings to all our friends and an affectionate greeting to you.

Pier Giorgio

[1] It was a period in which it was firmly believed that Catholicism was on a victorious and swift march among German intellectuals; the facts, however, showed the contrary.

[2] These meetings interested him very much inasmuch as he found realized in them the thing in which he believed: brotherhood between students and workers, which was an assumption of reciprocal understanding and collaboration on the same social level. Enthused by such an experience, a few months later on the occasion of the convention of FUCI (Federazione Universitaria Cattolica Italiana – the Federation of Italian Catholic University Students) held in Ravenna, Pier Giorgio proposed the merger of the Italian Catholic Youth Organization (whose members came mostly from the working class) with FUCI, an idea, however, for which the times were not yet ripe.

[3] It was meant to be a society of mutual assistance, moral and material, which would also serve to cement and strengthen many relationships and connections which life tends to undo. This idea which was constant in Pier Giorgio's mind, later found application in his society of the Tipi Loschi.

To Father Filippo Robotti[1]

Berlin, March 25, 1921

Just a few days ago I met Dr. Sonnenschein, a nice priest who takes care of the Italian Catholics living in Berlin, and who directs the Catholic students. He invited me to the meetings of the clubs which are a mixture of workers and students. I understand that unfortunately few will be able to come to Ferrara[2] because there's a lot of poverty in the student population. I entrusted the letter, which your brother so kindly gave me, to the Father Prior of the Dominicans in Berlin whom I have found to be very kind and congenial. A thousand best wishes for a Happy Easter and also regards from my father.

Pier Giorgio

[1] This letter was written to the Dominican Father who served as the chaplain of the FUCI club Cesare Balbo that Pier Giorgio belonged to in Turin.
[2] He was referring to a convention of both the FUCI and the Pax Romana. Pier Giorgio was very committed to uniting the German and Italian students to bridge the divide created by World War I which had ended in 1918. The convention, originally planned for Ferrara, actually took place in Ravenna.

To His Aunt Elena Ametis

Berlin, April 5, 1921

Dearest,

Since you left, the time here passes much more slowly, because you left a great void. Now I will apply myself to my studies in earnest and to my exams even moreso because soon I must go to Silesia.

A thousand best wishes and kisses. Kisses to grandmother and to papa, greetings to everyone from

Pier Giorgio

Berlin, April 6, 1921

Dearest,

Thanks for the telegram which pleased me very much. Last night I had dinner with a German family and I had good practice in German, because when I made a mistake in pronunciation the kids gently corrected me. A thousand kisses to papa and to grandmother and again to you a thousand best wishes and kisses.

Pier Giorgio

Berlin, April 7, 1921

Dearest,

Thanks for kindly thinking of buying me an alarm clock, but I should yank your ears a little, because as usual you are too generous. The telegram pleased me a lot and it was already enough for my birthday. At tea the other day I was really very amused at several people who were speaking Italian, especially some from South America. Yesterday we had lunch at Chiaraviglio's house together with the Honorable Bianchi, a socialist follower of Giolitti and De-Micheli. Greetings to everyone, kisses to grandmother and to you a thousand kisses and thank yous from

Pier Giorgio

Berlin, April 9, 1921

Dearest,

I received your clock, which works very well. Yesterday I was with a German family to hear a recitation of Dante in German. I felt very comfortable, because many nice people were there, among others three Italians. Tomorrow we're going to Werder in the boat, hoping that the weather favors us.

Wednesday morning I visited all the rooms of the national library.

Imagine there are eight floors completely full of books all very well organized and divided according to subject.

Again a thousand thanks for the fine gift; greetings to everyone from all of us, a thousand kisses to you and to grandmother from

Pier Giorgio

To His Grandmother Giuseppina Frassati

Berlin, April 11, 1921

Dearest,

It's been many days now that nothing is happening other than holding receptions. Thanks to the death of King Nicholas[1] they can't hold balls and big dinners, and this is fine with me.

I'm studying some German so that I can return to Italy knowing it well enough. I've made the acquaintance of two German students, and now I'll visit a bit of Berlin with them especially the more interesting parts.

A thousand kisses to you and a big kiss to uncle.

Pier Giorgio

[1] Nicholas Petrovich I, the former king of Montenegro and father of Queen Elena of Savoy, died on March 2, 1921.

To Antonio Villani

Berlin, April 28, 1921

Dearest Friend,

Excuse me if I'm late in writing to you, but it's the fault of my laziness. Yesterday I spoke with one of the heads of the student economic organization, who wanted an invitation to Italy from the Catholic Italian students; I told him that we're expecting a strong core group of Germans in Ferrara.[1]

Maybe in another week Dr. Sonnenschein will go to Rome and I'll write him a letter of introduction to Spataro[2] and also one to you because he'll probably pass through Turin on his return. I recommend that you prepare a wonderful evening like the one we had with the Germans and Poles who came to Turin for the convention of the former students of Don Bosco.[3]

I'm sorry that I can't be in Italy these days to bring my measly contribution to the People's Party, especially on behalf of Stella and the others of a decidedly popular character.

I should leave off now because I'm going to bring a cup of coffee to Dr. Engel.

Greet all our friends for me; and to you an affectionate kiss.

Pier Giorgio

[1] He was referring to the convention of the FUCI and the Pax Romana which actually took place in Ravenna.
[2] The president of the FUCI.
[3] St. John Bosco (1815-1888), founder of the Salesian Congregation and apostle of youth in Turin.

To His Aunt Elena Ametis

Berlin, May 5, 1921

Dearest,
   Yesterday evening I went to Berlin's great drama theatre to see A Midsummer Night's Dream. I didn't understand much of it, but I was very well entertained because the acting and the scenery were well done.
   Tomorrow morning I'll be seeing the beautiful sea at Hamburg and then maybe I'll return from Stettino.
   Greetings and kisses to grandmother, regards to everyone and to you a huge kiss from

Pier Giorgio

To Willibald Leitgebel[1]

Hamburg, May 7, 1921

   Hamburg is magnificent. Yesterday I went to Lubec where I admired an original City Hall and many old houses. My respects to your mother and my greetings to your sister, to your brother and you. Yours

Pier Giorgio

[1] This letter was originally written in German.

To His Grandmother Linda Ametis

Brake, May 8, 1921

Dear grandmother,
   This morning mama and Mrs. Marchisio left to go to Berlin, while I have set off for Bremerhaven to see a bit of the North Sea. I'm staying 4 hours here in Brake and then this evening I'll return to Bremen.
   Greetings to everyone and to you and to aunt a big kiss.

Pier Giorgio

This is the Weser.[1]

[1] A river in Germany whose photograph was on the reverse of this postcard.

37

Albissola Marina, May 17, 1921

Dearest,

I'm sending you this photograph of one of Hanover's most beautiful Gothic churches. I'm here by myself at the train station restaurant with just enough time to eat and then leave immediately afterward for Berlin. Greetings to everyone to you and to aunt a great big kiss.

Pier Giorgio

I wasn't able to send this from Hanover because I didn't have stamps.

To Gian Maria Bertini

Munich, June 5, 1921

Today I visited Munich with the head[1] of the Catholic student organizations of Southern Germany a very kind person whom I hope will come to Ferrara.

Greetings to all our friends from

Pier Giorgio

[1] A reference to Dr. Fritz Beck.

To Alberto Falchetti

Munich, June 5, 1921

Yesterday we were in the old art museum where there are some magnificent paintings, three rooms full of Rubens, some paintings by Rembrandt and others. We then visited the house of Franz Stuck[1] but the maestro wasn't at home. This morning we visited the Lenbach house[2] and then the gallery of modern art where we found "Plowing high up in Engadina"[3] among the beautiful paintings. A shame that you couldn't be here because I'm sure you would have spent some fine days here.

Kisses from

Pier Giorgio

[1] Franz von Stuck (1863-1928) was a popular architect and graphic artist of the time.
[2] The Lenbachhaus is a municipal art gallery in Munich.
[3] A painting by Segantini, an artist whom Falchetti had known and admired.

To Fritz Beck

Albissola (Savona), July 1921

Dear Dr. Beck,

It is just today that I am able to respond to you regarding the students whom we met in the Residenzpark. There is a student dining hall in Padua where one can have two meals a day for six lire;[1] a furnished room costs 60 or 80 lire a month.

University life is very cheerful. There is also a Catholic boarding house with a park and an athletic field for those enrolled in the University of Padua.

I also thank you again so very, very much for what you did for me in Munich. Thank you also for the book which I have not yet read, because reading takes a great effort.

Are you coming to Ravenna? If you are unable to come, I hope to go to Germany in September and meet up with you in Munich.

Now I am with my cousins in Albissola and I have already gone swimming many times. The sea is splendid. I ask you to excuse me if this letter is written with a few mistakes.[2]

Pier Giorgio Frassati

[1] The lira (plural = lire) was the Italian currency before the euro.
[2] This letter was written in German and ends abruptly because the second part has been lost.

To His Mother

Albissola Marina, July 20, 1921

If Andres gets permission for me to make a trip in the electric car from Savona to Genoa, if you allow me I would go as far as Recco to see Vittorio all the moreso because while in Turin Mrs. Bersezio invited me to spend two or three days with Vittorio. My back is all peeling because of that ointment and it was already very dark. My head is better. Greetings and kisses to grandmother, aunt, and to you a big kiss from

Pier Giorgio

To Antonio Villani

Albissola Marina, July 25, 1921

Dearest friend,

I'll be in Turin Wednesday the 27th in the morning. Yesterday I was in Recco to find Vittorio Bersezio. I've already been swimming a lot and I've already gotten very black.

Thanks again for all that you've done for the German students.

Regards and kisses from

Pier Giorgio

To Gian Maria Bertini

Albissola Marina, July 27, 1921

Dearest friend,

Excuse me for the disturbance, but you need to have patience and gladly put up with these little troubles in life. Thanks for all that you've done for Father Robotti and for the German students. Regarding the students I have been informed that the boarding house has put 20 rooms at their disposal.

Cordial greetings from

Pier Giorgio

To Antonio Villani

Pollone, end of July 1921

Dearest Villani,

As soon as I arrived in Turin I stopped by your house, but you had left many days ago.

Upon my arrival in Pollone I found letters from my German friends. Dr. Sonnenschein asks if the places in Turin can be ready and available from the 15th of August to the 15th of September. Write me right away making a complete report to me about what you've been able to arrange with the Catholic boarding house and then I can give a definite response about Turin.

Dr. Beck from Munich will be coming to Ravenna for the 28th with a lot of students from Bavaria; and asks me to ask Spataro if the promise of 4 weeks for free also includes him and Dr. Siegert, the heads of the Bavarian organizations.

I heard from Bertini that Spataro has promised room and board for 4 weeks, but Turin isn't included.

Please send me the text of the letter of invitation to the students from Munich; I must check the translation which Dr. Beck made so that I can write to him what is correct and that he understood it well. While you are writing, please thank the FUCI for their kind invitation on behalf of Dr. Beck and all those who have been invited.

Affectionate regards from

Pier Giorgio

To His Mother

Middle of August 1921

I don't envy your stay in the Mountains because of the bad weather. My foot isn't hurting anymore, but I need to give it a rest. Greetings to Berti[1] who I heard wanted to put me in The Abruzzi in Africa.[2]

Greetings to the Marchisios and kisses to you and to aunt.

Pier Giorgio

[1] Nickname for Alberto Falchetti.
[2] The name of a painting envisioned by Alberto Falchetti. Pier Giorgio and his sister were sometimes called upon to pose for Falchetti paintings.

To Antonio Villani

Pollone, August 16, 1921

Dearest friend,

I'm heartily congratulating myself because the Germans are in Rome and they are enjoying it, but the FUCI have sent a letter of invitation to Munich which Dr. Beck has kindly translated into German and then sent to me. Now I've retranslated it into Italian and I'm sending it to you so that you can compare it to the original and thus clear up any misunderstanding.

In Dr. Beck's letter from many days ago he wrote to tell me that he is coming to Ravenna together with Dr. Siegert and he asked me to put in a good word with the President of the FUCI so that in addition to the discount for the train, seeing that the conditions aren't good for German currency, they might be able to have room and board at the lowest possible price.

Now I've received another letter in which Dr. Beck expresses his regrets that he can't come to Ravenna due to an urgent job.

However the fact remains until the contrary proves true that Dr. Siegert will come to Ravenna and I hope that the FUCI won't want to make it difficult to house this leader of the Southern German Catholic student movement, all the more so if the translation of the invitation sent by the FUCI to Munich is correct.

Have you seen Dr. Sonnenschein in Rome?

Bertini has sent me the check and the card.

I've been in bed for a few days now because of a foot infection and I hope to be able to come for sure by the 24th to Reggio Emilia.

Is it really necessary to bring my bicycle? I would prefer to leave it here all the more so because I'm not going directly to Berlin from Rome, but first I'm returning to Pollone.

I'll send you a telegram giving you the precise time of arrival. Please answer right away.

Regards and kisses from

Pier Giorgio

To His Mother

Bologna, August 27, 1921

This morning I visited nearly all the churches of beautiful Bologna.[1] Maybe if I have a few minutes of time left before leaving I'll visit the art museum.

Many greetings and kisses.

Pier Giorgio

---

[1] His itinerary in a city always started with the churches, and not only for artistic reasons.

To Alberto Falchetti

Bologna, August 27, 1921

I'm sending you a postcard of Raphael maybe it will inspire some good ideas for your painting of Rhapsodist in Africa.[1]
Greetings from

Pier Giorgio

[1] This was a monumental painting which Falchetti had begun some time before and for which Pier Giorgio had also posed.

To His Parents

Ravenna, August 28, 1921

Dearests,

I arrived at 6 and I'm staying in a nice little lodge together with all my friends from Turin. Tomorrow the convention opens.[1]

I'm here at the station waiting for the arrival of the Germans.

Greetings and kisses.

Pier Giorgio

[1] He is referring to the convention of the FUCI and of Pax Romana, the International Union of Catholic Students, held in Ravenna from August 26 to September 1, 1921, on the occasion of the sixth centenary of the death of the Italian poet Dante Alighieri.

To Alberto Falchetti

Bozen, September 15, 1921

Today I visited the art museum of Brera in a hurry. I'm really sorry that I wasn't able to greet you before leaving for Germany. Tomorrow I'll be in Munich, where I'll be staying three or four days then I'll be going to Freiburg to study a little German. How's your painting coming along? Is there anything left of Bertino?[1]
Regards.

Pier Giorgio

[1] A nickname for Alberto Falchetti.

To His Mother

Brenner, September 15, 1921

Dearest,

I arrived safely in Brenner, where I received the sad news that my luggage had been unloaded in a station halfway between Verona and Brenner.

Tonight I slept in a first class car parked at the station, because the only hotel in this little town was closed.

I hope that it will arrive on the 12:10 train otherwise we'll file a complaint.

The train service is really indecent. Perugini, whom I ran into on the direct train from Rome to Berlin told me that his luggage was sent to Taranto instead of being sent to Terontola and then he had to spend over 300 lire to track it down.

I will arrive in Munich today at eight in the evening.

Greetings to everyone and a thousand kisses to you.

Last night I was very unhappy about this incident, but now I'm here in a warm place waiting for the noon arrival.

Greetings to Grandmother, aunt, papa, Luciana, Sister, Maria, Dora, Marta, gardener Italo[1] from

Pier Giorgio

[1] These were many of the domestic staff in the house whom Pier Giorgio thoughtfully greeted in his correspondence.

Innsbruck, September 16, 1921

My luggage finally arrived in Brenner this morning and so this evening I can go to Munich. I've already telegraphed to Count Tornielli so that a room will be prepared for me.

If you pass through Innsbruck stop to buy something because prices are really good for us there.

For 5 lire one can buy three knit ties.

Greetings to papa, grandmother, aunt, Luciana, Sister, Maria, Dora, and a thousand kisses to you from

Pier Giorgio

Regards from the Italian stationmaster in Innsbruck.

Munich, September 20, 1921

Dear mama,

Where are the Baedekers[1] of Germany? Write to me via general delivery in Freiburg, because I shall leave Munich Thursday morning. Yesterday I phoned Perugini and asked him to tell Dr. Sonnenschein to write me a special-delivery letter right away. As soon as I know your reply I will write to Perugini to send me the Baedekers to Freiburg in order to have a guidebook of the city. Today I went to the Stadt Gallery and for a good while I admired Segantini, Hans Thoma, Marée, Liebermann and others.[2] Tomorrow I shall visit the Deutsches Museum and perhaps also the Schloss Residence.

A thousand best wishes and kisses to everybody and a great big kiss to you.

Pier Giorgio

[1] A set of guidebooks Pier Giorgio wanted to use while touring.
[2] Pier Giorgio loved art and collected reproductions of famous paintings.

To Gian Maria Bertini

Munich, September 21, 1921

Dearest Gian Maria,

Thank you for your kind letter, and thank you also for what you have done for my Dante research. Here in Munich I saw again two very dear Germans whom I had met in Rome, Mr. D. Lueble and Mr. Dück. The family of Dr. Dück has been very kind to me. Last night I went with Mr. Dück and his sister, a nice young lady dark skinned and very Italian looking, to the Festwiese, a feast which takes place every year at the end of September and lasts two weeks and where you can find all amusements like merry-go-rounds, rollercoasters, etc.

Today from 10 to 12 I went to see the Deutsches Museum, a technical museum where you can find every machine, invented by human progress. One should stay in Munich at least a year and every day visit a small part of it in order to have some idea of every apparatus and to be able to obtain practical along with theoretical knowledge of the multiple problems of mechanics, physics, chemistry, geology, thermal mining machines, etc.

I am very sorry that your sister ended up with such a low ranking, but because of the great distance that separates Munich from Turin, I cannot personally speak to Prof. Staffetti. Reassure your sister that I shall write to Theologian Borla and in the meantime to console her I shall send her many postcards from the cities that I shall be visiting.

For the newspaper *Piave* give Bonini 70 lire on my behalf because here I don't have any Italian lire to send.

Thank you for all the information about the Club at the Crocetta.[1]

Best wishes to Ostraccione and all of my friends. To you a handshake.

Pier Giorgio

I was very upset after reading the interview given by Vuillermin,[2] because he did not describe the facts accurately, and mentioned only two or three people while everybody had acted in the same way.

[1] He is referring to the Milites Mariae club, of the Italian Catholic Youth, founded thanks to Pier Giorgio's insistence at his parish church in Turin.

[2] The lawyer Renato Vuillermin had given an interview about what happened in Rome during the 1921 convention of the Catholic Youth and the famous attack by the police and the Royal Guard against the marching youth. Pier Giorgio had been arrested while defending the banner of his club Cesare Balbo. Vuillermin in his interview mentioned mainly the bravery of Pier Giorgio, although many others were involved and Pier Giorgio wanted to share the credit.

To His Father

Stuttgart, September 23, 1921

Dearest,

I visited the city, which is not too interesting from the artistic side, but the surroundings should be very beautiful, all woods of beech, birch, chestnut, etc.

Now I am in here in the station waiting for the direct train from Stuttgart to Karlsruhe. Tomorrow evening I will be in Freiburg and then I will write you the address of my boarding house.

In Munich I enjoyed myself very much because I found the family of a friend of mine, whom I met in Rome, who took me twice to the Festwiese and once to the Isertal and then I spent several pleasant evenings with them.

Many greetings to you and to mama from that family.

Greetings and kisses to mama, aunt, grandmother, Luciana; greetings to Sister, Maria, Dora, Marta and to everyone and to you a big kiss from

Pier Giorgio

To Antonio Villani

Stuttgart, September 23, 1921

Have you received my special delivery letter from Civitavecchia? Have you gotten back my photographs? What have you done with my machine to sharpen razors?

In a few minutes I will be leaving for Karlsruhe and tomorrow I will be in Freiburg.

Cordial greetings.

P.G.

Write me in Freiburg general delivery.[1]

Regards to your parents, greetings to your sister.

[1] General delivery was a service more common in Pier Giorgio's day where the post office would hold mail at the main office until the recipient came to get it. This was a common method of delivery for people who were visiting a particular location and had no way of having mail delivered directly to where they were staying.

To His Mother

Freiburg im Breisgau, September 29, 1921

Dearest,

Thank you for your letter of the 27th. Today I also received the Baedeker, which however I have no use for, because, as I have already written to you, I bought another one so as to be able to visit Stuttgart and Karlsruhe well.

Up to now I do not know many people and have no companions, but perhaps on Friday I will leave this boarding house, where however I have been comfortable, to live with a German family, in which there is a young man my age. On Sunday along with a Dutchman I met in Berlin, I'll go to see a university professor, a friend of Dr. Sonnenschein.

Tomorrow I intend, if one can make the trip in one day, to go to Kostanz, to visit the city and then to take a riverboat from Kostanz to Lindau and in the evening return by train.

On the trip, the back glass of my alarm clock broke and the hands all fell out; I brought it to a watch repair shop and I hope to have it by Friday.

Yesterday I visited Colombischloss thinking I would find there paintings by Hans Thoma and Franz Stuck, like the Baedeker said, but instead aside from some drawings by Tiepolo and Canaletto there was nothing of great interest.

As for the Church, in the same house there is a small chapel and then a short distance from here there is a beautiful church.

The Cathedral is very, very beautiful. As a confessor I found a friend of Dr. Sonnenschein who speaks Italian well.

A thousand kisses to grandmother, to papa, aunt, Luciana, and to you a big kiss and an affectionate embrace from

Pier Giorgio

Thank Luciana for her postcard sent to me from Turin. Your letters arrive in two days.
You haven't yet received my letter of the 24th and of the 27th?

Freiburg im Breisgau, October 1, 1921

Dearest,

Today I moved from the house on Clara Street. I came to stay with the family,[1] which Dr. Sonnenschein through Dr. Vogenblach found for me.

The price of room and board is 2500 marks for the whole month of October; included in it is a daily lesson from the professor plus an hour of conversation with his son.

The family is numerous: there are father and mother, a young girl, a young man as well as 2 little boys and a little girl in addition to 2 sons who are away.

I would recommend that you tell Luciana to certainly visit the universities of Vienna and Prague which are the most ancient in central Europe and then comes the University of Heidelberg.

Surely at the nuns one would pay much less, but I had few occasions to speak, only at lunch during the day. I was always alone; I studied a lot and also took classes.

Yesterday evening I had a pleasing visit from a Dutchman I met in Berlin and together with another German industrialist and with a doctor of letters we had a sort of conference against militarism and the Jews; I did not understand much, but I thought of you who harbors these same ideas.

The room is very beautiful. Tomorrow I will go to Mass and after lunch maybe take a walk in the Black Forest.

Pier Giorgio

[1] This was the Rahner family. Two of the sons later became Jesuit priests; one of them was the well known theologian Fr. Karl Rahner.

To His Grandmother Linda Ametis

Freiburg im Breisgau, October 4, 1921

Dearest,

I have been at the new house for a few days, where it is very comfortable and from my window you can enjoy a splendid view of the Black Forest.

I am sending you a postcard of the Cathedral, because this is one of the most beautiful churches that I have seen here in Germany.

Thanks to papa, Luciana, aunt and Mama for the letter. I picked it up via general delivery.

A thousand great kisses to you and to all.

P. Giorgio

To His Aunt Elena Ametis

Freiburg im Breisgau, October 5, 1921

Dearest,

Since lunchtime is approaching I will take advantage of these free moments to write you.

The other night I was invited to go with my Dutch friend whom I met in Berlin, and with whom I had visited the homes of many poor people in Berlin. We spent 2 or 3 hours together and discussed the Catholic movement managing to understand each other.

Yesterday he left for Vienna passing through Constance and then through Munich in order to get a visa in his passport at the Italian Consulate, since he might have the intention of making an excursion to Italy to Venice; I wrote him a note of recommendation for Tornielli.

By the way if in Vienna you need something I know a student, rather, he should already have graduated, whose name is Domanig and who lives at Bäckerstrasse 9, Vienna I.

I would like to take a trip on the Rhine to Cologne next week; write me something, when more or less papa will be in Berlin, so that the unfortunate incident doesn't occur that papa comes to see me and I am in Cologne. I would stay about five days visiting Mannheim, Heidelberg, Koblenz, Frankfurt am Main, Bonn, Cologne, Düsseldorf and then on the return, Baden-Baden.

Today after lunch just after eating I am going to visit a professor at the University who knows Dr. Sonnenschein.

Thank Luciana for her letter and tell her that if she sees my friends to greet them all, but at this time I have nothing special to tell them. Also thank papa for his letter but tell him to excuse me if I don't respond to him, because I only write to one person at the house in Pollone, but the letter is for everyone.

Give a big kiss to Grandmother to you and to mama and papa and to Luciana thousands and thousands affectionate kisses from
Pier Giorgio

To His Mother

Freiburg im Breisgau, October 6, 1921

Dearest,

Today I took a nice walk in Schlossberg with Dr. Eiffler, a nice priest who is a friend of Dr. Sonnenschein. On the 20th of October, the family that I live with will celebrate their silver wedding anniversary; should I give them a little gift? If you think so write and tell me what I should buy. On the 21st I intend to leave for Cologne.

Write me something.
Greetings and kisses to everyone; to you an affectionate embrace.

P.G.

Freiburg im Breisgau, October 7, 1921

Dearest,

You can't imagine with how much joy I read your letter today, and more so because I found in it a photograph of my dear mama, which although is not a great picture is still a remembrance; so I'll have you closer and every night I will be able to see you through it.

By the way I have already written you a lot about the boarding house; Dr. Vogenblack found it for me with a family, where I have already been living for two weeks.

The price was 2500 marks for a month including a lesson each day; in Germany it is usual to pay in advance and when I moved from Klarastrasse to Zähringerstrasse I paid my room and board. I had already told Dr. Vogenblack my plan to take a trip on the Rhine near the middle of this month, so that he'd tell the landlord. I have been treated well here; Sunday I took a nice walk and this coming Sunday we are planning a trip to the Black Forest to the Titisee: we'll be gone the whole day.

As I wrote to you, on October 20th they are celebrating their silver wedding anniversary here; I need to give a small gift; if you think so, please write to me what I should buy.

For the Polytechnic there is nothing else to pay but the admission fee for the 3rd year of industrial mechanical engineering (find out at the secretary's office how much it is for returning students.)

The coat is not necessary, because it is almost summer here: 73 degrees in the shade. It's cool in the early mornings, but later in the day it is very hot.

Greetings and kisses to grandmother, my best wishes to the pastor, to you a big and affectionate embrace.

P.G.

Greetings to Giulio, Tonino, Camillo, Anna, Mario, Alda and to all.

To Pilade De Nicola

Freiburg im Breisgau, October 8, 1921

Dearest friend,

I left Ravenna without greeting you because I had many things to do.

I now find myself with the family of a professor. I'll be here until the end of the month. Please send me 2 or three photographs of the group of foreign countries and also let me know how much I owe. If you can send me that famous map please write me at: Professor Rahner, Zähringerstrasse 50.

To His Mother

Freiburg im Breisgau, October 10, 1921

Dearest,

Yesterday I took a beautiful walk in the Black Forest. I left with Miss Anna and Georg Rahner at 9 from Freiburg; we took the train to Waldkirche and then still in the midst of the trees I went up to Kantel (1200 m.)

The day was marvelous, not too hot, not too cold, the trees are mostly firs or pines, but from time to time you find enormous expanses of beech or of birch. At Kantel I drank a good liter of the exquisite German drink and then went down to Saint Peter, where there's a seminary for priests and from where I sent a postcard. Here I drank a characteristic German coffee and then again on foot to Kirchgard, from where a little train took me home.

Now, dear mama, I'll tell you what I am eating and how many times. I have breakfast at 7 in the morning; bread, coffee, milk, butter and marmalade, then at 10 bread and salami or something; at one we eat and there's always a soup, a plate of meat, vegetables and the usual potatoes and then almost always some dessert. At four in the afternoon coffee the same as at midday.

So, you see, dear mama, that I am very well; and the family is very nice.

Behind Freiburg there's the Schlossberg, which is part of the Black Forest, where there is now a diversity of colors between the green of the meadows, the green of the pines, the red of the pear trees, the yellow of the acacia and the reddish violet of the beech, which deserves to be seen.

Then in the gardens of Freiburg there are still beautiful flowers and between the houses there are placed bits of garden, where they grow beautiful vegetables.

Then a Cathedral half Gothic and half Renaissance, marvelous. And the Cathedral square: completely surrounded by little old houses, where on Saturdays there is a marvelous market.

Now Mama I'd like to buy a pipe for indoor smoking, the so-called student's pipe: it is a meter long and you smoke it comfortably when you study: it costs 15 Italian lire.

Greet Bertino and tell him that one of these days I'll write him a postcard.

Kisses to grandmother, to papa, Luciana, aunt.

Thank Luciana for the letter that I received just now along with yours.

To you a thousand affectionate kisses.

Pier Giorgio

To Maria Fischer

Freiburg im B., October 11, 1921

Dear Miss Fischer,

I read your letter today with great joy: joy augmented by the fact of learning that you wish to learn the beautiful Italian language. This will be extremely useful for the Christian International (Movement)[1] which started in Freiburg, Switzerland, and grew stronger in Rome and that, God-willing, we will bring to its completion.

But there are many bad people in the world and unfortunately also many who are Christian only in name, but not in spirit, so I believe that we must still wait a long time for true peace. However, our Faith teaches us that we should always keep the hope that we will enjoy it one day.

My friend Kaag has just left for Vienna and I have given him Mr. Domanig's address and yours. I am sorry that Mr. Domanig is not in Vienna. You'll see that my friend will drop by and may take up some of your time.

Freiburg is beautiful. On Sunday I went for a long walk with the daughter and the son of Prof. Rahner. We went up the Kantel through the lovely Black Forest and we reached St. Peter.

Miss Schwan is always talking about Rome and cherishes some fine memories of the eternal city.

You too enjoyed Rome, but when you returned to Vienna did you not perhaps tell your parents that you didn't like St. Peter's Square?

Forgive me for reminding you of this which already annoyed you in Rome, but I beg you, dear lady, not to hold it against me.[2] It was a real pity that in Munich I didn't have, then and there, Miss Martone's address, and so lost the occasion of attending the Fucini meeting.

I will be leaving for Vienna in November.

Warmest greetings and Pax tecum.[3] Yours

Pier Giorgio Frassati

[1] Pier Giorgio is referring to the International Union of Catholic students Pax Romana which began in Freiburg in July 1921 with the aim of combining all the energies of Catholic students to promote peace among the various nations by putting their intelligence to the service of God.

[2] Miss Fischer did not like St. Peter's Square. Pier Giorgio, even if just jokingly, never forgave her for it.

[3] This was the official Latin greeting of the members of Pax Romana meaning "peace be with you."

To Alberto Falchetti

Freiburg im Breisgau, October 14, 1921

Dear Berti,

Unfortunately just a few days ago the fine weather came to an end; and as I write to you the rain has set in.

After my stay in Munich, where I had lots of fun and where I met the charming family of a friend of mine, I spent a couple of hours in Stuttgart and Karlsruhe. But in these two cities there is not much to see in terms of the artistic, except for a Hans Thoma room, with some fine paintings, which would certainly have been of great interest to you.

It's already about three weeks since I arrived in Freiburg, but studying so hard makes the time fly which, on the other hand, seems eternal due to the separation from my loved ones.

The other day I was really pleased because I received a telegram from my dear father in which he told me to telephone him. I tried but unfortunately I could understand almost nothing he said.

Our lady travellers[1] are already in Vienna where they will stay perhaps 4 or 5 days then after a brief visit to Prague they will go on to Berlin.

There are no museums here, but there is a magnificent Cathedral: in Gothic and Romanesque styles; perhaps, together with the one in Nuremberg, it is one of the finest that I have seen in Germany.

At the end of this month I am going to make a trip on the beautiful Rhine stopping at Heidelberg, Mannheim, Frankfurt am Main, Mainz, Koblenz, Bonn, Cologne, Hamborn and then through Westphalia and Thuringia I will go on to Berlin.

I am glad your Rhapsodist in Africa is going well and I wish for you that it will proceed more rapidly.

Yesterday I went to a lecture on Dante, the prof. spoke very well, then a German read Count Ugolino, Sordello and St. Bernard's prayer[2] in German, but it was no longer Dante's lovely harmonious, musical poetry. Dante can't be translated, no translation can render the same effect as hearing the Divine Comedy in our own beautiful language.[3]

I am reading a very interesting book "The Kaiser in Exile," written by a Dutch countess. When I am back in Turin, I'll let you read the translation.

A thousand kisses from

Pier Giorgio

[1] He is referring to his Aunt Elena and Luciana.
[2] Pier Giorgio had copied out by hand this prayer "Virgin Mother, your Son's Daughter..." and pinned it up on his cabinet in his study where it could be easily seen.
[3] These observations of Pier Giorgio reveal a perceptive, thorough knowledge of Dante. Count Ugolino: *Inferno*, Canto 33; Sordello: *Purgatorio*, Canto 6; St. Bernard's prayer: *Paradiso*, Canto 33.

To His Mother

Freiburg im Breisgau, October 14, 1921

Dearest,

I received a postcard from Vienna from Luciana; I have already

written to Aunt Elena via general delivery in Prague.
  Tomorrow I am going with Prof. Rahner to hear a tribute to Dante. As a gift, I bought a fairly nice terracotta vase (60 marks) and I will also buy some flowers. Greetings and kisses to grandmother and to you a thousand from

P.G.

Freiburg im Breisgau, October 16, 1921

Dearest,
  Today I went for a very pleasant walk in the Black Forest, then I went on to a village above Gunstertal.
  This morning coming back from church[1] I was really hoping to receive a letter from my dear mother, who is so far away.
  The other evening an Italian student was here and I had a lively argument with him as he belongs to the Fascist party.[2]
  Today there was a silver wedding anniversary party: my gift was a terracotta vase filled with roses and a cyclamen plant; their children gave them a pretty copy of the Madonna by Luca della Robbia; others gave them plants or roses. The youngest of the children, who is 7, recited a short but very sweet poem.
  I received a postcard from Vienna in which Luciana tells me she has been with Mrs. Axerio's brother and her nephew Tonino II at a variety show and that she was leaving Vienna on Saturday morning for Prague.
  I was just finishing this letter when your own much appreciated letter arrived; you cannot imagine with what joy I read it. I get a lot of letters here from my German friends but those don't give me the immense pleasure as when I see from a distance Italian stamps and the handwriting of my dear mother, or the Italian coat-of-arms or my sister's writing or my aunt's.
  I still haven't done a thing about my trip on the Rhine, but as soon as I know something I will write out my itinerary so that you from far away can follow me on the map as, sadly, you're not with me to point out the essential things, you who already know the lovely German Rhine.
  Give my regards to Mrs. Alda and to Paola and tell them that I wrote a letter to Lalla in German and I'd like to know if it reached its destination.

Here the flowers are beautiful too; on Saturday mornings in the Cathedral square there is a big market to which all the local country people flock, bringing all kinds of God's gifts.

Greet grandmother in a special way and kiss her for me and to you an enormous and tight hug and thousands, thousands, thousands of kisses from

Pier Giorgio

[1] Even while abroad, Pier Giorgio never lost his habit of going to church every day.

[2] A firm anti-Fascist, he continued, even after Mussolini came into power, his unceasing, exhaustive (often highly animated) battle against the movement.

To His Father

Freiburg im Breisgau, October 17, 1921

Dear Papa,[1]

I have just come back from a walk. Together with Dr. Eiffler I went as far as Schönberg and from the top had a splendid view of the Rhine plateau and the Vosges Mountains and the marvellous Black Forest. My Mother writes that she has had no news from you. Luciana and Aunt are now in Prague.

Lots of kisses.

Pier Giorgio

[1] This letter was written in German.

To His Mother

Freiburg im Breisgau, October 20, 1921

Dearest mama,

Thank you for remembering me in Oropa, from beautiful Oropa so loved by everyone from Biella and especially by every Catholic.

Last night I had dinner with a German and I met two very nice Japanese people. We bombarded them with questions to learn how one lives in Japan right now. It's the same everywhere: there too there's a crisis, high cost of living, irreligiousness, however socialism is not as widespread as it is in Europe. On Monday I went for a wonderful walk with Dr. Eiffler as far as Schönberg, a hill not far from Freiburg, from where you enjoy a magnificent view of the Rhine plateau and the Black Forest.

Wednesday Prof. Rahner and his wife left for the Danube Valley celebrating their silver wedding anniversary with a trip; I am now having lessons with their eldest son.

I received postcards from aunt from Prague and Dresden and now I am expecting a long letter in which she will tell me all that she has seen.

Please thank Alda, regards to Bistolfi and Berti.

Perhaps on Sunday I will go for my last long walk in the Black Forest, because on Wednesday or Thursday at the latest, I will bid farewell to fair Freiburg.

I always look forward to your letters because when I receive them I feel as if I almost have my dear mother with me.

Special greetings to Father Pietro,[1] I will write to him soon.

Greetings and kisses to grandmother, regards to everyone and to you a tight hug and thousands of big kisses from

Pier Giorgio

[1] Unfortunately, most of the letters written by Pier Giorgio to priests were never recovered.

To Gian Maria Bertini

Freiburg im Breisgau, October 23, 1921

Dearest friend,

Forgive me for not having written, but since I have been in Freiburg I have been concentrating on my German and haven't had time to write to my friends.

The weather has always been fine, but now unfortunately it is raining so I haven't been able to go for a final walk in the Black Forest. The other week I went with Dr. Eiffler, a really nice priest, to Schönberg, a mountain not far from the city. It was a summer day; from the top we admired the lovely German plateau as far as the borders of our dear unfortunately French friends.[1]

I am very sorry that the P.P.I.[2] is only out for votes and as a result people are abandoning it, let's hope that at the next Congress they will make some concrete decisions because Italy expects a lot from this party.

I read the agenda³ and I thought it a big mistake to have left out agriculture by means of which Italy will eventually be rebuilt.

I am pleased that you have launched the fundraiser for our banner, ripped up on the orders of the Freemason government.⁴ Around November 15th I will be in Turin and I will bring you lots of postcards for your sister.

After dinner today I am going to the theater to see Mignon; Wednesday I leave fair Freiburg and go to Bonn where I will have the pleasure of once again seeing Miss Schwan, one of the German girls I met in Ravenna.

Regards to your parents, greetings to your sister and to you a handshake from

Pier Giorgio

If you reply right away write to me via general delivery at Koblenz. Otherwise, later via general delivery at Cologne.

N.B. This year the Club needs an energetic president with left-wing tendencies; certainly not Severi, because the "Cesare Balbo" Club would turn into a women's club. The ideal would be Villani, but Villani doesn't want to do it. Let us hope in God we're able to find a President who will carry the "Cesare Balbo" banner alongside the workers and the peasants in the struggle for the Faith, always keeping in mind the maxim that appeared to Constantine "In hoc Signo Vinces";⁵ with this conviction at heart, he wouldn't falter in leading the club into the bloodiest battle.⁶

---

¹ The reputation of the French for corruption and the effective moral degeneration into which France rushed at the end of World War I, the indignation about the treatment given to Italy during the peace of Versailles, and the haughty airs of the French officials who strutted around the streets of Berlin, had sorrowfully struck at Pier Giorgio's spirit.

² Italian People's Party.

³ The politics regarding the agendas established by the Italian People's Party at that time had begun to worry him.

⁴ The banner suffered damage in Rome that year, during a meeting of the Catholic Youth with 50,000 participants. As the young people were moving in procession towards the tomb of the Unknown Soldier, they were assaulted and charged by the Royal Guards. Blows, insults, arrests and torn banners were the distressing outcome of that encounter. During the clash, Pier Giorgio distinguished himself by his tenacious defence of his club's banner and afterwards, by his consistently brave, dignified behavior during his arrest.

⁵ A Latin expression meaning, "In this sign you will conquer." According to legend,

Constantine I had a vision of a sign in the sky while marching into battle and adopted this phrase as his motto.

6 When it came to matters of the club, Pier Giorgio became quite someone else. Even his own friends came in for severe criticism. Over and above everything and everyone, he placed the interests of the youth organizations destined to stand for, as he hoped and believed, the ideal of a Christian social life.

To His Mother

Freiburg, October 25, 1921

Dear mama,

I want to send you my love once more before I leave. This evening I go directly to Heidelberg and tomorrow afternoon I will already be in Mainz.

On Thursday at 10 I leave Mainz by boat to get to Koblenz where unfortunately I have to stay over for a day, because the French allow only one boat at a time to sail.

I will reach Bonn on Friday evening and then Sunday or Monday evening I will be in Berlin.

Luciana wrote to me that in Berlin on November 4th there is a huge commemoration of the Unknown Soldier.[1] I don't understand whether it is a celebration of the Allied countries which is impossible or a German celebration, because all the ambassadors including papa are taking part wearing uniform. I hope to receive a postcard from Luciana with some explanation.

I am taking my black suit, my blue suit and I will wear the tan one; plus lots of shirts and underwear.

I can't say yet when I will be back in Turin as it will depend on my stay in Berlin.

I am enclosing my photograph so that the distance between us will be lessened just a little.[2]

Greetings and kisses to grandmother, regards to Father Pietro and everyone and to you thousands and thousands of kisses from

Pier Giorgio

---

[1] Pier Giorgio is referring to a commemoration of the Allied victory of World War I in the Catholic Church of Unter der Linden. The baritone Mattia Battistini sang the Mass, which was attended by all the diplomatic and military authorities of the Allied countries.

[2] His inscription on the picture was, "To my dear Mother far away, with immense affection."

To His Father

Heidelberg, October 26, 1921

Dear Papa,[1]
   I have already visited a fine castle. This afternoon I will visit the churches of St. Peter and of the Holy Spirit then I will leave for Frankfurt am Main.
   Lots of love from the city where you once lived[2] from
                                                                    Pier Giorgio

[1] This letter was written in German.
[2] Alfredo Frassati took a post-graduate course at Heidelberg University.

To Alberto Falchetti

Frankfurt am Main, October 27, 1921

Dearest friend,
   I have just returned from the Museum where I saw lots of fine paintings among the modern ones 2 very beautiful Segantini. I am sending you a Velasquez to give you some good ideas for your Rhapsodist.
   A thousand greetings and kisses from
                                                                    P.G.

To His Mother

Bonn am Rhein, October 28, 1921

Dearest,
   I left Freiburg Tuesday evening with enormous regret as I spent many happy days there, especially together with the kind Rahner family.
   Wednesday at eight in the morning in Heidelberg I went for a really good walk along the Philosopher's Walk, then I had breakfast at a famous café, the students' café of the Veranschlagen Fechter. In the afternoon I left for Frankfurt am Main where I spent the night. That same evening I went to the theatre to see an operetta, in order to visit the theatre which is built in Italian Renaissance style.
   The next morning I had a good look around Frankfurt then at around 2 in the afternoon I left for Bonn.

I couldn't do the Mainz–Bonn stretch by boat, partly because of the season and partly because of those French, there is no longer any such service.

Last night as soon as I arrived I saw Miss Schwan who had very kindly found me a room in a good hotel. Today I went with her to Holy Mass at the Cathedral; I am now having breakfast, as soon as I have finished, I will visit the city a little with Miss Schwan.

At Mainz and at Koblenz I didn't have time to pick up my mail. Write me and tell me whether you had written anything and I will have it collected. Write to me via general delivery in Cologne. Greetings to everyone and to you and grandmother thousands and thousands of kisses from

Pier Giorgio

Bonn am Rhein, October 29, 1921

Dearest,

I arrived here in this fair city Thursday evening: I have never been on my own here because I have been seeing once again Miss Schwan, whom I met in Rome, and who has been very kind in giving up a lot of her precious time to show me Bonn's main sights.

This morning I visited the wonderful physics institute where she studies and is preparing to graduate in June.

After lunch I went to Cologne where I visited the art museum and then the magnificent Cathedral.

Tomorrow morning with Miss Schwan I'll see some more of Cologne then I leave for Düsseldorf where I have to visit a Catholic Student Association.

Tomorrow I'll get some advice about my return trip. I'll definitely be in Berlin Monday evening.

I must leave you now as I'm very sleepy. Tomorrow the 30th I have offered a Mass for the dead for Aunt Emilia and for great-grandmother.[1]

A thousand kisses to Grandmother and to you a tight, tight hug and a thousand kisses from

Pier Giorgio

---

[1] His aunt Emilia Ametis died before Pier Giorgio was born. His great-grandmother Angela Clavacci Copello died when he was four years old. Even though he did not know them during his lifetime, Pier Giorgio remembered the dates of their death.

Altenbeck, October 31, 1921

Dearest,

I send you my last greeting before arriving in Berlin. This morning I visited Cassel's marvelous art gallery and I was very glad I went because, apart from everything else, there was a whole room of Rembrandt. I telegraphed papa.

Greetings and kisses from

P.G.

Berlin, November 1, 1921

Dearest,

The other day I arrived in Berlin and with great pleasure immediately found your letter. I was in Mainz for just a few hours and I stopped there only to see the Cathedral and to pick up your letter, but then I forgot to pass by the post office before leaving. However as soon as I reached Bonn, I asked Miss Schwan to write 2 postcards, one to the head of the post office in Mainz and one to the head in Koblenz to have my mail forwarded to Berlin.

Today I received your postcard sent on from Mainz.

I enjoyed the Cassel art gallery very much; what a pity you weren't there because you'd have been delighted by it and would have spent many happy hours admiring the Rembrandts, the Rubens and other great works.

I have already seen Dr. Sonnenschein and Miss Kohlstedt again and tomorrow I'm going to see my friend Lietgebel.

I received a letter from the Rahners in which they ask me to thank you for your thoughtful card.

Tomorrow I'm going to look for a Zeiss stereoscopic camera for a friend of mine, but I think it will be difficult to find one, because these expensive devices are immediately sold abroad.

This morning we went to the cemetery to take flowers to the graves of the soldiers who died in the war in Berlin.

It is a splendid day and I'm going horseback riding with Luciana.

Greetings and kisses to grandmother and to you thousands and thousands of kisses from

Pier Giorgio

Berlin, November 7, 1921

Dearest,

Last night aunt left for Munich and while taking her to the station I thought how in a few day's time I too will be taking the train back.

It's a pity the weather is so awful, it is going to be very tedious visiting the city in the rain, but nevermind: I have to go because I have to see a student I met in Rome who needs to speak to me.

I have lots to do here looking up all my friends and this evening I am going to a lecture at the university: on Sunday together with Dr. Sonnenschein's group we will go for an outing to Spandau. Today I have to buy two or three precision instruments for doing drawings and making calculations.

After lunch on Monday unless I change my plans I am leaving for Prague where I will stay 2 days and then I will continue on to Vienna.

Now I must leave you; greetings to grandmother and to you thousands and thousands of affectionate kisses from

Pier Giorgio

Tetschen, November 16, 1921

With tremendous regret I left papa, aunt, Luciana and all my Berlin friends, but on the other hand I left willingly because in a week's time I will be seeing you again after so long.

Greetings to everyone to you and to grandmother a thousand kisses.

P.G.

Prague, November 16, 1921

Dearest mama,

I arrived today at four and at the station I found the priest[1] I met in Rome. Acting on my telegram he had booked a room for me in a Catholic students' residence. This evening I went to dinner with him and then he kindly invited me to the theatre to see a national opera: "Dve Vdorg" or rather the Two Widows. Early tomorrow morning I will go and see the main churches then the museum and around noon I will call on the Apostolic Nuncio.[2] At four I have to be at the station to meet Anselmi's brother with whom I will be making the trip from Prague to Vienna.

I sent you a postcard from Tetschen but I don't know whether you will get it as I didn't post it myself.

Greetings to everyone a thousand kisses to grandmother to you a tight, tight hug from

Pier Giorgio

[1] Father Nicola Levy.
[2] Clemente Micara, a priest from Rome who was appointed the Apostolic Nuncio to Czechoslovakia on May 7, 1920. In 1946, he was elevated to Cardinal. He died in 1965.

TO LUCIANA

Prague, November 16, 1921

Dearest,

I liked Prague very much more so because my friends were all so very kind to me. Last night I had dinner with Father Levy at the Catholic restaurant and then he invited me to the theatre to hear The Two Widows which was very well performed. Today Father Nicola Levy had to leave for his home town because he received the sad news that his mother is very ill.

This morning together with the president of Catholic students in Czechoslovakia I went to see Prague's major churches and then all the rest. After lunch I went to the station in vain to wait for Anselmi's brother, then later on I went to call on the Apostolic Nuncio. He is a very amiable Archbishop, a very simple man; he immediately offered me a cigarette[1] then we had a little discussion together. He kindly had the courtesy to accompany me to the front door.

Tomorrow I leave Prague and I will be in Vienna by three in the afternoon.

Greetings to everyone and kisses from

Pier Giorgio

Please don't forget to keep the stamp for Miss Kohlstedt to whom I've already promised it.

[1] As a teenager, Pier Giorgio picked up the habit of smoking inexpensive, small, black, Tuscan cigars from his mother who was fond of smoking them. Pier Giorgio joked that he was "weaned while my mother smoked Toscani."

To His Aunt Elena Ametis

Vienna, November 17, 1921

Dearest,

As soon as I got to Vienna at the station I found Miss Fischer, one of the people I met in Rome. She had kindly booked me a room at the Continental Hotel. Later on she and I went for a stroll around Vienna. The city is very beautiful and I liked St. Stephen's Cathedral immensely.

Greetings to all of you and kisses from

P.G.

As Anselmi's brother hasn't left, write via general delivery.

To Luciana

Vienna, November 19, 1921

Dearest,

With each day that passes I am more enthusiastic about Vienna. Today I went to see the modern art gallery; there wasn't much of interest except for a fine Segantini, a Bocklin and a Monet.

Tomorrow I've been invited by Miss Fischer to a party given by the Catholic women students. Last night I went to the opera which I enjoyed very much: I saw Don Giovanni; I was expecting to find a very elegant theater, instead one saw only a few men in black jackets and one or 2 in evening dress, otherwise everyone was in their working clothes even those in the private boxes.

I saw at a watchmaker's an Omega watch at K.[1] 21000 which is the equivalent of 80 lire, I think it is silver, it seems to me worth buying; also a pair of mountain boots at 23000 K and another at 11000 K. Write and tell me if I should buy the watch and the studded mountain boots for 11000 K = 50 lire; they're a gift and so is the Omega watch, if it is silver it is really very inexpensive.

Greetings and kisses to you all from

Pier Giorgio

P.S. Yesterday strolling around the streets of Vienna I ran into Caputo, who is the "La Stampa" correspondent and then Anselmi's brother, who had missed the train and that was why he had left me waiting in vain in Prague. Tell papa I won't be writing to him for the moment, because I have so little time, but writing to one of you I write to you all.

Greetings to all the staff.

[1] K is the abbreviation for Krone (crown), the currency in Austria.

To His Mother

Vienna, November 21, 1921

Dearest mama,

Last night I spent a really pleasant evening at a party at a boarding house for Catholic female students of Vienna.

Right now I am in a café having breakfast. Later on I am going to the Gallery of Ancient Art and then this evening to a Catholic students' Academy.

Greetings to everyone to you and to Grandmother a thousand loving kisses. Thursday I leave Vienna.

P.G.

November 23, 1921

Dearest,

I am writing to you on the train because I am on my way to Venice. You cannot imagine with what joy I left Vienna thinking that within four days I will see you again; but on the other hand I left this city with deep regret, because I had to part from dear friends who showered me with kindness. Write to me via general delivery in Venice. Greetings to you all to you and to grandmother a thousand kisses from

P.G.

To Maria Fischer

Venice, November 23, 1921

Dear Miss Fischer,

I have arrived in Venice after a fairly good journey. At Tarvisio we were halted for two hours by the customs who were very severe, and so I was able to admire the beautiful mountains. Venice is magnificent and even after having visited many other cities I think there is not another Venice in all the world, even if the Queen of the Sea has a lot of faults, such as, for example, the narrow streets and the bad smell that the stagnant water gives off. I have no words to describe this city. I hope to return soon and I also hope to visit it with you. I think you will like St. Mark's Square better than St. Peter's Square.

Today with the president of our group we sent a telegram for the commemoration of Dante. We signed with the name of Spataro, since we are very sure that he would be very happy about our idea.

Tomorrow I will leave Venice and immediately afterward I will renew my studies. My regards to your parents and cordial greetings to you.

Your

Pier Giorgio Frassati

To His Grandmother Giuseppina Frassati

Venice, November 25, 1921

Dearest grandmother,

Forgive my long silence. Yesterday I reached Venice. I who have seen so many beautiful cities in Austria and Germany have not seen any as beautiful as the queen of the sea.

Greetings and kisses from

P.G.

To His Father

Turin, December 13, 1921

Dearest papa,

Certainly I remember that my dear papa is in Berlin, but I have never had the time to write you; then I was thinking: Mama writes, I will write as soon as she leaves.

I have just returned from the station, where I said goodbye to mother for a few months; I am very sorry that Mama is going to Berlin, all the more so now that she is very tired and therefore not in the best condition to lead the active life she will have to lead in Berlin.

I have to study a lot because this year is a very difficult one. Tell Luciana that I have given Mama a list of errands for Berlin and that I beg her to do them as soon as possible so that she can give the stuff to aunt when she comes to Turin.

Tonight I have been invited to the Marchisio's to eat hare. When are you coming to Turin? Let's hope it will be soon. Now I shall leave you because I must go to school. Many kisses and greetings to you, to aunt, to Luciana, to Mama when she arrives, greetings to all the others from

Pier Giorgio

To His Mother

Turin, December 17, 1921

Dearest mama,

When I arrived home this evening I remembered that the 20th of this month is your feastday and so I want immediately to send you from afar my best wishes. Dear Mama, not being able on that day to tell you in person, and to kiss your forehead I will take Holy Communion for you praying to God that he give you good health for many, many infinite years and fill you with blessings.[1]

The trunk has arrived and I found everything except my postcards that I left in Berlin and that I would ask aunt to bring to Turin so that I can complete the Album. Find out again if one can buy drawing paper, slide rules, square rules, rulers, pairs of compasses, graph paper, pencils, etc. wholesale and what one must pay to the German and Italian customs. Send me an answer as soon as possible because I must tell the president of the engineering students' association.

Many good wishes from the sister as well as from Maria, to you a thousand good wishes and kisses from

Pier Giorgio

All the best and kisses for papa, aunt and Luciana.

[1] This type of spiritual bouquet was Pier Giorgio's preferred way and doubtless the best way to celebrate a precious anniversary.

To Dr. Max Greslig

Turin, December 20, 1921

Dear Mr. Greslig,
Excuse me for not writing sooner, but it is only today that I got your address.
Miss Danieli has sent you the Ravenna photographs and asked me to inquire whether or not you have received them. How are you? And the work of the Pax Romana? Let us hope that the Pax Romana does not remain only on paper. If all the People of every nation have an inner spirit, the Pax Romana will bring Peace and Justice.
Many cordial Christian greetings for Christmas!
May God bless your work with peace so that in the coming year all the delegates from all over Europe may reunite in your Freiburg in the Christian spirit, and that there may be no more delegates like the Belgians who were present at the feast of peace dressed in military uniforms.
Receive my warmest greetings extendable to the other Swiss just as cordially

Pier Giorgio Frassati

To Maria Fischer

Turin, December 20, 1921

Dear Miss Fischer,
Please forgive me for not having written anymore, but I had a great deal to do and now I find myself in the first days of the Christmas vacation with the prospect of having to work hard since a very difficult exam is waiting for me at the end of January. My friend from Genoa has sent me several photographs sent to him by the German delegate in Ravenna; they are not too nice and they are small, but I give them to you in the hope of being able to send you better ones.
Now I shall keep my promise and send you the recipe for the tagliatelle.
Take 700 gr. of white flour, three quarters of a liter of tepid salted water and one egg. The flour should be placed on a board and a well made at the center in which one puts the water and the egg.

Mix well. The dough should be cut into two sections and rolled out very thin. Allow the sheets of dough to dry out a little, then cut them into long ribbons and boil them for several minutes. Please let me know if the macaroni turns out as well as it did in Ravenna. Thanks for the nice postcard from Salzburg.

I think that the best wish I can send you is: that the new year bring real peace. When I think of the Pax Romana I always fear that it will only remain on paper. But I hope that God may reopen the hard hearts of men who sow hatred and that on my return to Austria I will find the old Vienna again.

Regards and best wishes to your parents and to you many cordial greetings and regards. Your devoted

Pier Giorgio Frassati

To His Mother

Turin, December 21, 1921

Dearest mama,

The days pass but they seem very long to me since you left us. Yesterday a card arrived from Lupo for your feastday – he has already sent the pastries for the poor.

I opened 2 letters of papa's because they weren't personal and I am forwarding them because I think they may be important. Olga has written you best wishes. Tomorrow I go with Alda to Mrs. Rosano. Grandmother is very well today and has been to Berti's. Ask Luciana if she has done the errand for the Galileo Ferraris.

Merry Christmas to all of you. I will be with you in spirit on that day. Many kisses to papa, Luciana, aunt and to you from

Pier Giorgio

To Luciana

Turin, December 23, 1921

Dearest Luciana,

I read in La Stampa how well you organized a lottery for charity that brought in a considerable sum; therefore I am asking you to give some thought to mine that will be for the benefit of the two

Catholic clubs, male and female. They are both penniless and so I trust that you will procure for me some small object in good taste and inexpensive; aunt can bring it down because the charity banquet will be in the first week of February.

Have you done my errands for the Galileo Ferraris? I have begun to study abstract mechanics and am being tutored by a professor whom Giulio recommended to me.

Every morning I make wonderful perfumes in the chemistry laboratory. Too bad that you are in Berlin or I would get the perfumes for you free.

Thank papa for his letter and tell him there was one sentence I couldn't decipher. Thank mama for her good words and tell her that I am present with all of my spirit and on holidays I go to Holy Communion and beg God to shed his blessings upon you all.

Thus I should wish that you too will take Holy Communion on the first of the year and so our souls refreshed by that Grace would be united even if a great distance separates us.[1]

Tell aunt that grandmother is very well and cheerful, later she can read the words grandmother wrote herself.

I am pleased that you are keeping my dear aunt there with you in Berlin to enjoy her for awhile. Later I will spend more time with her than you so aunt will be able to visit the museums and get to know Berlin a bit which she couldn't do before because she always had to be running errands.

Take care that Mama does not tire herself too much, because when she left she was already far from rested.

Maria has received the postcards from Marta; she had to pay the postage on the last one.

Best wishes to all of you so that you may begin the New Year with the blessing of the Lord. Greetings and kisses from

Pier Giorgio

Ida Maja, aunt Marinetta, Rina send you a thousand good wishes. Reviglio, Brinatti and Moccia send you a thousand more good wishes.

[1] According to Luciana, this was the only mild insistence that Pier Giorgio pressed upon her for her "not excessive attachment" to religious practices.

To His Mother

Turin, December 25, 1921

Dearest mama,

Yesterday I went to lunch at the Marchisio's with Berti who has a bit of a cold. Mrs Marchisio gave me the box of chocolates that you so kindly thought to send me for Christmas. You cannot imagine how happy I was not for the chocolates but because that object given in the name of my dear Mama shortened for a moment the long distance that separates us.

Yesterday I went to midnight Mass with my club to the nuns from the Immaculate Conception at Via Ormea 9 and during the Mass I prayed a lot that the Lord fill with blessings those of you who are far away. Believe me Mama that in those moments my spirit communicated intensely with yours.

After the Mass, the mother superior gave us a breakfast of coffee and milk and I offered my companions your chocolates. Then we accompanied Canon Bues to his seminary where the canon offered us a glass of Marsala, after which we returned home.

Now I am at Grandmother Frassati's to study a bit of mechanics and later I will go to Vittorio's and around 5:30 I will be at home to keep grandmother company for awhile.

This evening after dinner I will be going to the Marchisio's who are having a nun to dinner. The commander[1] is also to be present. He wants to get a license to carry a revolver because he is always expecting the tall man and the short man. Best wishes for a good ending and a good beginning and may you start the year with the peace of the Lord.

Give my best wishes to Chiusano and Cosmo and to everyone at the Embassy.

Best wishes and kisses to papa, aunt and Luciana and to you again a thousand kisses and a tight, tight hug from

Pier Giorgio

---

[1] Alberto Falchetti.

To Luciana

Turin, December 29, 1921

Dearest Luciana,

May the last letter of 1921 reach you with my best wishes for the New Year.

I wrote to all of you last night and I also sent a telegram to aunt hoping to persuade her to stay in Berlin a little longer. Certainly I would like to embrace her again as soon as possible, but I would be happier if she spent the end of the year with you, because that way she can be a bit of company for my dear Mama whom she will have to leave for a few months.

Chemistry Prof. Montemartini by way of his assistant, my friend D. Losanna, asked me to inquire in Berlin about the prices of the following books:

1° Zeitschrift für analytische Chemie from 1911 to the end of 1921.

2° Berìchte der deutschen chemische Gesellschaft years 1916-17-18-19-20-21.

Please find out as soon as possible how much they cost and let me know because they are books for my chemistry professor. Before buying the two books send me the price of each annual and I will let you know whether or not to buy it.

Once more a thousand good wishes from us to all of you and to you a big kiss from

Pier Giorgio

Have you received all my letters?

1922

To Luciana

Turin, January 2, 1922

Dearest Luciana,

Thanks for running those errands; I'm glad that you ordered the Nestlers[1] although 9 are a bit too many, but don't worry I'll sell them to my friends. I'm still scared of the huge number of curved lines; are they all for me or are the samples also for G.F. The German books have arrived in Rome and Seitun wrote to me that he sent them to me by insured courier. I saw the Berlin polytechnic school's program and please stop by the secretariat in Charlottenburg to find out if the exams I took here in Turin in the equivalent subjects are acceptable and if it's only necessary to take the exams in the subjects which I haven't studied here in Italy in order to enroll in semester VII (year IV).[2]

Your ideas for my raffle are very good, music, stationery, books, or even some of those little objects of good taste which don't cost a lot in Berlin but make a really good impression; do as you think best because you have enough wisdom to be able to decide; with your good taste and Mama's I'm sure that they'll be very suitable things. I really liked the inkpot for Vittorio.

Yesterday afternoon we were at the Banzattis for lunch. The previous evening we began the year together with the Marchisios and while we were raising our glasses to toast the new year our thoughts flew to those of you who are far away wishing that in another year we'll be able to finish it and start the new one all together.

As I'm writing to you it's 5.30 p.m.; outside the sky is like springtime and it's so bright that I don't need to turn on the electric light.

The eng.(ineer) Druetti has told me to pass on his many greetings to Mama and Papa. Greetings to everyone at the embassy to Perugini and tell Mrs. Perugini that her desserts are very good,

Italo, Marta etc., to you and Mama and Papa a thousand greetings and kisses from
Pier Giorgio

1. A brand of compasses for mechanical drawing.
2. Because his father was the Ambassador to Berlin, Pier Giorgio considered attending the university of Berlin in the following academic year. However, his father resigned his post shortly after Mussolini came to power in October, not wanting to represent the Fascist government. So Pier Giorgio continued his studies in Turin.

Turin, January 8, 1922

Dear Luciana,

I'm giving you another errand which is to get me a subscription to the best German magazine on techniques for mining engineers so that I can learn the technical terms, because Vosmera tells me that as far as the language is concerned I can now very easily attend Berlin's polytechnic school. Greetings and kisses from
Pier Giorgio

Dear papa, when will you be coming to Turin? I'll write to you soon. Many greetings and kisses to you and mama.

TO HIS FATHER

Turin, January 10, 1922

Dearest papa,

It's not that I've forgotten my dear papa who is so far away, but when I write to one of you I am writing to all of you. I'm glad that you will be coming soon and so we'll spend some time together and so for a little it will seem to me that the great distance, which unfortunately separates us, will be diminished. I'm studying a lot in the hope of attending year IV in Berlin, where studies are more practical particularly in the mining branch. Greetings to everybody to you to Mama and to Luciana thousands of kisses and greetings from
Pier Giorgio

To Luciana

Turin, January 17, 1922

Dearest,

I'm not writing long because I always have little available time but my thought often turns to Berlin and I have you in mind very very often. You ought to give a few marks on my behalf to Dr. Sonnenschein for the poor students. And when is papa coming? Has it snowed there? In two or three days I'll be able to go to school on skis. Berti is always working on his painting, in the evening he always goes to the club; he goes home late a lot and then you can find him at home asleep at 10:30 a.m. Write him a sermon.

Greetings and kisses to all of you from

Pier Giorgio

To His Mother and Sister

Turin, January 31, 1922

Dearests,

Thanks for the beautiful gifts for the raffle but I want to know whether the three or four books of music are for the raffle or should they be given to other people? Many people have responded to the appeal and even many businesses including Talmone, Carpano, Martini and Rossi and so I hope to be able to make a lot of money to replenish our club's[1] exhausted finances. If you have some more of those photographs brought by papa of the funeral ceremonies of His Holiness Benedict XV and, especially the ones where students can easily be seen, send them to me.

Many greetings and kisses from

Pier Giorgio

[1] He is referring to the Catholic university club "Cesare Balbo."

To His Mother

Turin, the end of January 1922

Dearest,

I read papa's telegram with great pleasure, within a few days I'll be welcoming my dear papa it's a pity that it won't be possible to embrace you too, be patient these months are passing by, I'll take my exams and then we'll be together a little.

Can you send me the ruler for drawing // and ||[1] because I need it. Thanks for the books I'll become a wise man when I've read all of Goethe.

Regards to everyone thousands of kisses to you and to Luciana from

Pier Giorgio

[1] Parallel and perpendicular lines.

To His Mother

Turin, February 7, 1922

Dearest Mama,

Yesterday I went to Berti's to tell him the happy news of the election of the New Pontiff[1] so I had a good opportunity to criticize a bit.

The painting is nice enough but it has one big defect, it doesn't come up to the frame. The artist's work is inferior to that of the framer (luckily he doesn't have to pass some jury's evaluation otherwise he'd be wide open to certain failure.) I told Bertino that it wasn't right to send a similar inkblot to Venice for an International Exhibition, a painting not even worthy of being shown at any of the many exhibitions of the Promoter or of the Artists' Club.

Bertino wasn't persuaded by anything I said to him and he believes that I am too passionate a critic, but unfortunately this is the truth.

Thanks for your letter which we've been awaiting for a long time and which finally arrived. And I'd like to be a little nuisance to you too and I believe that you would calmly put up with it just to have you nearby and to see you every day, but in this regard one must unfortunately always be doing what one does not want to do, therefore I will be patiently waiting for the time to pass and your return here to Turin.

Greetings and kisses to you and to Luciana from

Pier Giorgio

[1] Cardinal Achille Ratti was elected Pope on February 6, 1922, taking the name Pius XI.

To His Mother and Sister

Turin, February 10, 1922

Dearests,

I hope you received the previous letter where I gave Mama a ruthless critique of Bertino's painting which is unfortunately far inferior to the work of Michetti and Morelli.

Now we are getting the gifts ready for the raffle, Berti gave me 2 of your paintings and we also have some other things; we hope a lot of people will come and that we can finally straighten out the club's finances.

I'll leave you now because I should be going to the Sociale for the usual Friday conference.[1]

Greetings and kisses to all of you from

Pier Giorgio

[1] He was talking about the Social Institute of Turin, the school he formerly attended which was operated by the Jesuit Fathers. It was there that Pier Giorgio attended meetings of the Conference of St. Vincent de Paul to which he belonged. The commitment required meeting one day a week in a given place and then visiting two or three families every week. It was not necessary to pay dues in order to be a member; it was sufficient to have good will and nothing else. A collection was taken up at the end of the meeting for the group's needs, but everyone was free to give whatever he wanted. Pier Giorgio was extremely committed to this work.

Turin, February 21, 1922

Dearests,

On Sunday we had the famous raffle, big posters few people in attendance. But we had enough fun and it was a very happy day and we made 1300 lire.[1]

I had the immense good fortune of winning the gift donated by His Holiness Benedict XV,[2] then my buddies from Cesare Balbo[3] and the girls from Gaetana Agnesi[4] all crowded around me and you couldn't hear anything but "You should pay up, Frassati" and so they cleaned out my wallet which luckily wasn't very full. On Fat Thursday there was the big carnival at the Catholic Student Residence with a party for the incoming students and you ate cakes absolutely for free and other foods and tea with joy.

On Wednesday evening I'll go with my friends to hear Aida in the third balcony[5] and we'll take some food with us, and so goodbye;

lots of big kisses to you to papa and Luciana from

Pier Giorgio

1. In spite of everything, the results of the raffle were respectable, if one considers the value of money at that time. But Pier Giorgio hoped for something more.
2. It was a picture of the "Madonna della Seggiola" in a case with doors that opened. The Pope had sent it to the raffle a few days before his death. Pier Giorgio jealously guarded it his whole life long. When he received his last Communion just before his death, he wanted this picture to be nearby on the improvised altar.
3. The Catholic university club for men.
4. The Catholic university club for women.
5. Senator Frassati was at that time the ambassador to Berlin but he still had a front row seat in the theater in Turin; nevertheless, Pier Giorgio never wanted to be anything other than "one of the guys" among his friends and so he chose to sit in the seats much higher up.

To His Parents

Turin, February 24, 1922

Dearests,

Yesterday there was a huge uproar at the student residence and so did I begin the Carnevale;[1] the other evening I stood in line from 5:30 pm till 7:30 pm to hear Aida and to sit in the third balcony: we were a group of students, we brought food to eat and so the time passed quickly.

Now I'll leave you because I'm going to the Marchisios' house to greet them after one month (of not seeing them) and then to the Conference.[2]

Greetings and kisses to you all from

Pier Giorgio

1. Carnevale, from the Latin for "farewell to meat," is the name in Italian given to the days of celebration before the start of the Lenten season.
2. He was referring to the Conference of St. Vincent de Paul to which he belonged and was extremely committed to doing works of charity on a weekly basis.

Turin, February 28, 1922

Dearests,

Thanks for your letter; I've been spending these days of Carnevale studying Theory of Mechanics which luckily is already well underway. Last night I had dinner with the Axerios; Mrs. Axerio apologized profusely because Tonino was at San Maurizio and so was her husband, then Mrs. Micheli invited me for Wednesday I don't know whether for dinner or after dinner, but I'll make up an excuse about some cousin arriving because I don't want to waste my evenings.

This afternoon Msgr. Pini arrived and so we will have a cozy little evening at our club.

Greetings to you Luciana and papa and kisses to you all from

Pier Giorgio

Telegram to His Mother in Berlin

Turin, March 24, 1922

Mechanics Exam went well 90 points

Pier Giorgio

To His Parents

Turin, March 25, 1922

Dearest Mama and Papa,

Finally that blessed Mechanics exam has been taken, I'm very happy to have lifted such a huge burden off myself now I'm beginning to work on this summer's exams. They are in two hard subjects, but with a bit of good will and a bit of effort I will succeed in taking them. I received your telegram today, it arrived at eight this morning but I was sleeping soundly to give myself some rest after all the evenings of study and so when I had breakfast I found it there and with great pleasure I read about your 90 kisses.[1]

Thank Luciana for her letter and for that errand to the G.F. Everything is going very well. This evening I'm going to Vittorio's after about a month (of not seeing him); he wanted to send me the seconds,[2] but I told him that he did very well not to send them because it was a waste of effort.

Greetings and kisses to Luciana. Greetings to the Seituns to Michetti to Berti, Marchisio and to you all a thousand kisses and greetings from

Pier Giorgio

[1] The telegram sending 90 kisses to Pier Giorgio was in response to his telegram to his parents giving his exam score of 90 points.
[2] This was a dueling term and most likely an inside joke between Pier Giorgio and Vittorio.

To His Mother

Piscina, April 2, 1922

A thousand greetings and kisses from the Eucharistic Congress.

Pier Giorgio

To Alberto Falchetti

Turin, April 6, 1922

Illustrious Commander,[1]

    I am writing you a bit late to give you a thousand best wishes; let's hope that you become a bit less juvenile. I will pray to St. Albert that he sends you some good inspiration for future paintings so that you don't make any more paintings like The Rhapsodist.

    I recommend that you don't pass yourself off as such a famous artist, because the Germans aren't so naive, they will believe a bit, but then as soon as they see your painting in Venice they'll say: What a phony.

    Greetings and very best wishes from

Pier Giorgio

[1] When Senator Frassati was named commander, he despised to be called by that title. So, the family began the custom of "decorating" with the title anyone they wanted to tease.

To His Parents

Turin, April 6, 1922[1]

Dearests,

    Thanks for the nice letters and the best wishes which you have sent; thanks again for the gift, which you also shouldn't have bought for me, because you have done too much for me already, but which I will always treasure.[2]

    Today after some time for relaxation I began to study for the oral exam which I will take after vacation and for this summer's exams: the two most difficult subjects which will permit me to enter the fourth year. The weather is always magnificent with a summer sun. Maybe during this holiday if I have 2 days free I'll go to Pollone to see our village a bit after a four-month absence.

I'll leave you now thanking you again. Thank the Peruginis for their birthday wishes; greetings and kisses to you all from

Pier Giorgio

I'll pray to God that as a reward for all that you have done for me, He will send His Blessings down upon you.

A thousand thanks and greetings to Marina and Andrés.

[1] This was Pier Giorgio's 21st birthday.

[2] The gifts which Pier Giorgio received from his family were always few and of little value; yet they seemed to him to be many and very grand. Perhaps, it was because he always greatly regarded the spirit in which they had been given.

To Giuseppe Spataro[1]

Turin, April 8, 1922

Dearest Spataro,

With great regret I am unable to accompany you to Germany, because at the time of the Congress I should be studying so that a month later I will be able to pass the most awful of the third-year exams.

You can imagine how I welcomed your proposal, not only because of the great pleasure of being able to spend a few days in your company, but also being able to see my German friends again; there will be another time, first work then pleasure.

Here in our Polytechnic in Turin we must fight energetically against the anticlerical elements which have stooped to acts of vandalism, like those who destroyed our Club's display case more than 2 times, they force us to defend ourselves so that we do not fail in our dignity.[2] On the other hand we have to exert strong pressure on our director, because he is a person without dignity; he will give one reason to us and another to our adversaries. Luckily we have many Catholic professors in the Polytechnic; among them the most active is Prof. Colonnetti, who is always quick to defend us on every occasion.

This evening we leave for San Mauro where a course of Spiritual Exercises will be held for the University students both FUCI members and non-members; there are 40 of us.

When you go to Germany, can you make a side trip to Turin? We're hoping to see you.

The FUCI members of Turin together with our president Bertini have asked me to greet you.

Give my special regards to Mrs. Martone and receive a thousand cordial greetings in J.C.[3]

Pier Giorgio Frassati

[1] Spataro was President of the FUCI at that time. After 1950, he was many times a member of the Government.

[2] The defense of the display case at the University is a very famous episode in the life of Pier Giorgio. The display case was used by the Catholic students to tack up religious notices, alongside posters of every kind. Pier Giorgio stood up fearlessly to a group of assailants and, although he wasn't himself overcome, the display case was shattered and the poster torn. But the next day, the spiritual notice reappeared well-affixed.

[3] "Greetings in Jesus Christ" is a greeting Pier Giorgio began to use frequently at the end of his letters, often using the initials "J.C."

To His Mother

Turin, April 13, 1922

Dearest Mama,

Perhaps this is the first Easter that we are not spending together,[1] but on that day I will receive Holy Communion for you all and thus it will seem to me that the distance may be lessened and I'll pray to God that He blesses you along with all of the others. The weather is very unsettled these days; I've resumed my studies so that I can take the oral exam after Easter.

Best wishes and kisses.

Pier Giorgio

Greetings and best wishes to Berti, Marina and Andres.

[1] It was an exceptional event for him to spend that Easter far from the family. Indeed, in the Frassati house it was a tradition to spend all of Holy Week at the home in Pollone, up to "Monday of the snacks" (lunedì delle merende), as they called it in Turin.

To Mario Bergonzi

April 1922

Dear Mario,

I would like to be in your place to see the Holy Father every now and then, you know how I love the Pope; I would like to do something for him, but being unable to do so, I pray every day that Jesus would give him many consolations and blessings.
Long live the Pope, long may he live.

Pier Giorgio Frassati

To Maria Fischer

Turin, May 17, 1922

Dear Miss Fischer,

Excuse me for not having written for such a long time, but I have had a lot of work these last months. Yesterday in Turin, I witnessed a day of triumph for our Faith. My city is called the City of the Blessed Sacrament because on June 6, 1456,[1] a thief who had sneaked off with various sacred objects from a country church, including a chalice and a monstrance, had scarcely arrived at the houses on the outskirts of the city, when he saw his donkey kneel down before the Sacred Host which rose up toward the heavens. A bit later the Bishops, all the city Authorities and the people went to pray to God that He would never abandon the city.

On Sunday there was a solemn procession in Turin to commemorate this miracle. One can't say how many people gathered together from all the villages of Piedmont like a swarm of bees, nor describe their enthusiasm. I think that it was like Palm Sunday in Jerusalem, when the children and the people threw flowers on the streets as Jesus Christ passed by.

In my thoughts I am accompanying the gentleman who will bring you this letter, while I unfortunately must stay in Turin.

I always remember those beautiful days in Vienna. My best wishes to your parents, and a heartfelt greeting

Pier Giorgio Frassati

[1] The actual date was 1453.

To Antonio Villani

Turin, July 18, 1922

Dearest Villani,

The other day Prof. Marchisio from our Conference of St. Vincent recommended another sad case to me. It's the situation of a poor young woman who is graduating in fine arts and who needs to find a job so that she can support herself. I don't know exactly who I should turn to; I thought of you, because you always have good ideas and you already have more experience in life than I do. The idea would be to find a tutoring position with a family or else a job which pays a lot of money.[1]

I'm afraid that our recommendation has had little luck, because Facta will finally no longer be Prime Minister. Maybe if we have the 2 Filippos we can hope that at last our country can have a Ministry capable of commanding respect;[2] and which finally puts an end to the huge scandal represented by the Fascist movement.

I would hope for a government of the People's Party-Socialist. I can still understand the violent actions which the Communists have unfortunately perpetrated in some towns; at least they stood for a high ideal, that of elevating the working class which for so many years now has been exploited by people without consciences; but the Fascists what ideals do they have? Dirty money, paid by the industrialists and unfortunately even more shamefully paid by our government, they don't act unless prompted by money or dishonesty.[3]

Fortunately there is a Higher Justice in the next life; otherwise if a Good and Just God didn't exist, our life would be useless. Dear Severi is completely busy, because yesterday Miss Abati graduated, one of the numerous "hunchbacks"[4] who are forever leaving university life (Abati, Giuffredi and others).

I'm expecting you for sure on the 23rd; reply right away especially if you have some suggestion for that family.

Do you know anything about that Venetian family? Our conference[5] has agreed to assign them a periodical allowance, but for now we have no other information.

Greetings in J.C.

Pier Giorgio

[1] Despite Pier Giorgio's numerous good works, there are few references to them contained among his letters. However, when he was helping those in need, he never hesitated to turn to the many friends he had and practically imposed on them, always hoping for the maximum result.

[2] He is referring to the crisis of then Italian Prime Minister Facta; notwithstanding Pier Giorgio's hopes, Facta appointed his own Assistant Minister a little while later, thwarting the hypothesis of a coalition government of Populists and Socialists. It would have been an important historic event, because the political initiative of establishing a government would have been assigned to parliamentary groups. The deal fell through, opening the door for the Fascists to step in. (The "two Filippos" were Filippo Meda and Filippo Turati.)

[3] Pier Giorgio's political convictions, shaped under the scrutiny of an intense and sound Christian experience, decisively led him toward a left-wing Catholicism which must be considered in the proper context of the era. On the heels of the papal encyclical, *Rerum Novarum*, Pier Giorgio fought for raising the consciousness of the masses of working-class people toward a universal brotherhood in Jesus Christ. In his view of the Kingdom of God on this earth, the rich would have had to be the first to relinquish their own privileges in order to live a more intense moral life. This is why he justified Communism (the reader should bear in mind this was 1922 and not much was known at the time about Russian Communism) as opposed to Fascism, whose practice of violence and whose politics on the road to power seemed to Pier Giorgio to lack any spiritual basis.

Finally, it can seem strange or at least ironic that he, born and bred in a well-to-do family, would have pitted himself so very strongly against the industrialists and against a government which was clearly supported by the magnates of finance. But one needs to remember that in addition to claiming absolutely nothing of his father's estate for himself and taking no interest in his present and future rights, he had on several occasions publicly stated that once he had received his inheritance he would distribute it among the poor.

[4] "Hunchbacks" was Mrs. Frassati's playful nickname for girls attending Catholic university (because they were always hunched over their books studying rather than leading a social life.)

[5] Again he is referring to the Conference of St. Vincent de Paul.

To His Mother

Turin, July 19, 1922

Dear mama,

    I regret and it has caused me a lot of pain to know that you are having thoughts which just aren't true. A Mother's advice is always the wisest and always the best even when one is already old. This year you have been very far away from me and I have appreciated what it means to not have one's Mother close by to scold you every now and then, but also to kiss you and bless you in the evening; although I am not alone, as I have my dear aunt and a dear grandmother.

Unfortunately, dear Mama, I can't be with all of you in Pollone; it's a little bit my own fault due to the serious defect of being a bit too slow, but it's also a little bit the fault of having a lot of difficult studying to do.

This third year is a tough one and I need to make many sacrifices so that I can reach my goal. But let's not feel sorry for ourselves, because there are greater sorrows in this life.

Luciana will arrive on Saturday morning, the Banzattis left yesterday. There's a general strike today in Turin all because of those Fascist scoundrels.

Vittorio graduated with a final mark of 100 out of 110 which is very good especially because he had to prepare (for the finals) in a hurry while doing his military service. Should I send him the inkpot now or wait until this autumn?

Dear Mama, forgive me again for all the little sorrows which I have given you, but remain assured that, if I sometimes failed you, I will try to do better in the future, because I often think of you and I always pray to God for you, that He might grant you those consolations which I cannot give you due to my faults, even though I love you so much.

Kisses to you and to aunt.

Pier Giorgio

To Maria Fischer

Pollone, August 29, 1922

Dear Miss Fischer,

Thank you for your kind letter to which I haven't replied promptly because I've had a lot of work to do in Turin.[1]

It's too bad that my exams don't permit me to take part in the Pax Romana week in Vienna.

Finally after a long dry spell, the countryside is beautiful again and the flowers are blooming.

This year the students of Turin, both the guys and the girls, have collected our songs in a little booklet; I believe that you'll like them because they will remind you of the FUCI Conventions, and therefore I have sent you a copy.[2]

Do you know Mr. Domanig's address?

After my exams in October I'll be leaving for Germany and if there is snow I'll stay at Semmering for a week.

Regards to your parents, my greetings to your group of friends in Innsbruck and to you cordial greetings. Pax tecum from

Pier Giorgio Frassati

[1] His work wasn't only schoolwork. Every day in the scorching hot hours of the afternoon heatwave or in the cool hours of the evening, Pier Giorgio wore himself out for his poor, going all around Turin, to the homes of the very wealthy where he went to beg, and to the dwellings of the very poor where he went to give comfort.

[2] It was a promotional booklet with the FUCI anthem "Cantiamo Fucini" ("Let's Sing, FUCI Members") that Pier Giorgio had published.

To Antonio Villani

Pollone, August 29, 1922

Dearest Villani,

I've already started for the past 2 or three days applied mechanics and I've begun to repeat graphic Statics.[1]

Yesterday I was in Sordevolo, a little town close to Pollone, for the blessing of the Youth Club's banner. It was a pretty grand celebration particularly because the Sordevolo Club is one of the best in Biella.[2]

The weather is always menacing, but it can't ever decide whether or not to rain.

And how's it going with you? Decide to come and spend a few days here in Pollone, and so you can learn a bit about the Biella region. Unfortunately even here the dear... Fascists have arrived, naturally summoned by our great patriots the managers of Discount Bank. They've forced the mayor to submit his resignation and so Pollone's debt will increase because the citizens have to pay an office worker to direct the town's future until the next elections.[3]

Write to me right away and do remember to consider the possibility of coming up here.

My regards to your family, and to you a thousand greetings from

Pier Giorgio

[1] Statics: The equilibrium mechanics of stationary bodies.
[2] Pier Giorgio was one of the organizers of the Catholic youth groups in the region

of Biella. Besides having founded two groups in Pollone in 1923 (one for young men and the other for young women), he was often present at the Catholic parties and gatherings of the groups in the neighboring towns.

3 Pier Giorgio courageously condemned the methods used by the Fascists and didn't miss an opportunity to expose them to public contempt.

To Antonio Severi

Turin, September 16, 1922

Dear Tonino,

I arrived this morning at 10, I've already seen dear Bertini, who has been looking for rooms for our club, he hopes in the headquarters of the P.P.I.; but we would have our own special entrance there; we will need to reach an agreement about the price.

Tomorrow our banner will go to Alpignano with some of our members for the blessing of the Youth club flags.

I spoke to Bertini about the meeting in Novara in which a fairly large group of University students might take part. I plan on bringing a good number of booklets to try to sell; by the way don't you think that it would be opportune to give a discount as a deal with the members of our sister association?

Have you received my registered letter by express mail? Otherwise send me the authorization to sign the necessary forms for every subject on your behalf. The deadline for submitting applications is Saturday the 23rd.

That good Delpiano sold 23 booklets for me[1] maybe if I go back to Biella after Novara I'll leave some samples with Nino Caneparo president of the Biella Federation.

Have you already started studying and when do you become a citizen?

Answer me right away especially about your application because the deadline is approaching and a lot needs to be done in a hurry.

Regards to your family to you a brotherly greeting in J.C.

Pier Giorgio

[1] He is referring to the promotional booklets "Let's Sing, Fucini Members" which he had published.

Turin, September 19, 1922

Dear Tonino,

I received your forms, but you forgot to send the general application, I filled one out for you today; since the office boy at "La Stampa" had a copy of your signature, I tried to imitate it as best I could; be sure that you don't report me to any court.

Thanks for the good and long letter, I'm sorry that I made you write such a long letter and I sincerely admire you for your willpower. I have to admit that I couldn't have done it. Now I would like to ask you a favor. In November I'll be going to Germany and when I pass through Innsbruck I'll go to see Miss Fischer, at which time, through all the infinite kindnesses of her family, I'd like to give her as a present *I promessi Sposi*[1] and at this point you're now asking yourself "so what?", but now you can help me out if you can tell me where and in what book I can find a beautiful dedication. I don't know much about these things and so I'm asking you to look yourself or to tell me where I can find something that will be beautiful and will go well.

The application for the exams has already been turned in along with the form; now I'm letting you know the exam dates:

Elements of mechanical technology	6 October
Machine design	16 October
Political economics	19 October
Industrial construction	16 October
Hydraulics	6 October
Thermotechnology	28 October

Bertini has written you a heap of insults, don't take offense, because down deep he's a good guy; I'll very gladly be a go-between to make peace, I hope that it doesn't take a lot of meetings.

Tomorrow is the terrible day; as soon as Panetti will have decided something[2] I'll write to you.

Many greetings and hope to see you very soon.

Pier Giorgio

---

[1] *The Betrothed*, considered to be the greatest work by Alessandro Manzoni, a convert to Catholicism.

[2] That is, whether to allow Pier Giorgio to take his exam in Applied Mechanics.

To Antonio Severi

Turin, September 25, 1922

Dear Tonino,

The other day I was finally able to have a private talk with the engineer Modesto Panetti, luckily he was in a good mood and he was very courteous. He saw the table of gears and added that he saw an improvement and as the professor of Applied Mechanics it was sufficient and so I was able to take the exam. You can't imagine my joy especially because I worked on the table for three days; every ten minutes I washed my hands so I wouldn't get it dirty then I controlled the urge to keep correcting my work so that it would be finished well within the time limit available.

Now in these last few days I've completely abandoned Guidi[1] in order to dedicate myself fully to Applied Mechanics and I hope that I'll take this blessed exam on October 2nd.

Make sure you pray for me and my exam on that day, because I really need it.

Do you have news about the sale of the booklets? And can the loan[2] be paid at the end of the year or does some more money need to be sent now before sending the rest later? Write something to me.

I left your booklet with the doorman at Piazza Solferino 20, because when you arrive in Turin I will probably have returned to Pollone to study Guidi.

I don't know anything more about Villani.

There's nothing new about the Club except that in a few days we have to move and up till now no location has been found.

Write something to me and cordial greetings from

Pier Giorgio

[1] Construction Science textbook.
[2] It had been necessary to sign a promissory note so that they could publish the FUCI songbook. Naturally Pier Giorgio, being the soundest financially, signed the note.

To His Mother

Turin, September 28, 1922

Dearest mama,

It was Divine Providence that in these last few days I ran into my friend Villani, who is giving me the final help before the exam. On the morning of the 9th he'll come to Pollone where we will review together all of Guidi and then at the end of the month I will take the exam in Guidi.

I'm glad that you were able to see the beautiful glaciers.

It has rained so much here that certain parts of Corso Siccardi are so full of water that traveling by tram gives the illusion of being in a vaporetto[1] in Venice.

Write me something about the Rahners and how you like my Freiburg and my beautiful cathedral.[2]

Greetings and kisses to you and Luciana and to Papa when he joins you from

Pier Giorgio

[1] A small water taxi used to ferry passengers in the canals of Venice. Originally powered by steam (vapore in Italian), they are now motorized.

[2] Luciana and Mrs. Frassati had gone to Freiburg to meet the Rahner family whom Pier Giorgio had lived with during his stay in Germany.

Turin, October 3, 1922

Dearest mama,

I hope that you received my telegram where I announced that I am finally freed from the Applied Mechanics exam; now I need to concentrate all my strength on Construction Science and then I will join you in Berlin.

The other day I received a form from the Civil Committee against blasphemy along with the request to tell papa that he should express himself against such an ugly vice which is making Italy less civilized than so many other nations. I'm enclosing it for you with the request that as soon as papa joins you, he will give his opinion and then send it to Verona.[1]

On Monday the 9th, Villani will arrive in Pollone and then we'll study hard until the 29th, the night before roll call for the Guidi exam.

This evening I had dinner at the Banzatti's and then I kept Anna Maria company a bit, because Camillo had gone to study with one of his friends.

Tomorrow morning I'm going to see the professor who has

returned from the countryside. Friday afternoon I'll have lunch at the Bellingeri's at Cascina Vica.

Many greetings and kisses to you to Luciana to papa when he joins you from

Pier Giorgio

[1] Questionnaires of this sort often reached Senator Frassati through Pier Giorgio. He would fill them in only at Pier Giorgio's request; something Pier Giorgio's friends knew well.

TELEGRAM TO HIS FAMILY IN BERLIN

October 8, 1922

Mechanics 70 kisses[1]

Pier Giorgio

[1] This was considered a great triumph because sitting for an exam before Professor Panetti was a difficult undertaking.

TO LUCIANA

Pollone, October 9, 1922

Dearest Luciana,

I arrived from Biella late yesterday evening along with about ten members of "Pollone Youth" and the assistant parish priest; we were returning from the youth convention in Novara. It was a stupendous display of strength; about 20,000 young people marched through the streets of Novara processing with the Blessed Sacrament. The procession began at 1:30 p.m. and lasted until four and was made up entirely of young men; the girls didn't participate. We had 2 special trains from the government driven by white railway workers,[1] who made sure that we arrived in Novara exactly on time and we took up a collection to offer them a drink as a way of thanking them. On the other hand the Santhià-Biella Co. didn't allow us to have a special train and we had to spend 3 hours waiting at Santhià which terribly annoyed us.

The exam wasn't too boring; they only looked at the table which I had re-done in October, there was a discussion about the design, then a small exercise; it lasted half an hour of which ten minutes were without Panetti.

In an hour or so I'm going to Biella to pick up Villani and then I'll settle down to do some serious study of Guidi so that I can take the exam before the first of November and free myself of another heavy burden.

I hope mama received my letter from Turin which had a form for papa to fill in, so that he can give his opinion about blasphemy; make sure that he does it as soon as possible and then sends it to the "Civil Committee against Blasphemy" – Verona.

Greetings to you all and kisses from

Pier Giorgio

[1] This was the designation for workers in the Catholic union.

To Antonio Severi

Pollone, October 9, 1922

Dearest Tonino,

I've returned again for a few days to study here among the green grass and beautiful flowers. Yesterday I was at the convention in Novara together with Bertini, Delpiano, and others from the "Cesare Balbo" club. It was a demonstration which really touched me: passing through the streets of Novara, that recently witnessed the bloodshed of our brothers, were thousands and thousands of young men enthusiastic and full of Faith.

For Benediction, the Cathedral was packed, it's a bit shorter in length than Turin's cathedral: I think that Novara has never before seen a demonstration like this; the people didn't participate as much as they do in Turin: they were respectful but still a bit cold. There is a good awakening of the female youth; (mind you: we sold 2 booklets to their president) unfortunately many Fascist girls were there, but they backed off a bit mortified to see so many young men marching side by side under the banner of the Faith and praying throughout the streets of the city; let's hope that Providence gets through to their hearts so that these little lost lambs are brought back to the flock.

I brought 50 booklets with me fearing that I wouldn't be able to sell them but on the contrary only a few are left and so about a hundred were sold.

And what are you up to? Did you get my letter where I told

you about the good results of my exam? Now I'm concentrating all my strength on Guidi; because since up to now the divine Grace has helped me pass the most boring test, I may also pass the last one and thus be able to enter the fourth year.

Cordial greetings from

Pier Giorgio

To CARLO BELLINGERI

Pollone, October 11, 1922

Dearest Carlo,

I've been here in the region of Biella for two days and just my luck it's been raining and raining. On Sunday there was a demonstration which I will always remember: more than 20,000 enthusiastic young men marched before the Blessed Sacrament through the streets of Novara. Until Sunday I don't think the people there had ever seen such a marvelous army, preceded by the fine units of the vanguard, organized and disciplined like soldiers; exactly because of this the people maintained a respectful and dignified attitude, but they weren't very interested; they remained completely dumbfounded almost as if they didn't believe that in our day, 20,000 young men would have answered the summons and gathered to follow countless banners.

It was really bad of you not to come; the very Rev. Father Pesso asked me about you, I told him that you were studying a lot and for this reason you weren't able to come.

On Sunday we had to wait at Santhià for three hours, because the men in charge in Biella didn't want to have a special train and there were about 400 of us and so I arrived in Pollone at one in the morning.

Now I've returned to studying Guidi because time is passing and soon it will be time to return to Turin.

Thanks again to your parents for their hospitality; greetings to your sisters and to your brothers; to you a big kiss from

Pier Giorgio

To Luciana

Turin, October 28, 1922

Dearest Luciana,

Tomorrow I'll leave Turin to go back to Pollone and this time I'm leaving willingly, because I need the tranquility of the countryside so that I can distance myself from the whole atmosphere that's here all around the city. But today I didn't get much studying done, not because of me, but because our feelings can't remain unspoken in the face of such a tragic hour.[1] So many thoughts were going through my head that they didn't allow me to concentrate on Construction Science anymore.

Alda is totally shocked, she's very nervous and sad: I can imagine the atmosphere at the Embassy.

Now I'll leave you because otherwise my pen might push me to write something imprudent.[2]

Lots of kisses to papa and again a thousand congratulations[3] and to Mama and to you whom I hope to see again very soon finally all united and at peace.

Pier Giorgio

[1] Pier Giorgio is referring to the political turn of events on October 28, 1922; specifically, the March on Rome and the rise of Benito Mussolini to leadership of the Italian government. Discouragement overcame Pier Giorgio momentarily, which was a combination of his feelings for his friends and his fears for his family in Berlin.

[2] He is making a reference to the possible censorship of the mail, now that the Fascists had triumphed.

[3] His father had recently received one of the highest orders of knighthood in the kingdom of Italy. (Italy became a republic in 1946.)

To the Members of the "Milites Mariae" Club[1]

Turin, October 30, 1922

Dear Members,

As you know this year during the Convention of Italian Catholic Youth, held in Rome, the deplorable disorganization of our students has been noticed; accordingly the heads of our movement have decided to unite, within the Catholic Youth Society, these young people, who need special instruction, adapted to their abilities, and a solid foundation in apologetics in order to face the continual dangers to which they are frequently exposed in the public schools which are unfortunately very corrupt.

The very active Federation of Turin, convinced more than ever of the need to organize the students to strengthen them in advance against the dangers in their life, had already formulated a bold and magnificent program last year. Unfortunately the students have hardly responded to the generous appeal of the Federation thus showing that they are not aware of the lofty mission entrusted to them by Divine Providence.

And even more in this grave moment which has confronted our nation, we Catholics and especially we students have a serious responsibility to fulfill: our own formation.

We, who by the grace of God are Catholics, should not waste the most wonderful years of our life, as unfortunately do so many unhappy young people, who are preoccupied with enjoying the good life, which does not result in good, but which brings the fruit of immorality into our modern society. We should steel ourselves to be ready to carry on the battles we shall certainly have to fight in order to fulfill our program and thus to give to our country, in a not-too-distant future, happier days and a morally healthy society. But for all this is needed: continual prayer to obtain from God that grace without which our efforts are in vain; organization and discipline so that we can be ready for action at the opportune moment and finally, sacrifice of our passions and of ourselves, because without this it is impossible to reach the goal.

Concerning the organization this year the Federation, taking up this difficult task again with greater vigor, has extended a warm invitation to all the Clubs, so that they can work together toward this goal. If the students respond generously to the appeal, the Federation promises to hold a class after school, where they can complete their cultural formation, which at present the state school, so lacking in seriousness, is unable to give more; and at the same time they will receive teaching in religious and philosophical matters.

Complying with the wishes of the Federation, in the name of the Board of Directors of the "Milites Mariae" Club, as a delegate of the students, I address a warm request to you, to promptly send to Mr. Chiesa the secretary of the Club or else to the Club's headquarters some precise indications about the school and the classes which you attend, so that this list can be forwarded to the Federation in as short a time as possible.

Meanwhile I thank you for what you will do, certain that you will be generously rewarded in life. I greet you in a Christian way. Long live Jesus. The student's delegate

Pier Giorgio Frassati

[1] The Soldiers of Mary was an association of Catholic youth that Pier Giorgio started at his parish church in Turin – not to be confused with the Legion of Mary.

TELEGRAM TO BERLIN

November 6, 1922

Guidi 75 kisses.[1]

Pier Giorgio

[1] This was his way of telling his exam score with kisses meaning points.

TO LUCIANA

Turin, November 7, 1922

Dearest,

Yesterday I took this year's last exam I was pretty lucky because I picked a thesis that I knew pretty well.[1] Now I am regularly enrolled in Year IV, but this year I again have a lot to do because I have a lot of compulsory subjects but much easier ones. When I come up I'll think about a gift for Villani's graduation; if you have a chance these days to find something go ahead.

Greetings and kisses to all of you and I'll see you soon.

Pier Giorgio

[1] When he went for his exam, he was presented with a bag from which he drew a number corresponding to a thesis to explain, dealing of course with a specific part of the exam material.

To Maria Fischer[1]

Innsbruck, November 13, 1922

Dear Miss Fischer,
   It is really too bad that you left for Munich, because I didn't have the pleasure of greeting you.
   I was in Rome on Friday, the weather was beautiful and I greeted St. Peter's for you. I liked Innsbruck a lot. The city is really beautiful.
   Yesterday afternoon I took a walk to a village where one enjoys a beautiful view of the countryside.
   The novel I brought you is by one of the best authors who is also a good Catholic.
   The Rosary[2] (I don't know how to translate this word) was made in the country with seeds from my garden, and it's already blessed and it has all the indulgences (I don't know the word in German).
   Did they have the Catholic Convention in Munich or not?
   Write something to me in Berlin.
   Many cordial greetings from

Pier Giorgio Frassati

Pax tecum.

[1] This letter, as were all those to his German friends, was written in German.
[2] Pier Giorgio made rosaries with seeds from a plant in the family garden at Pollone (called Lacrimae Jobi – "Job's Tears") and he gave one to her as the highest token of moral solidarity.

To Gian Maria Bertini

Berlin, November 15, 1922

Dear Bertini,
   I arrived in this gray, but always beautiful, Berlin yesterday after a very fine trip. I stayed in Innsbruck 2 days but unfortunately I wasn't able to see Miss Fischer; she had left for Munich, where there may have been a Catholic convention, and is staying for a few days.
   I left her the book with this dedication "In remembrance of days full of Faith and enthusiasm, spent together in Italy, to the kind young lady... this book is offered by...." it's not very beauti-

ful, but I didn't know the correct thing to write; I even forgot to write the date.

Today I'll go to see Dr. Sonnenschein and then my friends and so I will enjoy a bit of the quiet life of Berlin.

The shops are still full of nice things, but the Germans can't buy them anymore, because life here is very expensive.

The cost of living is also high in Austria even for us Italians, things cost the same as in Italy; here it's much less expensive for us, not to mention using the trains; it costs nothing to travel.

Every day that I spend here I fall more and more in love with these wonderful people, hardworking people who unfortunately are suffering terribly, but we who are Catholics know that God doesn't abandon good people and if evildoers are on top of the world today, tomorrow God will put such weapons into the hands of the righteous that they will wage war against the Sons of Darkness (the French).

Write something to me about the Club. Greetings to you all from

Pier Giorgio

To Antonio Villani

Berlin, November 19, 1922

Dearest Tonino,

I'm here all by myself because my family went out for lunch; I'm writing to you, but for the last time, because you don't reply and so I'm a bit angry with you.

I glanced at Mussolini's speech[1] and all the blood boiled in my veins:[2] believe me, I've been so deceived by the really shameful behavior of members of the People's Party. Where is the fine program, where is the Faith which motivates our people? Unfortunately when it is a question of climbing after worldly honors men trample upon their own consciences.

I wish that school would never start again. I would like to have my degree so that I could stay in this beautiful country, where men still feel a sense of responsibility and still have a very well-formed conscience.

Today more than ever we must reluctantly recognize that the

Christian poet Dante was and unfortunately still is right when he exclaimed:

> "Alas, thou enslaved Italy,
> thou abode of grief,
> A ship without a pilot in a great tempest,
> Mistress not of a province,
> but of a brothel!"

Now I'm going to find my friends and chat a bit about our matters.

Believe me how good it is here, where it is peaceful because it is far from our poor country fallen into the hands of a band of scoundrels.

---

[1] He is referring to Mussolini's famous speech delivered in November of 1922 in the Italian Parliament after the March on Rome, on the occasion of presenting his first Government, when he described the House as "a filthy, dirty chamber."

[2] Pier Giorgio suffered through the rise of Fascism with moral and psychological backlash. The hope he had cultivated was now brusquely revealed to be an illusion, and he grieved in an unbelievable way: it didn't seem possible to him that Faith wouldn't give light to the politicians. Even more than the events themselves, he lamented this unforeseen collapse of the spirit and moral responsibility.

To Maria Fischer

Berlin, November 20, 1922

Dear Miss Fischer,

Thank you for your kind letter; I'm here for a week where the weather is very overcast. I always like Berlin, but it is not as beautiful as Innsbruck, whose valleys remind me of ours in Piedmont. Unfortunately I had to leave. I would willingly have stayed a bit to ski, but I had to reach Berlin because my father is returning to Italy soon[1] and I wanted to spend a few days with him.

When my parents leave, I will remain in Germany for a few more weeks, because I want to visit the mines in Upper Silesia. I'll be happy to pay you a visit when I am passing through Munich, because I will make my return trip through Switzerland.

I'm sending you the postage stamps that I promised you in Vienna.

I forgot to write the date in your book, but when I pass through Innsbruck I'll put it in.

My regards to your parents and to you cordial greetings.
Yours

Pier Giorgio Frassati

[1] His father's reaction to the March on Rome was immediate. He submitted his resignation to Mussolini on the 4th of November.

To Antonio Severi

Berlin, November 23, 1922

Dearest Tonino,

I received your letter just now and I'm hurrying to answer you because it's about something urgent.

Mr. DeAgostini really doesn't keep his word and I'm not surprised, because, as soon as our contract was signed, I heard bad things about him, but I didn't really believe that he would go this far.

When we went to see him in July he promised to fix the billiard table, give us a new cue-stick holder and new cue-sticks and I believe also new balls, all for 1500 lire; but you could also ask Villani, who was with us one time.

Now if the Club's board of directors agrees I would say not to pay him for the moment and to wait for me to arrive in Italy, and then I'll go and find Mr. DeAgostini and tell him off. Write something to me or if you think it's okay I will write a fiery letter to him personally.

Yesterday I sent you a postcard from Berlin, it wasn't very pretty but I didn't have any other; I'll buy some and then I will send you another and when I don't write it's because I'm lazy.

When I was in Rome I gave the booklets[1] to my friend Curio with the letter and I think that he's taken them to their destination; but please send me Miss Capparoni's address, so that I can give my apology for not having come myself.

Greet all of the fucini and fucine[2] for me, you get a cordial greeting from

Pier Giorgio

My sister and my mother thank you and send their greetings in return.

[1] This is another reference to the promotional booklets with the FUCI anthem which Pier Giorgio had published.

[2] FUCI was the organization of the Federation of Italian Catholic University Students. Here, Pier Giorgio is greeting separately the guys (fucini) and girls (fucine) who were members.

To Antonio Severi

Berlin, December 4, 1922

Dearest Tonino,

With deep regret I learned from your letter that Mr. DeAgostini doesn't want to give you the billiard table for 1500 lire as he assured both of us, in charge of "Cesare Balbo," that he would.

I would like to be in Turin so that I could go with you to DeAgostini and personally clear up once and for all what has come up, because it's seriously hurting our Club, because now, as you say, you have a billiard table you can't play on, because there are no balls, which DeAgostini should be giving us along with the repaired billiard table for L.[1] 1500.

I think, if the Club's board of directors is in agreement, that you should go to Mr. DeAgostini and tell him, that I am really astonished that there are these kinds of difficulties which didn't exist in July, because otherwise we wouldn't have taken on such a huge responsibility on behalf of the members of our club, who have the right to claim the billiard table.

I don't like any of your ideas about the P.P.I.;[2] as far as I am concerned it's better to be alone, but with a clear conscience, than be together with all the others but with a huge stain on one's conscience.

As far as the unfinished sentences go I would like an explanation otherwise I won't accept them; why is it such an extraordinary thing that I greet a young lady, whom I was with during the conventions in Ravenna and Rome. Especially now that I don't know when I will return to Germany.[3]

Your Reitz-brand pocket-sized ruler has already been purchased; please warn Pasquali that they don't have the Nestler 37 Electro ruler in Berlin anymore and so having to order one and not knowing the date of its arrival in Berlin, I cannot bring it to him.

Greetings to our friends, to you a cordial handshake.

Pier Giorgio

Persuade Bertini to stay at his post[4] or if Bertini really doesn't want to, make the good Negroni do it, I wouldn't object to vote in your favor if it weren't for the fear that our club will become a club that is dependent on the girls' club; don't take it the wrong way.

[1] L = Lire, the Italian currency at the time.
[2] The Italian People's Party, in Italian the Partito Popolare Italiano.
[3] In a letter to Pier Giorgio, Antonio Severi had made subtle insinuations about Pier Giorgio stopping to see Maria Fischer in Innsbruck. This irritated Pier Giorgio because he had no tolerance for humor on these subjects.
[4] Bertini was the president of the "Cesare Balbo" Club.

To Carlo Bellingeri

Berlin, December 14, 1922

Dearest Carlo,

Thanks for your letter: I sincerely admire you, because I wouldn't have had the strength to write so much.

As soon as I read it, I was really surprised to hear your account of the new problems of that unlucky family.

I thought that by this time Mr. Zanatta would already have had a job in Rome in his cousin's office and that he would already have begun to earn some money but unfortunately it was only a nice dream.

Carlo, if you really want to know, one of my ideas is that I would abolish certain conferences of St. Vincent; when there are men from another generation, so full of Christian zeal, who don't even know how to warn the parents about the alleged misconduct of their daughters and thus try to do good work, but instead they prefer to abandon that family, it's better that the conference didn't exist; not because the members are acting out of bad faith, but because it's not adapted to modern times.

I don't know what to suggest to you for the Zanattas but if you want to advance them some money, I give you a free hand to do so also on my behalf.[1]

In a few days I'll write my letter of resignation[2] to the attorney Bertagna.

Pardon the terrible handwriting, but I'm writing to you while in bed, because I've had a slight flu. Now my fever is gone and so I hope to get up a bit tomorrow.

I planned to go to Danzig and then to Poland, but unfortunately I have to renounce. As soon as I'm better I'll leave for Katowitz in Upper Silesia, where I'll visit a coal mine, and after I've seen all of my friends, scattered around various German cities, I'll return to Turin.

Regards to your parents, greetings to your sisters and your brothers and a big kiss to you.

Pier Giorgio

1. This was the very sad case of a poor man whose family was reduced to destitution. The members of the Conference of St. Vincent de Paul at first attempted to help them but then gave up because, given the immoral living of the daughters, they felt it was no longer right to take care of them. Pier Giorgio disagreed with how this case was handled.
2. In 1922, Pier Giorgio resigned from the St. Vincent de Paul Conference at the Social Institute of Turin and transferred to the Conference sponsored by the Cesare Balbo club at the university he was attending.

To Maria Fischer

Berlin, December 22, 1922

Dear Miss Maria Fischer,

I don't know if you received my letter.

My parents are departing from Berlin on Saturday because they want to spend Christmas in Turin. I am staying here in the beautiful city, partly unhappy about not spending the Holy Feast with my family, but partly happy about being able to spend it with my German friends.

I may leave for Danzig on the evening of the 25th to visit this part of Germany and to have a look at the Baltic Sea.

Then I'd like to go on to Katowitz and visit a coal mine. Perhaps I'll push on to Krakow which I unfortunately was unable to visit with my sister because I was ill.

If I go to Krakow most likely via Vienna I'll go to Munich again and thus I'll be able to see you and your parents and to see that very beautiful city once again.

If I will be coming, I'll send you a telegram.

Are you going to Midnight Mass? I'll be going with my friends and I'll pray for you and for your Fatherland and I'll ask God to send many Blessings upon your Country and your Family.

Accept a wish for a Merry Christmas, deepest regards to your parents and cordial greetings to you from

Pier Giorgio Frassati

To His Mother

Berlin, December 25, 1922, 8 p.m.

Dearest mama,

We've finally packed all the bags with Perugini's help and while I'm waiting for dinner I'm writing a couple of lines to you. Last night I spent the evening first at the Chiusanos' house and then at Leitgebel's house with whose family I went to midnight Mass. I've been invited to lunch at the Gugenheims' house at noon on Sunday and today at the Rofis' house. This evening at 10:44 I leave for Danzig 2nd class ticket sleeping car for 4500 marks. Tomorrow I'll visit Danzig and then I'll go to Katowitz.

Dear Mama believe that I leave this beautiful city unwillingly and I leave only in the hope of returning soon.

Perugini told me that you forgot Elisabetta in distributing the Christmas gifts and so I gave her 100 L.[1] then I paid for Papa's last pair of shoes.

If you want to write, write via general delivery to Freiburg im Breisgau, Baden.

Many kisses to grandmother to Papa to Luciana to Aunt and to you.

Tell Luciana to telephone the headquarters of the Italian People's Party giving my Christmas greetings for the Cesare Balbo club.

Greetings from Perugini. Greetings

Pier Giorgio

[1] L = Lire, the Italian currency at the time.

To Maria Fischer

Katowitz, December 28, 1922

Dearest Miss Maria Fischer,

Yesterday I arrived in Katowitz but the Polish customs officials gave me so much trouble that I had to go back to Berlin again in order to return to Katowitz.

Today I visited the Ferdinand's mines, but I only saw the upper level installations and unfortunately I can't stay any longer to see the lower level too.

This evening I'm taking the express train to Breslau and it'll truly be a joy to sleep in a bed again.

The trip from Berlin to Katowitz was very unpleasant: from 10 until 4 in the morning I had to stand most of the time and then I got a seat between two women, crammed into a position where I couldn't sleep even for one second: I had a bit of room on the way to Breslau, but it was already six and so I slept for only three hours.

Tomorrow afternoon I leave for Regensburg. I'll visit the city and then I'll go on to Munich. I regret to have had such trouble with the Poles. I will have to give up the idea of going to Vienna via Krakow, because time is flying and I should return to Italy soon.

I'm sad about having to leave Germany and Austria in a little while, but I leave your Fatherland and Germany in the hope of returning.

My best regards to your parents and cordial greetings to you.

Pier Giorgio Frassati

Pax tecum.

To His Mother

Katowitz, December 28, 1922

Dearest mama,

After a horrible night I arrived this morning in this somewhat dirty city. I really should have arrived in Katowitz yesterday morning on the express train from Danzig to Katowitz but I had a thousand problems with the Poles; I spoke German and they didn't answer or rather they hardly answered and then they tried to cheat me.[1]

So from Danzig I returned to beautiful Berlin making a huge

surprise for Perugini and my German friends, who were thinking that I was already very far away from the German capital. By taking this indirect route I saved 2000 German Marks and a lot of inconvenience. Today the Polish customs agents at the border made me open my bags, which has never happened to me neither in Germany nor in Austria nor in Czechoslovakia until today.

I can hardly wait to leave this stretch of Upper Silesia which unfortunately has fallen into the hands of such a villainous people and to return to Germany, where the people are very kind and nice.

I wanted to push on all the way to Krakow, but I decided not to because it just isn't good to travel with the Poles.

This afternoon I'll visit the coal mine and then this evening I'll leave for Breslau where I'll stay until tomorrow at noon then go on through Regensburg to be in Munich for the end of the year.

Ask Papa if he can give 2 senatorial tickets[2] to Bertini who ought to go to Rome to represent our Cesare Balbo club before the high council which is meeting in assembly toward the first half of January. If you want to write, write via general delivery Freiburg im Breisgau.

Best wishes to all of you for a good ending and a good beginning and many kisses to you to Grandmother to papa, aunt, Luciana from

Pier Giorgio

[1] For political reasons, the Polish people had a deep dislike for the Germans. Therefore, it was not well received when Pier Giorgio addressed them in German.

[2] In his capacity as senator, Pier Giorgio's father received some tickets for free train travel for the family's use.

1923

To Antonio Villani

Munich, January 1, 1923

Dear Tonino,

You will be more upset than ever at my long silence, but for your part you have hardly ever written.

Last night I ended the year happily with a German family: the evening passed in an instant.

Unfortunately the time is now drawing near to leave this beautiful city and Germany,[1] leaving without knowing the day of return is very sad; but my heart tells me that my separation from this beautiful country will be brief. Tomorrow morning I will leave for Freiburg where I will only stop for a day to greet the family,[2] where I learned German so well and where I spent some unforgettable days.

Saturday January 6th I hope to be in Turin to again begin my intense life of study.

And what are you up to? Write to me sometime in Turin. When will you show up?

I hope that you have begun well the New Year which, let's hope, will bring true peace to all of Europe.

Regards to your parents, greetings to your sister, to you a thousand kisses

Pier Giorgio

---

[1] Educated in the German language from earliest infancy (recall his first little letter in this foreign language when he was 10 years old), and having grown up in a household which certainly was not opposed to German culture, Pier Giorgio had begun to consider Germany as a second spiritual fatherland, won over as well by that group of committed Catholics whom he had known in the course of his first journeys.

[2] This was the Rahner family.

To His Mother

Freiburg, January 3, 1923

Dear mama,

Today I was at the central post office in town and I was sure that I would receive a letter from home. It was a great joy for me to receive news of you all and to know that you have all begun the year well.

I started the year in Munich with the Dücks and we toasted it with punch; and at that moment I thought of all of you so far away physically, but very near in spirit.

Tomorrow or the day after I will unfortunately leave this last beautiful city of Germany; but I reluctantly leave Germany, where I have had to leave very dear friends who have treated me with so much kindness.

The other day I had a magnificent day and so the trip from Munich to Freiburg was stupendous.

Georg Rahner has again returned from Italy, where he was hoping to get a job, but unfortunately he didn't find anything.

Today I'm going for a walk in the neighborhood of Freiburg to give a farewell to the beautiful Black Forest.

Greetings to all my friends, to all of you a thousand kisses and I will see you soon.

Pier Giorgio

Greetings from the Rahner family.

To Maria Fischer

Freiburg, January 4, 1923

Dear Miss Fischer,

I'm sorry I didn't stop by Vienna, but time has flown by. After Christmas I traveled around Germany a lot and now I'm almost tired of traveling.

Tomorrow I have to leave the beautiful city of Freiburg and unfortunately I will have to say goodbye to Germany and to your Country.

I offer you my congratulations on the fact that the Crown[1] is finally improving. I hope that the New Year will bring much good to Austria.

I will send you from Turin some crowns that I have left over from my stay in Innsbruck. I ask you to distribute them as charity without saying who they are from.[2]

Give my greetings to the beautiful cathedral of St. Stephen and everywhere in the city of Vienna. I ask you to greet Miss Halledauer for me when you are in Innsbruck.

Regards to your parents; again many greetings to Miss Luisoni and to you cordially

Pier Giorgio Frassati

[1] He is speaking of the currency in Vienna.
[2] Pier Giorgio's acts of charity were not confined to the streets of Turin. It was a way of life for him, even when he traveled. Anonymity was always his preference.

To Antonio Villani

Turin, January 10, 1923

Dearest Tonino,

Unfortunately here I am again in this not-so-peaceful country; believe me I left Germany with great regret because I am a great admirer of the character of the German people.

Here in Italy the people change opinion at every change of the wind and then there isn't any more freedom; I find myself more of a foreigner in Turin than in Germany.[1]

I can't read the newspapers anymore because they only make our blood boil; have you seen the disgrace that the French are committing in the Ruhr?[2]

The occupation of that section of Germany is a disgrace because it means the ruin of the most Catholic part of the German population, but on the other hand it will be of much use to Germany because it will draw the sympathy of the free nations.

Now I am beginning my studies which I had interrupted and within two years I will also be, if God grants me life, working in the Ruhr; and as a Catholic I will help the Germans as much as possible in its recovery, because I consider the war against France to truly be a Holy War since France is the nation which is the daughter of Darkness, enemy of Peace.

So as not to be inferior to the Communists of all of Europe, we Catholic university students of Turin are preparing a letter of protest against the infamy of the military occupation in the Ruhr; a letter that I will send to Miss Schwan, so that she can convey it to the Catholic students of Bonn.³

I know that words accomplish little but at least we will make them understand that Catholic university students do not agree with the Italian government, but that they are indignant against the European policy that will lead all nations to a bad end.

In a few days now we will go to Canon Barberis to protest against the infamies of the Students' Residence, where the majority are Fascists; and therefore our friends must continually cope with abuses of power and live in an environment that I cannot describe to you in a letter.

Greetings to your sister, regards to your parents and to you a thousand kisses from

Pier Giorgio

Kind regards from all my family.

[1] Mussolini's Fascist government had come to power in Italy in October 1922.

[2] On January 11, 1923, France proceeded to occupy the principal centers of the Ruhr valley, in reaction to Germany's failure to pay the reparations expected from the Treaty of Versailles (having fallen prey to increasing inflation). The German government responded by organizing "passive resistance" and on January 22nd proclaimed a general strike in the Ruhr. The occupation also gave rise to violent clashes which culminated, on March 31, 1923, in the shooting of thirteen German workers by French soldiers. Opposed as he was to every form of violence, Pier Giorgio saw, with the occupation of the Ruhr, the fall of another bulwark of Catholic social activism and German democracy.

[3] This gesture was a sign of Pier Giorgio's moral strength and political convictions. At so delicate a moment, to protest against the government about the development of French political maneuvers planned under the pretext of assuring the greatest possible peace in Europe, was truly an act of courage.

To the Catholic Men and Women Students of Bonn[1]

Turin, January 12, 1923

In these tragic and painful moments when your country is trampled under foreign feet, while your adversary occupies your hearths as an enemy of your country, we Catholic students send you an expression of our fraternal love.

We have no possibility of changing the sad situation, but we feel within ourselves the entire strength of our Christian love which unites us in brotherhood beyond all national boundaries.

Governments today are not heeding the Pope's warning: "True peace is more a fruit of Christian love for one's neighbor than it is a fruit of justice," and they are preparing new wars for the future of all humanity.

Modern society is drowning in the sorrows of human passions and it is distancing itself from every ideal of love and peace. Catholics, we and you, must bring the breath of goodness that can only spring from faith in Christ.

Brethren, in these new trials and terrible griefs, know that the great Christian family is praying for you; act in such a way that your sufferings and trials might become lighter for you to bear.

Since peace cannot return to the world without God, at least may you, as men of good will, cherish in your hearts Him Who in the stable was announced by the Angels as the Savior of Humanity.

Pier Giorgio Frassati
University Club "Cesare Balbo"

[1] This letter of Pier Giorgio was written in German and printed in the *Deutsche Reichs-Zeitung* (a German newspaper) as a protest against the French occupation of the Ruhr.

To Charlotte Kohlstedt

Turin, January 13, 1923

Dear Miss Kohlstedt,

I have been in Turin for two days since returning from Germany.

It was very painful for me to leave your Country, because of the many dear friends that I know there.

Yesterday my association sent a letter to Bonn to the Catholic students to protest against the terrible occupation by the French troops.

Today France has carried out an insane action; people who have a clear conscience must vote against the French. Today France has gravely wounded the heart of Germany, but I believe that it will be wounded by the same sword.

As for us Catholics, our hearts are breaking because we know that the entry of the enemy troops, especially of those Frenchmen, is the signal of the beginning of the demoralization of the Ruhr. I who have seen the entry of the enemy troops on the Rhine, understand the pain of the German people. But we cannot do anything else but pray that in these sad times God will grant the necessary patience to the German people, and everything will turn out for the best. I hope that God will listen to the prayers of all true Catholics. My greetings to the Seituns and the Gambettas, and in these sad times, may you in a special way be cordially greeted by a friend of Germany.

Pier Giorgio Frassati

Have you received the package for Christmas?

To Maria Schwan [1]

January 1923

Two days ago I received a letter from my good friend Mr. Domanig, who is the representative of the Austrian Students in Pax Romana.

In this letter he laments the urgent needs and misery that exist in Austria. The Union of Catholic Charity (founded by Chancellor Seipel four years ago) has started the Youth Protection Association.

It looks like this Association will be dissolved because the necessary funds are lacking. There are many children and women workers in Vienna today without a roof over their heads, left prey to hunger and misery. My friend is begging me to assist them with a collection.

In the spirit of Pax Romana I thought that you would be able to do the same in Holland.

I know you and your kind heart and I am certain that you will do it with joy.

I beg you to reply to me immediately and then I will send your address to Mr. Domanig and my friend will correspond directly with you.

Many grateful thanks in anticipation, and I cordially greet you

Pier Giorgio Frassati

Pax tecum.

---

[1] The name of the addressee is missing in the letter, but it is fairly certain that it was written to Maria Schwan.

To Maria Fischer

Turin, January 23, 1923

Dear Miss Fischer,

Thank you for your lovely letter. I have resumed my studies and I have to work very hard.

Yesterday I was in the mountains with my friends! We had a wonderful ski trip: it was magnificent.

If my studies permit me I will go to the mountains for Carnevale.[1] Mr. Domanig has written me a letter asking me a favor: I would have to take up a collection for the poor young abandoned girls in Vienna. It would be a great joy for me to be able to do something for Austria, but I'm afraid that I won't get much because here in Italy we're also going through a difficult period and there are also many poor unemployed people here and the people are also sinking down morally more and more.

Today's Heads of Government do not heed the warning of the Pope who says: "True peace is more a fruit of Christian love for one's neighbor than it is a fruit of justice," and hence is born the destruction of the world. But we need to have patience because the people know not what they do.

I who have traveled a lot across Germany admire the attitude of the German people today more than ever.

Today the German people are an example for all nations of true love for one's Country and of taking life seriously. At this time when all human rights are being trampled on by the French, may the German people receive prayers from us who are powerless to send material aid.

I'm sending you 90 thousand crowns that I had left over from my trip and I ask you to use the money as you wish. In this *my name should remain secret.*

Let me know again how you are doing.

Many cordial greetings and pax tecum from

Pier Giorgio Frassati

Greetings to Miss Halledauer.

[1] Carnevale was the period before the start of the Lenten season.

To Antonio Villani

Turin, January 24, 1923

Dearest Tonino,

The elections for the "Cesare Balbo" club were held a few days ago; I and all the members of the old administration decided not to accept any more offices no matter who was elected but it still turned out that Bertini was elected with 31 votes and I with 27, but we immediately submitted our resignations.[1]

The old administration had put up Pinin Brusasca as a candidate for the presidency, but that failed miserably because that evening those put forward by the Catholic Student Residence came into office. Guardia Riva is now the president; the club is in the hands of the student residence because the old friends have disappeared.

And what are you up to? Are you coming to spend Carnevale in the mountains with the Sucai?[2]

I sort of wanted to go but last night I was in a total crisis because I'm leading a good-for-nothing life[3] and so I don't know if I'll be going to the Little St. Bernard as much as I'd like because from now on I'd prefer to find myself in the company of young women as little as possible.

I've not yet started studying; I'm losing a lot of time but now I'll seriously concentrate so that I won't repeat what happened last summer. Write something to me because especially in these times I enjoy receiving nice words from friends.

Regards to your parents, greetings to your sister, to you a thousand kisses from

Pier Giorgio

[1] This was the first public display of clear and decisive opposition to the growing infiltration accomplished by Fascist elements, or those sympathetic to Fascism, in the bosom of the Catholic associations. Pier Giorgio resigned, knowing well that if he had accepted office, his adversaries would have exploited the situation.

[2] Sucai was the abbreviation for the Sezione Universitaria del Club Alpino Italiano (University Chapter of the Italian Alpine Club).

[3] During this period, Pier Giorgio began to experience an interior struggle brought on by his love for Laura Hidalgo, a member of FUCI and a member of the group that went on outings together to places like the Little St. Bernard.

To Willibald Leitgebel

Turin, January 28, 1923

Dear Willibald,

Please forgive me if I haven't written to you more, but unfortunately I always have a lot to do.

Although I write little to the Germans, I think of them a lot.

The days spent in Germany are for me amongst the most wonderful of my youth[1] and it is with profound sadness that I observe, unfortunately helplessly, your Country's harsh and difficult situation.

We too have lost the most beautiful and best thing that God has given to all men, namely freedom, without which life becomes difficult.

The Governments, above all that of France, don't want to recognize the Pope's warning: "True peace is more a fruit of Christian love for one's neighbor than it is a fruit of justice," and so hatred is sown in the world today instead of Charity.

War has annihilated moral sensibility in all Nations and we become helpless witnesses of France's brutality, while our Catholic conscience trembles in the face of this infamy.

But we can do nothing about foreign policy, since Catholics in Italy have unfortunately lost their freedom; with a bleeding heart we watch our Government help France and we cannot stop it. But we are sure that God will reward Germany for her harsh sufferings.

A friend of mine has finished University and would like to enroll at Rentlingen near Stuttgart in the school of textile arts. He has asked me to inquire in Germany whether the school is still open and if they make difficulties for foreigners.

Please, when you have time, ask the professors in Charlottenburg for some information. My friend, being from Merano, speaks better German than he does Italian.

When you have a reply, please write to me.

Many greetings to your brother and your sister and my regards to your parents and a cordial greeting to you from

Pier Giorgio Frassati

---

[1] The huge impression Germany made upon Pier Giorgio is mentioned in his letters several times. There he came into contact with a Catholic world of moral and social zeal, very different from that which he knew in Italy which had, much to his disappointment, succumbed to Fascism.

Turin, February 3, 1923

Dear Willibald,

I hope that you have received my letter sent from Turin.

At this time, which is so hard for your Country, we Catholics must pray a lot to God that He may again give true peace to men. Our Faith helps us with the great hope that this life is short and that only afterwards comes the true Life, in which Justice will triumph.

I've wanted to do a lot for the Germans, but unfortunately I can't do anything. Take this money, please, for the poor children of Berlin: it's only a little, but it's better than nothing.

Kindest regards to your mother. Greetings to your sister and your brother and cordially to you.

Pier Giorgio

To the Board of Directors of the "Cesare Balbo" Club

Turin, February 12, 1923

The Undersigned would like to have some explanation regarding the contract for the billiards table, applauding the Board's initiative in opening the room for the Members, thus discouraging our members from playing in certain places that are not very favorable to morality and creating a certain income which can contribute to restabilizing the desperate finances of the "Cesare Balbo Club."

With profound esteem in J.C.

Pier Giorgio Frassati

To Antonio Villani

Turin, February 1923

Dearest Tonino,

I arrived in Turin the other day after having spent Carnevale at the Little St. Bernard with the Sucai: there were 16 of us but we all got along very well. The weather wasn't very nice, but on the bright side we had a magnificent snowfall. Now I am into studying applied chemistry, because I plan to take the exam within a month along with third year machine design and then during Easter vacation I'll study Grassi[1] so that I can take the oral exam around the end of April.

We have a new presidency in the Club; it's a bit military, but on the whole it's doing well and so I've retired from the life of the Club and so have all the old guard; we only offer our services as simple members. The contract for the billiards table has been concluded and the Club is committed to paying 1700 lire within two years.

The P.I. Party convention[2] will be after Easter; where we hope that a sure path to follow will finally be outlined; I am happy that you are coming and so I am inviting you to be a houseguest from now on and thus we'll have many more hours to talk a bit about our things.

I'm sending you a package, which is a modest present that I'm giving you for your graduation; you'll have to excuse the lateness due to many reasons not excluding my own disorder.

My parents thank you for your greetings and they send theirs to you.

Excuse the brevity of this letter, but I don't have any more time for now and I'll write you a longer letter in a few days.

Regards to your parents and a thousand kisses in J.C. to you.

Fra Girolamo[3]

P.S. Bertini found one of your books in his house The Disciple by Bourget and I'm taking it upon myself to ask you if you want him to donate it to our Club Library in your name.

[1] This was the textbook for his course in electronics.
[2] It was one of the last free congresses of the Italian People's Party, which led to the exit of the Party's members from government.
[3] This is the first of many times that Pier Giorgio signs with the name "Fra Girolamo." This name (Brother Jerome) was the one he had chosen when he made his vows as a Dominican Tertiary on May 28, 1922. It was based on his admiration of a fiery Dominican preacher named Girolamo Savonarola who was hanged and burned on May 23, 1498, in Florence.

To Marco Beltramo

Little St. Bernard, March 4, 1923

We really had a good time today; we had a wonderful ski trip with a magnificent view from Mont Blanc over the Aiguille Noire de Péteret. I left my heart on those mountains with the hope of finding it again this summer climbing Mont Blanc.
Cordial greetings.

P.G. Frassati

To Maria Fischer

Turin, March 7, 1923

Dear Miss Fischer,

You must pardon me if I am not replying to your letter until today.

I spent Carnevale in the merry company of young men and women, students who make up the greater part of the Catholic Clubs. We spent a week of spiritual peace, far from the noises of the world. We skied all day, we only left our skis for an hour at midday and sat down at table where the meal was prepared by the girls, so that almost every one of us had our own cook.

We returned on Ash Wednesday. The weather was splendid and during the trip we enjoyed the splendid sight of Mont Blanc, the highest Peak in Europe.

Now the good weather has passed, we are in Lent and we also unfortunately have to study. God has divided up our life very well because He gives a joy alternating with a serious time.

I read today in the Italian newspapers the speech given by the Chancellor Dr. Cuno. Dr. Cuno has made a good strong speech and I believe that we Catholics should support it because he as a Catholic spoke as a Catholic.

He could have responded to foreign action with harsh words, but instead he wanted to denounce France's crime to civilized people, using more compassionate words, and I am sure that this desperate cry will find an echo of agreement in the conscience of all men.

With best wishes that a better time may soon return for your

Country and for Germany, I greet you cordially

Pier Giorgio Frassati

Pax tecum.

Have you received the January and February issues of "Studium"?[1]

[1] Pier Giorgio bought her a subscription to this Catholic monthly which is still published in Italy today.

To Antonio Villani

Santa Croce,[1] March 26, 1923

Dearest Villani,

Thanks for your letter and the nice words contained therein.

I'm writing to you while I have open before me that wonderful book of St. Thomas Aquinas and when I read those sublime concepts, I always think of you who were the first to instill in me the desire to know the great truths contained in this work written to exalt, to glorify Divine Providence.[2]

During these days when we gather to pray in the tranquility of this house, I will also pray for you, and please pray a lot for me, so that, if unfortunately in this earthly life we shall have to be far apart because of the necessities of our careers, at least the day that the Lord will choose, we'll find ourselves together again in our true Homeland to sing the praises of God.

As soon as I return to Turin if my good intention doesn't leave me, I will resume my studies because I intend to take the oral exam in Grassi and then Thermotechnical Hydraulics and metallurgical chemistry in July. In fact if you have some notes on these subjects please bring them to me when you come to Turin.

A few days ago I took the exam in machine design (I got 60%, I didn't deserve any better not having finished the designs), and in applied chemistry. This last exam went well in the beginning but not so well toward the end and so I had 65%; too bad, next time I'll study harder and so I'll deserve better marks.

And what are you up to? Do you always have a lot to do?

I think you'll miss university life with all its attractive features.

Farewell dear Villani and see you soon.

Best wishes for a happy Easter to all of your family and to you in particular in J.C.

Fra Girolamo

[1] This was the location of a retreat house conducted by the Jesuit Fathers in the hill country outside of Turin.
[2] It was his habit to do spiritual reading, and from this he drew nourishment for his faith.

To Fritz Beck(?)[1]

How goes it with the Catholic organization? Although a big storm may have passed over us, may the well-sown seed bear good fruit.

It will be Easter when you receive this letter of mine and I hope that just as life rises anew at Easter, so the world will arise to a more intense Christian life.

Receive as a greeting the interior peace which only men of good will can have and whose possession is for us Catholics what is best.

Pax tecum.

Pier Giorgio Frassati

[1] This letter was undated and had no addressee. From its contents, it seems to have been written shortly before Easter either in 1923 or 1924, and its reference to the world situation indicates that it may have been sent to Germany.

To Antonio Villani

Turin, June 20, 1923

Dearest Tonino,

While I have some time I'm writing to you, because I'm nauseated by all the events that have happened in Italy these past few days. You've seen that the organ of the Cathedral of Borgo D. Donnino played the Royal March and the hymn Giovinezza,[1] while the Prime Minister was visiting the church. It takes a lot of gall to get to the point of profaning with such hymns the temple, the house of God, where O.L.J.C.[2] is truly present in the tabernacle; and then have you seen what the Turin Fascists have done? I have only one hope, and that is in Providence, that He will give better times to Italy, we hope, but I'm afraid that these bad events may be chastisements sent by God to atone for all our sins.

On Saturday I'll take the exam in Electrical technology and so I ask you to remember me in your prayers on the day of my exam, and so, God willing, another huge load will be taken from me. Soon after I've taken this exam I'll find out how I can take the exam in Machine Construction toward the end of the next month otherwise I won't have enough time to prepare for Chemical Metallurgy.

I've already spoken to Falchetti the painter regarding you, but as soon as he comes back to Turin I'll remind him;[3] we hope that you can come to Turin soon and so we can again spend some time together.

Greetings to your sister, kind regards to your family, and to you a thousand greetings in J.C.

Pier Giorgio

I received your letter this morning, I'm already at the Polytechnic but Collonnetti is away from Turin, he won't arrive until Saturday, June 23, 1923; I'll drop in on him on Saturday and as soon as I will know something I'll write to you.

[1] This hymn was the anthem of the Fascist movement.
[2] Abbreviation for Our Lord Jesus Christ.
[3] He refers to a recommendation Villani wanted in order to obtain work with the telephone company.

Forno, July 8, 1923

Returning from Levanna's glacier I thank you for the magnificent service rendered to me by your ice-axe.

Christian greetings.

P. Giorgio Frassati

Turin, July 9, 1923

Dearest Tonino,

Yesterday I was up 3500 meters high to breathe a bit of good air and to get new energy in order to be well ahead for the Montel exam. On Saturday evening we got wet from some rain which was rather annoying, because then we had to sleep in our wet clothes in the place where we stayed that night. Then Sunday was one of those magnificent days and from the glacier my thoughts went to my distant friends; I would like to have had all of them here to enjoy this marvelous spectacle with me.

The last bit was the most enjoyable, because we made the climb on the side where the rocks were steeper, but at the same time more solid.

And now I must not think anymore about these beautiful things and unfortunately must return to my study of thermotechnology.

And what are you doing? Are you always building?

After the 15th I'll call on Colonnetti again to hear if there is any news about you.

Again a thousands thanks for your ice-axe, which served me very well.

Regards to your parents, greetings to your sister and a thousand kisses to you.

Pier Giorgio

I hope you will receive the postcard which I sent you from Forno.

Thursday, July 19, 1923

Dearest Tonino,

Yesterday I went by the Polytechnic to speak to Prof. Colonnetti on your behalf, but he's out of Turin for a few days.

On Monday my sister got her law degree, her thesis being on public water legislation, and she graduated with distinction and full honors.

Today I attended the burial of a Bachelor of Arts, Bertini's friend and Turin correspondent of the newspaper "Nazione." He died of tuberculosis in St. Louis Hospital and today I saw him before they put him in the casket. He was in a pitiful state; I wasn't able to stay in the room more than 2 minutes, because he was already nearly decomposed and therefore it wasn't convenient to stay any longer.[1] But it was good for me to see this. I reflected and thought that within a few years I will also be in that same state; I will then also arouse a sense of compassion mixed with disgust and yet I have sometimes been ambitious. And for what? Just for death, this great mystery, the only just one which spares no one, which will dissolve this body of mine and in a short time will turn it into dust. But beyond the material body there is the soul to which we must dedicate all our energy, so that it can present itself before the Supreme Tribunal without fault or at least with little faults, so that after having served some years in purgatory it will be able to go up to Eternal peace. But how does one prepare oneself for the great Transition and when? Since one does not know when Death will come to take him away, it is very prudent to prepare oneself every day as if one is going to die that same day; and so from now on I will try to make every day a little preparation for death, so that I shouldn't find myself unprepared at the point of death and have to regret the beautiful years of youth, wasted from the spiritual side.[2]

And what are you doing? What do you say about these resolutions of mine, which I hope I will be able to keep with the Grace of God?

This year I am disheartened about myself, because until now I've only taken the exam in principles of Electrotechnology, then I tried "Machine Construction," but that didn't go well and now I'm back studying Thermotechnology, but the heat kills me; I stay at the desk for many hours without accomplishing anything; I don't know if I'll be able to take the exam. In any case this summer I will study intensely in order to make up for the wrong done, otherwise this hoped-for degree will never arrive.

Fun is okay in the winter, but when winter is ending one must get down to studying because one doesn't accomplish anything in the heat of summer.

These are all resolutions that I go making every year and then the next year I make sure to forget them. You see how my morale is low this year. Now as soon as I have finished this exam I will go to climb Mon Viso and I'll have another chance to use your ice-axe which for now is in my care since the good Severi left for Modena this morning.

Regards to your parents, greetings to your sister.

To you a cordial greeting in Jesus Christ.

Pier Giorgio

I received the letter of the 18th; as soon as I know something I'll reply.

[1] Thus he encountered the death of a young man whom he had visited some days beforehand along with Bertini. His name was Spalassa, and he didn't have anyone who cared about him, except the nurse and some acquaintances. When Pier Giorgio and Bertini went to find him he didn't have more than a few days left to live, but Spalassa still had hope; he wanted to live! Pier Giorgio gently sought to instill in him a spirit of resignation to God's will and to prepare him for death in a Christian way. Unfortunately, when he returned to visit him again, he was already dead.

[2] These words demonstrate a remarkable spiritual maturity, especially considering the fact that they were coming from a young man who was in the best of health and who was only twenty-two years old. Pier Giorgio could not have known at the time that his own death was less than two years away.

To His Mother

Monviso, July 26, 1923

Returning from Mon Viso climbing the south wall (without a rope) under the best mountaineer guide my friend Paolo Gilli I send you a thousand kisses.

Pier Giorgio

To Antonio Severi

Pollone, July 29, 1923

Dearest Tonino,

Yesterday I left the beautiful mountains to come back here to start my studies again.

I am very happy to have been at Mon Viso so much so that next year if I'm still alive, I'd like to camp out in those regions for a couple of weeks to get myself into shape to climb Mount Cervino the day of my graduation.

Today there is a big celebration in Pollone, half the people of Biella will take part in the blessing of the flag of the boys' and girls' club. I am also the godfather of the flag of the girls' club.[1]

This morning at 6 there was a Mass and General Communion:[2] there were about fifty young men and also many young girls. In the afternoon at 3 there will be the reception of the clubs from the surrounding villages and at 4 the blessing of the flags and then a march through the streets of the village with three bands. I think it will be a beautiful demonstration of faith; at the end of the march there will be a meeting and in the evening a play.

In spring of 1924, if we are still alive, I and Beltramo have decided to try to climb Rognosa through a crest which up till now it seems has never been done: we need to overcome 7 rocky peaks, but that doesn't present a great difficulty.

Every day that goes by I fall deeply in love with the mountains; their charm attracts me.

Thanks for the postcard, regards to your parents thousands of kisses to you.

Pier Giorgio

[1] It was a custom to have a godfather or patron for a group's flag on the occasion of its blessing.

[2] In those days, most people received Holy Communion infrequently, due to a sense of unworthiness and a deep reverence for the Eucharist. A "General Communion" was often a part of a special celebration sponsored by a church group such as a sodality or confraternity. In preparation, the group's members went to confession before receiving Communion together at Mass. They wore the group's insignia and sat together as a body in the church.

To the Members of "Catholic Youth" of Pollone[1]

Sunday, July 29, 1923

Young people of Pollone,

Today God's minister has blessed your prayer, and he has invoked upon you the blessings of heaven, so that every one of you may be worthy of this flag and may defend it against every attack.

Because this flag, young people, represents in a symbolic way a divine doctrine, given by Jesus Christ for our redemption.

Young people, I see on your flag the motto "Prayer, Action and Sacrifice." These are three words which summarize a very vast program whose implementation requires our energies and those of generations to come.

Prayer is the noble supplication which we lift up to the throne of God. It is the most efficient means to obtain from God the graces which we need, and especially the strength of persevering in these times, in which the hatred of the sons of the devil is breaking out violently against the sheep who are faithful to the fold.

In recommending heartfelt prayer to you, I am including all the practices of piety, first of all the most Holy Eucharist.

And remembering that apostle of the Holy Eucharist, the Holy Father Pius X[2] of venerable memory, I urge you with all the strength of my soul to approach the Eucharistic Table as often as possible. Feed on this Bread of the Angels from which you will draw the strength to fight inner struggles, the struggles against passions and against all adversities, because Jesus Christ has promised to those who feed themselves with the most Holy Eucharist, eternal life and the necessary graces to obtain it.

And when you become totally consumed by this Eucharistic Fire, then you will be able to thank with greater awareness the Lord God who has called you to be part of His flock and you will enjoy that peace which those who are happy according to the world have never tasted. Because true happiness, young people, does not consist in the pleasures of the world and in earthly things, but in peace of conscience which we can have only if we are pure in heart and in mind.

After having fortified our spirit by applying ourselves with great diligence to works of mercy, and after having intensely studied the questions which are troubling us, then we can throw ourselves into the apostolate. And there are three distinct apostolates.

First of all there is the apostolate of good example. We Catholics must strive to have our whole life guided by Christian moral law. Then there is the apostolate of charity by going among those who suffer and comforting them, among the unfortunate and saying a comforting word to them, because the Catholic religion is based on charity which is nothing other than the most perfect Love.

The Apostle St. Paul says, "The charity of Christ needs us," and without this fire, which little by little must destroy our personality so that our heart beats only for the sorrows of others, we would not be Christians, much less Catholics.

Finally there is the apostolate of persuasion. This is one of the most beautiful and necessary. Young people, approach your colleagues at work who live their lives away from the Church and spend their free time not in healthy pastimes, but in vices. Persuade those unfortunate people to follow the ways of God, strewn with many thorns, but also many roses.

But if every one of you were to possess these gifts to the highest degree, and did not have the spirit of sacrifice in abundance, you would not be a good Catholic. We must sacrifice everything for everything: our ambitions, indeed our entire selves, for the cause of the Faith.

In order for our life to be Christian, it must be a continual renunciation, a continual sacrifice which however is not burdensome when only we think about what these few years passed in sorrow are, compared with a happy eternity, where joy will have no measure nor end, and where we will enjoy a peace beyond anything we could imagine. And so, young people, learn how to sacrifice from our Lord Jesus Christ. In order to atone for our horrible sins, He sacrificed Himself as an Innocent Victim on Calvary, and He renews this wonderful Sacrifice every day in every part of the world during Holy Mass.

From this day forward you have become part of the great family of the "Italian Catholic Youth." Hold high the place that the Lord in His Goodness has wanted to award you.

The times which we are going through are difficult, because persecution against the Church rages as cruelly as ever. But you fearless and good young people, do not be afraid because of this small problem. Bear in mind the fact that the Church is a divine institution that cannot end and will endure until the end of the world, and "the gates of hell will not prevail against her." Therefore keep this beautiful white flag immaculate, and if the occasion should present itself tomorrow, defend it, because from now on it is sacred: it not only represents your club, it also represents the most beautiful patrimony of our Italy and of the civilized world.

And in order to bring these poor words of mine to an end, let me cry out with you: Long live Jesus Christ! Long live the Pope!

Pier Giorgio Frassati

[1] Pier Giorgio gave this speech on the occasion of the blessing of the flag of which he was the godfather.

[2] When Pier Giorgio was just two years old, Pope Pius X took office. One of the changes implemented during the pontificate (1903 to 1914) of St. Pius X was most significant for Pier Giorgio. He advised everyone to receive Holy Communion daily, if possible, and he recommended that children should make their First Holy Communion not long after reaching the age of reason (around seven years old). Until then, it had been the practice to wait until one had been confirmed, around the age of 12 or older. This enabled the daily reception of the Eucharist to become a part of Pier Giorgio's sacramental life from a very early age.

To Antonio Severi

Pollone, August 2, 1923

Dearest Tonino,

I have just gotten to this peaceful place and now my vacation is coming to an end.

The other day we blessed the flags of the boys' and girls' club (but I and Miss Billotti were the only godfather and godmother for the young people's flag).

Great enthusiasm reigned in the hearts of those wonderful young people and more than a thousand of the brothers and sisters flocked to Pollone to honor these new flags. I believe that Pollone hasn't experienced enthusiasm like this for a long time: the 2 clubs are flourishing well enough now. There is a lot to be done now and the hardest work is that of founding the sister organizations near these 2 clubs, namely, one for Catholic men and another for Catholic women; but we shouldn't be afraid and we should always have faith in the goodness of God Who will give us the necessary help to establish these 2 important branches of Catholic Action.

I marched in the procession wearing your beret which was admired very much and we had also a photo taken of the flags together with the godmother and godfather and as soon as I have it I will send it to you.

And what are you doing? Are you thinking of studying this coming summer or have your plans already vanished?

N.B. – I found a young lady in the Quintino Sella mountain chalet who had certain qualifications to be a good wife for you because she is a fairly good mountain climber and a first class talker; but other defects made me abandon this idea straight away because she does not have such good morals as you would have liked. I wanted to send you a telegram, but the fact that she was a girl or lady of little Christian sensibility prevented me from doing so. There'll be another time.

Greetings and regards to your parents.

Pier Giorgio

To Marco Beltramo

Pollone, August 6, 1923

Dearest Marco,

I've just received the photos of the trip to Monviso from Reviglio; they turned out fairly well: but for the moment I cannot send them to you, because Reviglio printed only one copy of them for me. I have written already to Turin and I hope to have more in a few days; your photo didn't turn out too well, too bad, there will be another time.

I've already started to study; the subject is rather hard but I want to apply myself with a good attitude, because the day of reckoning is approaching, when one will reap what has been sown.

I hope to be able to make the trip to Mont Blanc next week and then I won't move from this place anymore; it's a bit hot, but peaceful enough, made just right for studying.

Have you already thought about the gift we'll give to Gilli?[1]

Up until now I haven't had time, because studies and other little things have kept me very busy.

Thanks for the money order, but it wasn't necessary to send it to me, you really could have waited until my return to Turin.

Do you still intend to climb to the top of the Rognosa by the crest this spring, if God gives us life? I'm always ready because every day I fall in love with the mountains more and more and, if my studies would allow me to do it, I would spend entire days on the mountains contemplating in that pure air the Greatness of the Creator.

Greetings to your brother regards to your family cordial greetings to you.

Pier Giorgio

---

[1] Gilli was their guide for their climb of Mon Viso. As a thank you, they gave him a water canteen. The money order mentioned in this letter was in reference to Marco's regulation regarding payment of expenses for the trip.

To Antonio Severi

Pollone, August 8, 1923

Dearest friend,

Villani left the other day and I cracked the books, because I have little time and a lot of material to cover.

I've wanted to go to Mont Blanc these days along with Delpiano and a club from Biella, but my father doesn't want to let me go, because he says that it's too dangerous: too bad; this means that I'll stay at home and my studies will get along better.

I have very few distractions here in this pleasant place and so I can concentrate on my books and meanwhile time flies by terribly fast.

Yesterday we formed a group of young men and women to put on little plays to defray the huge expenses incurred by the parish priest in the repairing of the Club's music hall. Believe me, I don't really like these little plays being done by a mixed group, but I'll look into it, maybe we could put on a play that is very serious.

In all of my outings I haven't written to the young ladies as I had told you I would; I haven't written to Laura for obvious reasons[1] nor to the others so as not to make her upset and so I can't really tell you what is going on with them.

The photographs taken at Monviso turned out very well so I'm enclosing my photograph for you in remembrance of our outing together and of our common love for the mountains.

You tell me to come and visit you and I would come very willingly if these four blessed exams didn't keep me here at Pollone, no matter what I have to take them within a month and a half. I'm very sorry but it really is impossible to visit you this year.

I ought to pull your ears a little bit, because you start distracting yourself instead of putting into practice the good resolutions which you made in Turin.

And so Tonino you have to make yourself proud this October by taking at least two exams and then this winter apply yourself seriously because the years are passing by and we're getting old and so we have to become wise.

Regards to your family and a thousand greetings to you.

Pier Giorgio

[1] The "obvious reasons" were the deep feelings that had sprung up in him toward Laura Hidalgo, his friend and fellow FUCI member. Although he shared his feelings with his closest friends, he had not shared them with Laura.

Pollone, August 13, 1923

Dearest Tonino,

Thanks for your postcard from St. Pellegrino and please thank your kind sisters and all the others who signed it. May I ask a question: aren't the Boschetti girls from Alessandria? I'd like to know because I was very surprised that their signatures appeared on the postcard.

Did you see the tragic end of the poor lawyer Loretz? Unfortunately he was killed at the Chateau des Dames, a very easy glacier, which I scaled 2 years ago with the guide Carrel's son without noticing the dangers from falling stones. But this year the thaw is stronger because it's so hot and so the rocks are more easily dislodged.

It's lucky that your goddaughter hasn't climbed the Grivola, because this year it should be much more dangerous than other years.

This is what will happen to me in a few years' time and so the moral is: when one goes into the mountains one should sort out one's conscience first, because one never knows if one will return. But despite all this I'm not afraid and on the contrary I want to climb the mountains more than ever, to conquer the most daring peaks; to feel that pure joy, which one can only have in the mountains.

My studying is going along fairly well, Hydraulics doesn't seem too hard, but on the other hand Chemical Metallurgy is very boring and difficult.

Should I send you your beret?

Regards to your parents, greetings to your sisters and to you a cordial greeting in J.C.

Pier Giorgio

Pax Domini sit tecum.[1]

[1] A Latin greeting meaning, "May the Peace of the Lord be with you."

To Costantino Guardia Riva

Pollone, August 14, 1923

Dearest friend,

I just received your nice circular letter in which you very reasonably insist that our flag be escorted by a good number of members. I would very willingly like to be able to be at the side of our flag in that very beautiful and mystical city.

I would not only like to be able to spend some days in the peace of Assisi, but I would be very happy to again see all of you and our friends from all parts of Italy whom I haven't seen since the day when we defended our beautiful flags in the streets of Rome.

But while I'll be with you in spirit in Assisi another duty keeps me here: my exams, which I must prepare for October.

Being unable to take part please greet all of our friends for me and I hope that the Convention results in a new Affirmation of our Ideals and writes a truly glorious page in the history of FUCI.

Pier Giorgio Frassati

Pax Domini sit tecum.

I may try to attend the Eucharistic Congress in Genoa but even if I can't go there I'll commit myself to attending the Regional Convention of Novara's G.C.I.,[1] which will be held in Varallo on September 2nd.

[1] He is referring to a meeting of the Italian Catholic Youth, in Italian the Gioventù Cattolica Italiana.

To Carlo Bellingeri

Pollone, August 15, 1923

Dearest Carlo,

After having left Turin I went to Crissolo to climb Monviso with Beltramo and Gilli. On the 26th of last month having a beautiful day we left the Quintino Sella hostel at 3:30 a.m. and by 8:30 a.m. we reached the summit taking the easier way up, but after having gone up another way toward the left, without using the rope.

It was a wonderful trip: then we wanted to climb Visolotto, but Gilli couldn't do any more climbing and it wasn't prudent to go on our own.

Then I came here to enjoy the fresh air, instead it's terribly hot, I need to shut myself inside the house so that I can study; otherwise I accomplish nothing.

On the 29th of the past month there took place the blessing of the flags of 2 Catholic clubs in Pollone. I was the godfather of the boys' flag. A huge number of boys and girls came together with their beautiful white flags from every village of the strong Biellese people to bring a bit of their great enthusiasm to this cold town. A thousand people marched along the streets of the village and I think Pollone has never seen such a huge number of people for any other flag; if one wants a well-done celebration it has to be a Catholic one.

I've already begun studying now and my study is going along well enough and in the coming month I'll increase the hours, hoping that the next rain will bring a bit of fresh air.

Maybe next week I'll go to Courmayeur to climb Mont Blanc along with Delpiano and the Alpine Club of Biella, but up until now I haven't yet decided.

I would have gladly gone to the FUCI Convention, which this year will be held at the end of this month in pleasant Assisi, but I have to give it up for a greater cause[1] (my studies). Maybe I'll go to that Eucharistic Congress in Genoa and if my studies don't permit even that, I'll go to the meeting of the G.C. of Novara, which will be held in Varallo on September 2nd.

In any case as soon as I've decided something about Genoa, I'll write to you and so you write something to me too. We could travel together from Turin to Genoa.

Thanks for your nice postcard. My regards to your parents, greetings to your sisters and brothers and to you a thousand things in J.C.

Pier Giorgio

Pax Domini sit tecum.

---

[1] It was a tremendous sacrifice for Pier Giorgio to have to give up these conventions which were the big celebrations of his life. But his sense of duty regarding his studies cancelled out every other consideration.

To Antonio Severi

Pollone, August 20, 1923

Dearest Tonino,

I should have climbed Mont Blanc with Delpiano last Saturday, but we didn't understand each other very well on the telephone and so Delpiano left on his own.

At first I was very displeased, but today I saw that this misunderstanding was a plan of Divine Providence, because the other day my uncle, already sick for a long time, got worse and so I would have been infinitely more upset to have been away.

And today while I write I am so sad and I need to write to you who, like me, trusts in the great Goodness of the Lord, not to lift up my spirit which, although stricken, is resigned only because of that Faith, which I learned from childhood and which I have strengthened through contact with all my friends in the club. My uncle, who loves me so much was so moved to see me, that today I couldn't approach his bed for fear of upsetting him too much, but now my task has been accomplished. Although unworthy I was an instrument of Divine Providence, along with my good mother and the nun who lovingly cared for him, because I was able to get him to perform all his religious practices. Believe me that when he received the Sacred Host tears of joy mixed with those of sorrow streamed down my face. As soon as he received the Host, our merciful God soothed his pain and afterward my uncle made us call the parish priest of the village to tell him about his satisfaction in having received the Blessed Sacrament.[1]

In His Infinite Mercy, God has surely not kept my innumerable sins in mind, but He has heard my prayers and the prayers of my family, and has given my uncle the great grace of receiving the last Sacraments while fully conscious.

I believe that life should be a continual preparation for the next life, because one doesn't know the day nor the hour of our passing.

Poor Loretz is actually the vice president of the G.M. and I think about the grief of his poor sister, who was there when he had his accident.[2]

Speaking of Grivola the other day a worker from "La Stampa" stopped by to see my uncle, a few days ago she had climbed Grivola on the rocky side. She said that it is a mountain that she wouldn't climb again, because it is a gamble. It's all crumbling rock, she barely passed a place when an enormous hunk fell off, and if it had cracked off a second earlier it would have killed the entire group of climbers tied together.

I'll send you your beret, if possible, by parcel post insured for L. 100.

I will not take part in the convention in Genoa either. Affectionate greetings in J.C.

Pier Giorgio

Pax Domini sit tecum.

1 His Uncle Pietro Frassati wasn't practicing the Faith but he had a great respect for religion. He experienced a deathbed conversion because of the encouraging words of Pier Giorgio.

2 Loretz, an attorney, was the president of the Catholic mountaineering association Giovane Montagna. He fell to his death at the Chateau des Dames. (Pier Giorgio also mentions this event in his letter to Antonio Severi on August 13, 1923.)

To Antonio Villani

Pollone, August 31, 1923

Dearest friend,

I'm responding to your 2 letters now for reasons that you well know. The first part of your last letter is almost mysterious; I can't understand the meaning of certain parts very well; I'll ask you for an explanation in person.

I'm very glad that you want to become a member of the great family of St. Dominic, where, as Dante says, "You grow fat if you don't rant and rave." The obligations are very small otherwise you must know that I wouldn't be able to belong to an order that required a lot.

When the Saint started the third order he instituted it as an army to do battle against heretics and thus it had very strict rules, closely following the ancient rule of the first order, but now that it has been modernized there are no traces left of the strict obligations. We need to recite the Dominican Office of Our Lady or the Rosary every day, but if you deliberately omit this for one day or for a few days you don't commit a mortal sin.

I hope that you can have your investiture in the magnificent temple in Turin and then I'll be close to you to give you the fraternal embrace;[1] since you are already tied to me by the bond of brotherhood through the Blood of O.L.J.C.[2] you will be doubly a brother to me through our common Father St. Dominic.

I would be very pleased if you take the name of Fra Girolamo, not because it is the name that I have as a son of St. Dominic, but because it recalls a figure who is dear to me and certainly to you as well, since you share my feelings against corrupt morals, Girolamo Savonarola, whose name I most unworthily bear. I am a fervent admirer of this friar, who died on the scaffold as a saint, I wanted to take him as a model when I became a tertiary, but I am far from imitating him. Think about it and then write to me with your ideas regarding this.

I haven't decided anything yet about going to Genoa.

Thank you also on behalf of my family for the kind words which are especially appreciated at this time[3] since they come not only as thoughts but as feelings from the heart since your heart is so close to mine in these hours.

Regards to your family and a thousand best wishes to you in J.C.

Fra Girolamo

[1] This is a ceremony where a new religious receives the habit. In the case of the Third or Secular Order, new members in those days were actually clothed in the full habit, which they were entitled to wear on special occasions and also when they died.
[2] Abbreviation for Our Lord Jesus Christ.
[3] He is referring to the recent death of his uncle, Pietro Frassati.

Pollone, September 13, 1923

Dear Tonino,

I've returned to the quiet of Pollone after having spent unforgettable hours in Genoa. Although I was tired and really worn out I will always have fond memories of Genoa.

Thousands and thousands of men, women, Catholic girls, boys and Fucini (the university female students were notably absent due to petty quarrels; and it's really a shame not to give God the honor due to Him because of internal problems, like one person wanting someone else's place) they processed through the streets of Genoa to give witness to their Faith before the whole world.

At the Catholic University Center I again met the representative of the Hungarian Catholic Association; you can imagine how very happy I was to be able to spend a few hours together after not having seen him for such a long time.

We marched from 1 until 5 in the afternoon, then the Most Blessed Sacrament was lifted up on the Grand Barge and the Procession on the sea began, lasting for two hours and then the march on the land began again and at 9 in the evening the Blessed Sacrament hadn't yet arrived in the Piazza di Francia, where the Legate of the Pope was to impart the first of the three Benedictions.

Now I'm intensifying my studies, because the day of the exam is approaching. I will be in Turin on the 26th of September and I will stay there until I've finished the exams.

Now I have a goddaughter,[1] who is 20 days old, I held her at the baptism the other day; she is pretty enough as far as babies are; at that age they're more or less all the same.

And when are you returning to be a Taurinus?[2]

Regards to your family and to you a thousand best wishes in J.C.

Pier Giorgio Frassati

The peace of the Lord be with you always.

[1] Elena Garino
[2] Taurinus was the Latin name for a citizen of Turin. It had been a Roman colony in ancient times.

To Tina Aimone Cat

September 1923

Dear Miss,

As I promised on Monday I have brought for you the timetable for all the trains to Biella.

It's really not my custom to perform favors for young ladies, but because you are coming to Biella it is my duty to provide all the necessary directions.[1]

This morning I returned from Genoa full of enthusiasm.
Cordial greetings in J.C.

Pier Giorgio

[1] Pier Giorgio was only joking about the inconvenience. At the bottom of this letter, he wrote out the train schedule.

To His Father

Turin, September 27, 1923

Dearest papa,

Tomorrow is your feast day and I am very sorry that I can't personally express to you all the feelings of my soul.

But tomorrow I will be close to you and I will pray for you, that God may give you all possible consolations for the Good that you have done and that you are doing.

I am studying here with great intensity, because the exams are approaching with big steps.

Yesterday Villani was in Turin, and on the 1st of October he will join the General Allgemeine Electric Company of Milan, because he was able to get a position with Toeplitz's help.

It is still hot enough here in Turin.

See you soon and best wishes and kisses from

Pier Giorgio

To Costantino Guardia Riva

Turin, October 24, 1923

I am really upset that you hung the Flag – which so many times, as unworthy as I am, I have carried in religious processions –from the balcony in honor of a man[1] who undoes works of mercy, who doesn't keep the Fascists under control but even allows them to kill Ministers of God like Father Minzoni, etc., and allows them to do other filthy things and then tries to cover up their misdeeds by putting up the Crucifix in the Schools, etc.

I accept full responsibility for taking the Flag down although I was late in doing so and as of now I submit to you my irrevocable resignation. With the help of God I will continue my work outside the Club as well, even though this causes me deep sadness, and I will do what I can for the Christian cause and for the Peace of Christ.

I wish that this letter of mine written in haste but dictated from the depths of my soul be read out publicly at the next meeting.

With profound esteem.

Pier Giorgio Frassati

[1] Pier Giorgio is referring to Mussolini's visit to Turin in 1923.

To the Board of Directors of "Cesare Balbo" Gathered for the Meeting of the 26th of October 1923

The members Frassati and Bertini, the former resigned and the latter in a state of protest, wishing to clarify the incident of the display of the Flag, went to His Excellency Monsignor Pinardi and they have learned that:

1) The Diocesan Committee did not deal with the above situation during their meeting, but when privately questioned Msgr. Pinardi expressed his disapproval of the participation of Catholic Associations in the reception of His Excellency Mussolini and he requested that the Flag be displayed, referring simply to the flag of the Catholic Associations' Headquarters.

2) Consequently the President's rationale that he was "just taking orders from on high" has no real foundation.

3) Furthermore the President, having known, some evenings ago, the mind of the members, acted illegally and on his own exclusive initiative displaying the Club's banner gloriously damaged in Rome.

However, not intending to start a personal quarrel, the 2 members nevertheless profess their deep affection for the President, and they are sad to have come to this point, compelled by pure love of sincerity. They declare that they want to preserve the life of unity free of bureaucratic and secret dealings between all the members and those who are actually invested with social responsibility, and not self-assumed authority. They recall the episode of the Flag as a simple but significant indication of a way of conduct they cannot and should not approve.

Awaiting the written response of the Board of Directors, they declare themselves fraternally in J.C.

Pier Giorgio Frassati
Giovanni Maria Bertini

To the Board of Directors of "Cesare Balbo"

In keeping with what I have previously said, I am returning to you my membership card and badge which legally no longer belong to me; I shall join the A.C.I.[1] as a member of the G.C.I.,[2] which followed a proper line of conduct on this occasion, because it could not honor him who, as head of the Government, is incapable of controlling his subordinates and allows them to continually do violence to the Clubs and their members.

One should not be surprised after all. J.C. himself has said: *The Sons of Darkness are more cunning than the Sons of Light*; but he also has said: *Be on guard against false prophets and wolves who come to you in sheep's clothing.*

I ask you to calmly judge this act of mine which I must do in order to be obedient to an obligation of my conscience.

With profound esteem in J.C.

Pier Giorgio Frassati

[1] Italian Catholic Action, in Italian the Azione Cattolica Italiana.
[2] Italian Catholic Youth, in Italian the Gioventú Cattolica Italiana.

To Gian Maria Bertini

Pollone, October 31, 1923

Dearest Fra Girolamo,[1]

Still in regard to the events in the Club I learned from Severi that the girl FUCI members are practically in mourning, because there is a war in our Club against the President. I'm protesting at the top of my voice and if you see any of the girls you could express my feelings to them because why should they be interested in the life of our Club? Other news includes as always Guardia-Riva's politics, it seems that he has simply remained in Turin and has maneuvered just like he did a year ago.

Now I'm calmly awaiting the Board's response[2] ready as always to do battle to the bitter end because I'm convinced that Guardia has acted illegally, even if under the advice of Canon Bues, displaying the flag after having known the contrary opinion of a few members who were present some evenings beforehand, and then I can't approve of Guardia-Riva's method of leadership, he hasn't known how to be popular with his advisers and he has always acted out of political or diplomatic motivation, very good qualities, but really out of place in a Catholic club, where actions ought to be as clean and clear as spring water.

My conscience like yours cannot bring me reproach for having given such a fatal president to the Club; we had thought it was better to propose Brusasca, but the shameful campaign run by certain elements whose principal exponent was perhaps Guardia-Riva himself has produced these fine results:

I - The internal life of the Club practically doesn't exist anymore;
II - The external life is miserable;
III - Bureaucratic ties with FUCI are at their best;
IV - Diplomatic intrigue and perfect secrecy.

Although I recognize Guardia-Riva's merit in having worked for the Club I cannot in good conscience approve of his methods and from now on I'll move to the firm opposition side and I'll spread the maximum propaganda so that he will no longer hold office in the Club to which, even though I have resigned, I'm still attached by so many fond and happy memories.

As soon as I get to Turin I'll speak to Canon Bues and then I won't hide anything but I'll tell everything so that truth and the good of the Club can triumph and if I've been wrong about many things I'll be happy to be corrected.[3]

In J.C.

Fra Girolamo

[1] Following the example of Pier Giorgio, his friend Bertini also chose the name Fra Girolamo upon the occasion when he was invested as a Third Order Dominican.

[2] The Board of Directors met to decide what to do about the situation. Pier Giorgio's resignation was rejected in the course of an ambiguous meeting of the Board which neither accused Guardia-Riva of wrongdoing nor reproached the rebels.

[3] Pier Giorgio asserted his point of view with the greatest strength and defended it to the end. In his humility, however, he was always ready to acknowledge his mistakes in judgment, if any had been made.

To the President of "Cesare Balbo"

Turin, November 14, 1923

Dearest Guardia-Riva,

Severi has told me that my position with the Club is still uncertain; now I am clarifying it for you.

So that there may be no misunderstandings, and my action is not interpreted as opposition to one individual or arising from other intentions, yet still strongly protesting the display of the Flag, for the good of the Club I withdraw my resignation.

Even if we don't agree on some issues believe me that I am yours most affectionately in J.C.[1]

Pier Giorgio Frassati

[1] This letter is an act of humility in the name of Jesus Christ, wiping the slate clean after a blazing quarrel and bringing the matter to a conclusion. Considering Pier Giorgio's temperament and the love he had for the Club, there could have been no other possible ending.

To Antonio Villani

Turin, November 16, 1923, 10:30 p m.

Dearest Tonino,

I just returned from the Conference of St. Vincent and finally found some news from you. Up until now I've taken the exams in Metallurgical Chemistry (75) and Machine Construction (70) and tomorrow Saturday the 17th I have to take the exam in Hydraulics. I hope to pass this one too although I know very little.

As far as my coming to Milan I don't plan to come so soon because perhaps I should be going to Innsbruck for Miss Fischer's graduation around December 15th. I've planned to stop in Milan for a few days to see you and talk with you.

They're getting ready for elections in the Club: we're making Severi president because we're all upset with Guardia Riva the undersigned most of all because he displayed the Flag for Mussolini; I had handed in my resignation as a member but then I withdrew it for the good of the club.

What do you think about these turncoats who are selling themselves to Fascism every day as "Il Momento" has just done?[1]

Every day I'm more disgusted and if I didn't have the certainty that my Faith is Divine I'd surely give in to some crazy action. But the thing that dismisses these thoughts from my mind is the certainty of a better afterlife if we work by doing Good so let's get to work and remain united comforting one another and urging one another along the path of Goodness. I have before me the portrait of that wonderful Minister of God Father Luigi Sturzo[2] and in the hours of discouragement I look at it drawing from him as well as from Religion the strength to carry on.

These days I'm working eagerly behind the scenes to set up the new presidency and it's a very troubled situation, just this evening I learned that Guardia-Riva has withdrawn his candidacy, leaving only Severi and Ferraris di Celle.

The Hydraulics exam turned out rather poorly 65% but now I'm enrolled in the 5th year with five exams to make up and five 5th-year exams because Sanitation is cancelled for now since Prof. Pagliano isn't with us anymore.

I plan to take Thermotechnology before March as an oral exam if possible and then in the March term which will be rather long I'll take Practical Geometry, Einaudi,[3] and Geology and then in July I'll take the oral exam in Electrotechnology and then Metallurgy and thermal Machines (the general course) and in October mining Geology, mineral preparation, mining technology and so I'll have finished all the exams; this would be the best plan. I know that to accomplish it I have to have good will which I hope won't fail me.

I'll send you De Mori's address soon.

Do you know that the Engineer Scotti, Pierino's brother, is in Milan? I think he's staying at the Cardinal Ferrari Foundation but I'm not certain.

And now I'll bring my work to a good conclusion.

Write me something and I'll see you soon.

Cordial greetings in J.C.

Pier Giorgio

---

[1] *Il Momento* was a Catholic daily newspaper at first very widely distributed by Pier Giorgio. It began publishing articles that were sympathetic to the Fascists while continuing to be close to the bishops of the Piedmont region.

[2] Fr. Sturzo was a priest from Sicily who founded the Italian People's Party.

[3] This was the text for his course in Economics.

To the Editorial Staff of "Giovane Piemonte"

Turin, December 17, 1923

Esteemed Editors,

I was amazed to receive the latest issue of the newspaper, given the absolute prohibition of the Supreme Head of Piedmont's Ecclesial Authority, His Excellency Archbishop Gamberoni. Please do not send "Giovane Piemonte" to me anymore, it doesn't represent G.C.I.'s political platform,[1] not only due to your act of insubordination against the Supreme Ecclesial Authority of Piedmont, but also by being a newspaper which represents the views of the Piedmont Regional Council, which, weeks ago, unconscionably agreed to sell the newspaper under an undignified contract to the administrators of a daily newspaper which once was Catholic. The contract fortunately didn't go into effect, but as far as I am concerned just to have accepted it, I believe, was not dignified.

I will send this issue of "Giovane Piemonte" to His Excellency Archbishop Gamberoni to show him how the Regional Council defers to Piedmont's Supreme Ecclesial Authority.

Pier Giorgio Frassati
Member of "Cesare Balbo" and of the "Milites Mariae"

---

[1] Pier Giorgio was fearless in denouncing the enemies of Catholicism and was capable of expressing himself with decisive language. He accomplished much more than merely canceling his subscription.

1924

To Margherita and Maria Palomba

Sauze d'Oulx, January 5, 1924

Sitting before a beautiful bowl of soup thinking of the capon of Novara which unfortunately I was unable to taste because of you, I send you a thousand gastronomic greetings hoping that God will preserve the good appetite you had in Novara.

P. Giorgio Frassati

To Antonio Villani

Turin, January 9, 1924

Dearest Tonino,
I hope you have already received the letter Guido brought to you in which I was telling you that my father thanked you for that matter regarding the budget and he would have spoken to you when you came to Turin.

Last night I was at the Club where I did battle on the question about the newspaper but believe me I really lost my self-control and I exaggerated a bit but my soul rejects these deceptive ways of acting.

I am enclosing the receipt for the skis, you already took back the sleeping bag. Write me something.

Have you had any news from Negroni?

Greetings and more greetings in J.C.

Pier Giorgio

To Nora Figna

Little St. Bernard, February 10, 1924

Skiing and singing in these happy hours a grateful thought goes to the violin deserter who in vain will regret it her whole life long. Youth will return no longer.

P.G. Frassati

To Antonio Villani

Pollone, April 15, 1924

Dearest Tonino,

I'm only now answering your letter, political worries have prevented me from responding before now.

Now the elections are over with a satisfactory result for our party. We had to fight against every kind of violence, but we successfully gained a fairly large victory. The struggle was really rather difficult in Turin: without a newspaper, with betrayal among our own and with bitter hostility outside, we reported 4000 fewer votes than in '21 when we were having political gatherings with maximum freedom. I'm glad that Marconcini was elected one of the deputies for Piedmont, I'm sorry about Stella who would have been an excellent member to fight the Farmers' Party which notably asserted itself in these elections. Also successful unfortunately was S.E. Bertone who is one of the deputies who is sympathetic to the Fascists.

Even in Piedmont there has not been complete freedom of voting and in the centers where there was no intimidation and the people were able to vote fairly freely it was a reproof for the dominating party.

In the faithful Val d'Aosta our people were prevented from voting and so the Fascists won the majority in towns where a victory by the People's Party was expected. But by this method and worse the Fascists obtained a free consensus; the violence perpetrated against the Catholic clubs should teach many people what kind of religious spirit is molding the majority party.

I'm sending you L. 50 for that German man which will help you to complete that good work you have begun.[1]

During this present month I plan to take three exams: practical geometry, political economics, and geology.

Then during the summer I intend to take exams in general electro-technology, hygiene, metallurgy and electrical measurements, for October I would be left with the three mining exams and mechanical terminology (a general course.)

It's a grandiose plan and I hope with God's help to be able to bring it to a conclusion.

Best wishes for a Happy Easter to you and your family from me and my family.

Greetings in J.C.

Pier Giorgio

[1] He was speaking of a needy young German boy. Villani had asked Pier Giorgio for help and Pier Giorgio didn't keep him waiting.

To His Mother

April 25, 1924

Dearest mama,

I took the Economics exam 90/100; yesterday I took the driving license exam from the engineer who also licensed Luciana. Being a colleague of his he didn't ask me anything. Everyone is well.

Greetings and kisses

Pier Giorgio

To Antonio Villani

Turin, May 15, 1924
Anniversary of *Rerum Novarum*[1]

Dearest Tonino,

I haven't had any written news from you for a long time but Misses Tescari and Bertola have told me about you. Yesterday I sent you the Thermodynamics textbook along with your notes by registered mail: now I'm studying General Electronics at high speed which I expect to take around the 20th of June. The other day I saw Fr. Cesarini who gave me news about the good Negroni, who hasn't for a long time given a sign of life; he's become a big shot in the

Catholic movement in Marino.[2] In April I took the exam in Political Economics and I had 90/100. Now I only have 9 more exams which I'd like to take by October as a very ambitious program hoping to graduate by March of the Holy Year.[3] And what good things are you up to, how is your time in Milan? Won't you take a quick trip to Turin to see your friends again? If you have some free days in August come to Pollone so that we can spend some time together to talk about the big changes that have happened this year. Were you happy with the outcome of the elections in Reggio Emilia? I was fairly happy with the general elections; given the near absence of freedom, we obtained a lot.

Greet Guido and tell him that I'll send him my subscription to *Domani d'Italia*[4] in a few days. It's really a little late but what do you want I'm always a bit disorganized. Write to me soon and affectionate greetings in J.C.

Pier Giorgio

Pian della Mussa, May 18, 1924. Picnic for the "official" founding of the Tipi Loschi. Pier Giorgio is sitting on the far right. To his left, facing the camera, is Laura Hidalgo.

P.S. – I've just received your letter and I send heartfelt condolences with the assurance of my prayers for the soul of your poor Grandmother. Farewell and let's hope to see one another soon.

[1] Pier Giorgio had an exceptional memory for dates of important events and, as a Catholic with a strong social sense, he would not allow the anniversary date of such a significant event to pass by without mention. (*Rerum Novarum* was an important encyclical letter written by Pope Leo XIII in 1891 about the Church's concerns for the working class.)

[2] Marino was a municipality in the vicinity of Rome, where the engineer Zaccaria Negroni had become the director of the Catholic youth movement Gioventú Cattolica.

[3] For the most part, he did follow this schedule with some variations due to circumstances beyond his control.

[4] Pier Giorgio subscribed to nearly all of the Catholic periodicals and newspapers in Italy.

To Luciana

Turin, May 28, 1924

Dearest,

I'm writing to you in a hurry so that I can send you at least 2 lines. The other day I was visiting Mrs. Bonelli who let me know when the Bellias are leaving for London and so Tina could plan to leave with them. I thought I could get myself out of it with a telephone call but Mr. Bellia invited me to his house and this very evening there was a soirée at their house; I was bored for an hour like a fish out of water.[1] Now I believe Tina will decide to leave on Sunday. We'll all go to the station to say goodbye and to give her our last bits of advice. She would have liked to travel alone to prove that she can do it on her own, but her mother is really afraid and doesn't have confidence in her. Although I'm not convinced that she wouldn't have problems I sided with her in front of her mother.

I advise you to be very good and learn English right away and then you can return soon. Say a little prayer for my exams and on my part I pray that God blesses you and always makes you better.

Pier Giorgio

[1] Mundane evenings like this were a nightmare for Pier Giorgio. He was bored to death and had to summon up all his strength to sometimes attend these events at the Embassy in Berlin. He said, "It's good enough that I show up in time to say goodbye when they're leaving."

Turin, first days of June 1924

Dearest Luciana,

    I'm going to Bergamo on Sunday with the Mining school to see two zinc mines. I don't know if Tina will have told you how the candies that Beltramo and I gave her were sown together one attached to the other.[1] Thanks for the letter. Toward the end of the month I'll take the most difficult exam in year V, general electronics, and first hygiene then the other 2 and then I plan on coming to Pollone. Now I'm going out on my own in the automobile to run errands and I'm bringing the letter to papa so that he can write something.

    Greetings and kisses to you and a thousand things and very loud cannon blasts[2] to Tina from

                                        Pier Giorgio

[1] Pier Giorgio and his good friend Marco Beltramo were fond of practical jokes. On this occasion, Pier Giorgio went with Tina Bonelli to the train station, attracted everyone's attention by a deafening racket, and then offered her a huge box of candies. However, they were all tied up one to the other in such a way that, when Tina attempted to offer them to the elegant Mrs. Bellia on the train, they came out of the packet in a long chain, to the surprise and laughter of everyone present.

Pier Giorgio wasn't satisfied to simply have played this trick: he also wanted to know how it turned out and what everyone's reaction was; he wanted to enjoy the whole thing, and so he wrote to Luciana inquiring about the outcome.

For her part, Tina Bonelli had been the initiator of a great prank on Pier Giorgio and Marco Beltramo in April. She conspired with her friends to organize an outdoor lunch at a villa near Mongreno in the hills near Turin. Pier Giorgio was absent because he had stayed home for family reasons. As a result, Marco became the sole victim of the prank. He was taken to Mongreno by car and was left there with a basket of what he thought was food. Instead it was firewood, a darning egg and a bib with the words, "Buon appetito" on it!

[2] "Cannon blasts" was a friendly expression used among members of the "Tipi Loschi Society" formed by Pier Giorgio and his friends on May 18, 1924. There is more about this group in later notes.

To Franz Massetti

June 13, 1924

Dear fellow citizen,

    I'm in the city of Petroleum and so my thoughts turned to you O Citizen Petrolius.[1] I hope that you have continued to study the rotating field[2] during my absence. On Saturday morning we'll meet again and we'll resume the studying which was very forcibly interrupted. Greetings from citizen

Robespierre[3]

[1] Franz Mazetti was a member of the "Tipi Loschi Society" formed by Pier Giorgio and his friends in May 1924. Each member had a nickname. Mazetti was called "Citizen Petronius" because of the care he took in dressing stylishly. (The name was based on Gaius Petronius, Emperor Nero's adviser in matters of luxury and extravagance.) Here, using a playful change of consonants, Pier Giorgio altered his nickname to be "Petrolius." This was also intended to be a slight pun by alluding to the supposed hair-growing properties of certain kinds of petroleum.

[2] This was some type of engineering term.

[3] "Robespierre" was the name Pier Giorgio had as a member of the "Tipi Loschi Society." (The name was based on the French Revolutionary leader Maximilien Robespierre who was noted for his role in the Reign of Terror. In Pier Giorgio's way of thinking his nickname was certainly a joke; as leader of the group, he had no other intentions than to portray the character of the incorruptible Robespierre in a light-hearted way. Pier Giorgio, as "Robespierre," along with his friend Marco Beltramo, as "Perrault," were known together in the Society as "The Terror.")

To Marco Beltramo

Piacenza, June 13, 1924

Dear fellow citizen,

In a few days we'll see one another. Tomorrow I'll go to Montecchio and I'll take advantage of the petroleum to make my hair grow.[1]

I sent a few postcards to all the members of the Tipi Loschi Society[2] and the associate members and especially to the citizens Miss President, Miss Secretary, and Miss Director of Excursions. Hail, O fellow citizen, Citizen Robespierre sends you terroristic cannon blasts. Boom!

P.G.

[1] In the letters to Marco Beltramo, one often encounters spirited jokes and purposely funny phrases and memories of pranks of every kind. The rapport between the two friends was warm, caring, and joy-filled.

[2] The "Tipi Loschi Society" (pronounced tippy lowski) was started to keep his friends connected together spiritually in joy. They were all members of the Catholic clubs and they loved the mountains. Both men and women were members, titled respectively "swindlers" and "swindlerettes." All of the Society's rules and directives were written in a joking manner. The pranks embellished the excursions in the mountains and the city life of the various "fellow citizens," "swindlers" and "swindlerettes." Being united with one another as much as possible was the aim of the Society to which all their energies and their "laws" were directed. Correspondence among them was written in a very tongue-in-cheek manner and often concluded with "terroristic cannon blasts" and/or "Boom!"

To Lea Raiteri

Turin, June 16, 1924

Dear Miss Raiteri,

I would have liked to write to you and to learn directly from you how you are doing in your town, but laziness has prevented this. Now I'm in Turin studying, but our souls are shaken about the monstrous things that are happening in Italy. One lives in a worried state not knowing what one is up against. Only Faith gives one the possibility of living.

Cordial greetings

Pier Giorgio Frassati called Robespierre

To Antonio Villani

Turin, June 21, 1924

Dearest Tonino,

In these moments, while all that is evil reveals itself in its most disgusting aspects my thoughts turn to those days we spent together; I remember the first elections in the time after the war, the coming of Fascism, and now I also recall with joy that we haven't been on the Fascist side not even for a single instant of our lives, but we've always fought against this scourge of Italy; and now while this party goes to ruin, we can thank God that He made use of poor Hon. Matteotti in the sight of the whole world to smash the infamies and the filth that are hidden under Fascism.[1]

We lucky ones, we can call ourselves that, who through the Goodness of God have been traveling upon the path, that if we have sometimes abandoned momentarily, have immediately taken up again, a decidedly different path, the path which does not give us the pleasures of the world, which one can obtain only by selling off one's conscience, surely if we continue on to the end on the way traced out for us by the teaching of O.L. Jesus C.[2] one will arrive at the triumph of the Future life.

---

[1] Matteotti was a Socialist deputy kidnapped in Rome on June 10, 1924, who paid with his life for his courageous struggle against Fascism.

[2] Our Lord Jesus Christ.

Turin, June 23, 1924

Dearest Tonino,

I'm writing to reassure you: you will read in the newspaper that yesterday we suddenly had a little invasion at home by the dirty Fascists. It was a cowardly undertaking but nothing much. We were quietly sitting at table and it was a quarter to 1 when we heard someone ringing the doorbell. Mariscia went to see and from the window she saw a young man who was dressed well enough; so thinking that he was a friend of mine she opened the door a bit. He suddenly asked for "Comm. Frassati"; she replied in the negative he pushed the door open and then yelling out "Come in" he came into the house along with five others. We were quietly eating when we heard Mariscia's screams. At first I thought it was thieves, but on reaching the hall and seeing one of them about to cut the telephone wires, I immediately realized that they were the Fascists. My blood raced in my veins. I threw myself at that scoundrel shouting rascals, cowards, assassins, and delivered a punch. Courageously, as soon as the swindlers heard the voice of one man, they ran for the door and fled hastily outside followed by me and Italo.[1] Outside they made off in a car that was waiting for them. All they managed to do was to break 2 mirrors. Afterward there was a coming and going of police inspectors, military police, investigating judges, Royal District Attorney, etc. They were too late but now I think that those guys won't dare to do this any more, all the more so because they arrested Mariotti one of the leaders of the group of assassins.[2]

They are shameless people; after the events in Rome they shouldn't be seen in public and should be ashamed to be Fascists but instead they continue to give proof of what they have always been and will be.

These are their last accomplishments, the accomplishments of a final agony because now the government is so corrupt that if it doesn't intervene immediately to surgically remove the party that is becoming a cancer there will be no more hope for us not even a little bit. We're fortunate that today we can glory in this event and boast about it since we've always been opposed to this party, made up of a union of delinquents or thieves or assassins or idiots, in short today's Fascism.

I'll end now, I've poured out my soul to you because I know

you share the same ideals, I leave you yelling
>Long live Matteotti. Long live Liberty.
>Long live Christian Democracy.
>Death to the tyrants.

Pier Giorgio

[1] Italo Pavoni was the family chauffeur.
[2] News of this attack by the Fascists and Pier Giorgio's bravery appeared in the Italian newspapers, and even those in England, Germany and the United States.

THE LONDON TIMES,
Tuesday,
June 24, 1924

THE MATTEOTTI CRIME.

TEN ARRESTS.

FASCIST DISORDERS AT TURIN.

(FROM OUR OWN CORRESPONDENT.)

MILAN, JUNE 23.

Serious disorders occurred in Turin late on Saturday night and early on Sunday morning. Bands of Fascisti appeared in the streets and entered the cafés and restaurants, terrorising and assaulting the occupants. Many persons were injured, some 20 being removed in a serious condition.

Fascisti held a meeting in the Balbo Theatre yesterday. After the meeting a strong column of Fascisti tried to storm the offices of the *Stampa*, but were driven back by the Carabinieri. At the same time, some Fascisti in a motor-car raided the private residence of Senator Frassati, proprietor and editor of the *Stampa*. The Senator was out of town, but his wife and his son, a young student, were indoors. The Fascisti began breaking up the furniture, but the young Frassati succeeded in disarming one of the assailants, and finally they left. Senator Frassati, lately Italian Ambassador in Berlin, is a Constitutional Liberal, a friend and supporter of Signor Giolitti. Minor Fascist violence is reported from other parts of the country.

To Antonio Villani

Turin, end of June 1924

Dearest Tonino,

Yesterday I had my first exam for this year: Health Engineering and I got 75%; I studied very little for it therefore the result was pretty good.

On July 12th I will take the Geology exam, and around July 22nd I will take General Electronics and therefore until then I will stay in Turin, then I am going to Pollone to prepare for Thermal Machines (general course) and possibly Checco Bonini will come with me. I would like to sit for the Thermal Machines exam around August 24th. My parents will go to the beach on August 1st, but I am not going with them since I want to study hard this summer in order to complete all my exams by October. I truly regret not being able to spend my vacation with you but the duty comes first.

I would like to sit for the Mines exam around mid-September and for the Mining Technology and Mineral Preparation around the end of September. I would like to test for Metallurgy around October 20, then Applied Geometry in November and thus I will have finally finished.

By the time of the Social Week[1] I think I will already be in Turin to study for the exams, but I will try to be there anyway, unless other important duties keep me somewhere else, because the discussions will be important, especially in regard to the current moment.

If you can stop by Turin from June 16th to 26th you will make me happy, and we can talk a little about the current situation.

Bye, dear Villani. Long live freedom.

Long live the Oppositions.

Long live the Christian Democracy, in J.C.

Pier Giorgio

---

[1] The Social Week of the Italian Catholics was an event held in Turin. In 1924, its theme was the social authority according to Catholic doctrine.

To Clementina Luotto

1924 (July 19th-20th)
before the trip to the Ciamarella

Dear President,

Please, do not expect from me a letter in the style of the 300s; we miserable mortals, immersed in those arid and abstract math problems, unfortunately cannot quench our thirst in the pure springs of the beautiful Italian Style, but I know you are so indulgent, so you will understand![1]

First of all, when opening this package, you will ask yourself what are these candies tied one to another;[2] these are candies we brought for the excursion of June 29th up the "academic" path on the Pagliaio coast and kept for those who, although they enthusiastically supported the trip, were compelled not to attend.

I am also enclosing 2 handkerchiefs with the "L" initial, which I think belong to you; I ask you to please compare them with yours. I am also enclosing the plan for the excursion to the Ciamarella, and I hope to be fortunate to include your name among the list of participants. However, we would like to make a little variation (not an academic one) that is to leave on the morning of Saturday 19th in order to arrive more rested at the Gastaldi Refuge and be able to rest a few hours more, so the next day we will have enough strength to go to the glacier. What is your opinion about this semi-academic variation?

I hope you can give me by the end of this week or the beginning of the next if not a definitive reply at least an almost.

Pier Giorgio Frassati

[1] Because of her style of speaking, Clementina Luotto was, at the same time, admired and laughed at by all of the members of the "Tipi Loschi Society." This is the meaning of Pier Giorgio's reference to the "style of the 300s." (I.e., the 1300s, the time of Dante and Petrarch.) It was a recurring joke in nearly every dialogue, in person or in writing, with Miss Luotto.

[2] A similar joke of candies tied one to another by the wrappers had also been done to Tina Bonelli when she took the train to go to England.

PROCLAMATION III – TERROR SECTION[1]

Turin, July 26, 1924

A war shout "Keep going…"[2]

In the Year 1924 ruling by the Grace of God and the Will of the Nation we the Terror,[3] Robespierre, invite you to a Tipi Loschi meeting on Sunday the 27th at 12:15 p.m., which will take place in the home at 70 Corso Siccardi where we presently live.

At 12:30 p.m. there will be a modest lunch prepared personally by Robespierre and I believe you O Perrault[4] will be so kind as to accept this humble invitation that Robespierre is making with all his heart. Come and we will spend an hour together discussing very important issues regarding our Society.

With love, we send you our terroristic regards. The citizen
Robespierre

Terror omnia vincit[5]

[1] Letters regarding matters of the Tipi Loschi Society were issued by Pier Giorgio as proclamations and used the plural pronoun "we" when referring to himself as a way to give them an august tone. His sense of humor and creativity are at their finest in his proclamations. In addition to the names he assigned to the members of the Society, he also created various sections to which they belonged; the Terror Section consisted of Pier Giorgio and Marco Beltramo.

[2] A reference to the saying, "Keep going, you're on the right road, so long as Mussolini is carrying the load," from the weekly satirical magazine *Il Becco Giallo* (The Yellow Beak) which made jokes of Fascism, censorship permitting, and was Pier Giorgio's favorite magazine.

[3] The Terror was made up of both Marco Beltramo and Pier Giorgio.

[4] Perrault was the name given to Marco Beltramo. It was based on the French scholar and writer Charles Perrault who was best known for his edition of children's stories such as *Cinderella*, *Sleeping Beauty* and *Little Red Riding Hood*.

[5] This is a Latin expression meaning, "Terror conquers all." Again, the proclamations of the Tipi Loschi Society were filled with double meanings, inside jokes and various puns for the members. This would have been a play on the expression, *"Omnia vincit amor"* (Love conquers all.)

To Gian Maria Bertini

Turin, July 29, 1924

Dearest friend,

Thank you for the postcard and your wishes. On Monday I was going to sit for the exam, I went to the Polytechnic after lunch when I learned the bad news that Prof. Grassi[1] had suspended the exams because not all the students registered for it showed up on Saturday night; fortunately now it all seems to be all right and so I hope to sit for the exam on Thursday or Friday August 1st. I implore your prayers,[2] but these things are little inconveniences compared to all the other battles that are taking place inside me. I need prayers because I am going through a critical moment in my life – you understand me, I am on the verge of concluding my student life, which is nice because without worries, in order to begin the hard climb in life, a much harder road, especially since something has changed in me, something that anticipates a very sudden storm. The last trip to the Ciamarella left me with good and sad memories which alternate indefinitely in me. Unfortunately, I think it will be the last trip I take with the group and this gives me a little sorrow since I felt I was very close to the group and for other reasons that you know very well. But if I have to make this extreme choice, I will make it not without regret on my part, the only thing I would wish is that she can quickly better her situation and be forever happy. My photo album will be for me a sad collection of memories of my life. Anyway, I will face the difficulties, I hope, by turning to prayers and in the hope that one day or another I will pass to a better life.

My illness is such that no human intervention can make it cease.[3] Human interventions can give me remedies to alleviate the crisis but they cannot eradicate the cause of evil; only Faith can be my hope and my comfort in the next life; hence I ask you to pray a lot for me so that every day I can solidify my Faith and have the strength to bear the difficulties that in these latest years of my youth have been impeding my path. You might find this letter a little strange but you will certainly excuse the feelings I am going through. Greetings to Matta and a hug to you in J.C.

Pier Giorgio

P.S. I don't really care for the title of Commander.

[1] Professor of Electrotechnics at the Polytechnic University.
[2] Whenever he had a big obstacle to face in life, Pier Giorgio turned to his friends for prayers. He knew the power of prayer and it was the only thing capable of assisting him during the sad moments of life.
[3] Pier Giorgio's internal struggle is in regard to his growing affections for Laura Hidalgo and the knowledge that he would have to forego any possibility of happiness with her. This is discussed in greater detail in future letters.

End of July 1924[1]

PHARMACEUTICAL CATEGORY
DR. ROCCHIETTA
"PROTON" PINEROLO

    We inform you that the famous young Englishwoman Tina[2] has gained weight STOP We ask you to tell us how many quintals of Proton she ordered from you STOP We need urgent reply STOP

MECHANICAL CATEGORY
FIAT FACTORY
LINGOTTO, TURIN

    I inform you that my daughter is visibly gaining weight STOP Please send truck because I cannot bring her back home by the usual car.

Eng. Bonelli

[1] This is a classic example of Pier Giorgio's sense of humor, although difficult to understand because of the numerous inside jokes. It is a playful telegram probably distributed by Pier Giorgio to the Tipi Loschi Society.

[2] Ernestina Bonelli was the Director of Excursions for the Tipi Loschi Society. At the time of this telegram, she was spending time in England to learn the language.

TO GIAN MARIA BERTINI

Viareggio, August 2, 1924

    Yesterday I finally passed my exam with 70/100 and now I am waiting for the tram to Forte dei Marmi. Please write me about when you want to go visit Luzzi. X will leave on Sunday from Turin for Quercianella (you understand well).[1] Greetings to you and Matta in J.C.

Pier Giorgio

[1] Here he is alluding to Laura Hidalgo who was in Quercianella. He was very cautious as to whom he shared this information with.

To Marco Beltramo

Forte dei Marmi, August 5, 1924

Dear Marco,

Your letter and the proclamations[1] restored my good mood: I thought about the beautiful excursions to the mountain and all the laughs at the Gastaldi refuge.

On Saturday I would like to go to Marina di Pisa to meet with Bertini and then perhaps I will proceed to Quercianella to see the Luzzi's and say hello to Miss Hidalgo. But I am not sure that I will go to Quercianella, because I received a letter from Bertini and it seems that, if I understood well, Luzzi is in Prato.

In regard to the photo, I will send it to you in Varazze as soon as possible, but you have to be patient, because as soon as I have a moment of calm I will write a dedication that must be worthy of a "Tipo Losco"[2] and especially of the "Terror."

Unfortunately, I also came to the beach with a stack of books and I spend many hours a day in my room, but every now and then I look out the window and contemplate the sea which is magnificent; then I go back, because the voice of my duty nails me to the chair with a few pleasant books in front of me; but the thought that with effort, quite enormous, in a few months I will be able to rest in the sweet tranquility of the Little St. Bernard gives me courage to continue studying. Can you imagine your Robespierre, this winter, free from exams, skiing down the steep slopes of the Little St. Bernard and at night drinking a good bottle together with the pleasant Rector?[3]

I am still writing to you in Turin, because I see that it takes one day for the letters to get there and so I hope that you will receive the reply by Thursday at the latest.

Do you know anything about our Distinguished Director of Excursions?

Has she already responded to our proclamation-report about the excursion and to the letter sent to her on Sunday?[4] And what about our pitiful state?[5] As soon as you have news about the young Englishwoman, write me something. I would like to write her that she should come spend some time at Forte dei Marmi, because here she could satisfy her desire to cut her hair short, because here it seems fashionable, especially among the American girls; she could pass for

163

a cross between America and England: what do you think? Perhaps she will not write anymore, because she will no longer understand Italian and so I am afraid that we made a mistake by not sending her the proclamation in English.[6]

Regards to your family: and to you a thousand terroristic regards.

Pier Giorgio

[1] The letters written by the members of the Tipi Loschi Society were called proclamations.
[2] "Tipo Losco" was the masculine singular form of "Tipi Loschi" and was used to refer to just one member rather than the whole Society.
[3] Everywhere, even on the Little St. Bernard, there would be a priest, even to have a drink together. The ironic thing about this part of the letter is that Pier Giorgio was practically a teetotaler. Once, when he was a child, he claimed to have drunk a finger of liquor (the equivalent of an inch of liquor). Later, his mother discovered that he had merely put one of his fingers into a bottle of liquor.
[4] The members of the Tipi Loschi Society agreed to undertake the mutual task of informing the others about every detail of their trips. This was the proclamation-report Pier Giorgio was referring to. When they wrote to Ernestina Bonelli, the Director of Excursions, the reports were filled with jokes and friendly teasing.
[5] This is another inside joke in which Pier Giorgio is referring to a lunch he had at his home with his friends Severi, Bonini, Delpiano and Beltramo. After lunch, they claimed to be in a pitiful state and sent a message to Tina exaggerating their condition, telling her about abundant food and drinks, etc. She responded by calling them "little beasts" as we will see in a subsequent letter.
[6] Tina Bonelli was in England and was sometimes attracted to worldly pleasures. They teased her about this. Also, she usually did not respond to the letters much to Pier Giorgio's dissatisfaction.

To Marco Beltramo

Forte dei Marmi, August 1924

Tipi Loschi Society, Terror Section
Proclamation

We had just finished the proclamation when we received your very welcome cannon blast and we from Tuscany, and precisely from Forte dei Marmi, will promptly respond to you with a torpedo blast.

You have stated very well that there will always be an indissoluble bond which will unite us forever and this bond we hold is Faith, which made us companions on beautiful trips and made it possible for our Society to be founded on solid rock. And this is the only consolation that we have considering the pain of having to be separated from you; if we didn't have this hope how could we still live when we see that every human joy brings sorrow and that almost every human sorrow brings joy.[1]

On this basis, O Perrault, we must solidify more and more our Society; it is our responsibility to accomplish this hard task, we who had the honor of foreseeing the desire of that swindler Luotto, who then became President, expressed in words which in that moment moved us so intensely to make us fall over like a corpse.[2]

The Presidential Council[3] places reliance on the fact that such a bond will truly be a very powerful one, and we believe that also when we are close to death we will always be remembered in the prayers of the "Tipi Loschi."[4]

Robespierre will gladly send to the citizen Gritti in London,

```
       COMPAGNIA DEI TIPI LOSCHI     1924
       ==========  ====  ============
           INDUSTRIE TURISTALPINISTICHE E AFFINI
           ------------------------------------
        SOCIETA' CON CAPITALE INTERAMENTE VERSATO
                      ( tanto versato che non c'è più )
                 == S T A T U T O ==
                 ------------------

   1°) - E' fondata la Compagnia dei Tipi Loschi, composta di soci e socie, che
         si dividono nei due gruppi di LESTOFANTI e LESTOFANTESCHE.
   2°) - La Compagnia è retta da un Consiglio Direttivo formata da :
                 Un Presidente --
                 Un Direttore di gite e affini --
                 Un Segretario --
                 Un " Figaro qui - Figaro là ".
                                  ┌fanti
   3°) - Per essere accettati come Lesto<           occorre una domanda regola-
                                  └fantesche
         re ai Lestofanti fondatori e l'accettazione da parte del Consiglio Di-
         rettivo.
   4°) - Il motto della Compagnia è :
                   " Pochi ma buoni come i maccheroni "
         e a questo motto deve inspirarsi ogni azione della Compagnia e dei
         singoli soci.
   5°) - La compagnia è posta sotto la ⁺ celeste protezione della
                   " SANTA PECE DE' PAZZI "
   6°) - Le solennità della Compagnia si celebrano al :
                   29 Aprile - ERA NOVELLA
                   18 Maggio - FONDAZIONE
                                        ┌fanti
   7°) - E' assolutamente vietato a tutti i lesto<           di portare cani di
                                        └fantesche
         qualsiasi razza, specialmente Mongrenica.
              Inoltre è proibita ogni importazione di pepe e simili insetti.

                      ==================
```

now famous for the exploits accomplished by the D.d.g.,[5] the pictures of the Ciamarella, however you must write to the citizen Gritti that he must wait until we go back to Turin to be able to access the pictures.

We send you our heartfelt thanks for the President's address: we had already requested it from the secretary, but since it is so complicated, we could not remember it by heart.

We must congratulate you for the greetings you left when departing the city that is the seat of the Terror: you could not have done better than that. We also like the coat of arms, and hence we seal this proclamation with it.

We embrace you terroristically.

Pier Giorgio Robespierre

[1] In this letter, the inner nature of the Terror and that of the whole Tipi Loschi Society begins to be revealed: it was a society with an indissoluble tie, it was a society based on Faith. This is what Pier Giorgio wanted. He always tried to realize this goal, with simple but appropriate means for those characters: cheerfulness and youthful vitality. Faith, the solid rock upon which the Society was founded, would keep the relationships alive and in contact.

[2] Clementina Luotto, the President of the Society, was respected and teased at the same time because of her sophisticated style of speaking, like a literature professor.

[3] The Presidential Council was composed of Clementina Luotto, Marco Beltramo and, of course, Pier Giorgio.

[4] This was, in fact, the most secret but substantial intention that Pier Giorgio had: to create, via the Tipi Loschi Society, a society of mutual spiritual support, founded on the indestructible power of prayer. It was a fundamental weapon, in order to both solidify friendships and make the bonds indissoluble, and to give more substance to the human relations. Through prayer, each member of the Society would have helped another to overcome an obstacle, to win a battle, and to reach a goal.

[5] This is another reference to Tina Bonelli, the Tipi Loschi Society's D.d.g. (Italian abbreviation for Director of Excursions), who was spending time in London to learn the language.

To Laura Hidalgo

Forte dei Marmi, August 11, 1924

Dear Miss Hidalgo,

I please ask you to forward my apologies and offer my thanks and my regards to Mrs. Randich.

After leaving the beautiful town of Quercianella I went to

Marina di Pisa intending to be home before evening but my friends and two nice priests kept me company until nine in the morning. At night I took a little walk with the nephew of Cardinal Maffi, a person as friendly as the abbot of Little St. Bernard. I have now started my studies anew, but I have changed my schedule since it is impossible to study at night with the dance music coming from the windows below. Therefore, I sleep and in the morning when it is not yet dawn I tie myself to the chair in front of my books; to think that I am so stupid as to rob myself of the summer in order to hasten my graduation day and that I want to cut short these unique days that remain of my, alas, all too beautiful life as a student.[1]

Then when I think about our Society destined to miserably break up like everything on this earth, I am overcome by a sense of regret; farewell beautiful trips to the mountains, what will Robespierre do without Perrault? The only thing that remains is a bond that we hope, with the Grace of God, will bind all the Tipi Loschi in this life and in the next: this sacred bond is Faith, the only powerful bond, the only sure rock without which nothing can be undertaken. And let us hope that this Faith that we have received in Holy Baptism, and that has made us companions on beautiful mountain trips will accompany us until the last day of our earthly journey and will be the connection through prayer to spiritually bond all the Tipi Loschi scattered all over the earth.[2]

Again, a thousand thanks. Greetings to all the young ladies and to you a handshake.

Robespierre
(Terror vincit).

[1] Pier Giorgio feels the presence of time which is quickly passing by and is transforming youth into maturity, always bringing with it new and heavy responsibilities, burdens and sorrows.

[2] Here there is the recurrent theme, the recurrent pain. Pier Giorgio thinks about the Tipi Loschi Society destined to split up, of the proclamations, of the trips, of the jokes, of the cheerful arguments destined to cease, leaving in their place the responsibilities of life. The original goal of that Society returns: Faith, the solid rock which enables the purest friendships and the most licit pleasures to be enjoyed, the rock which will allow old bonds to stay alive and to reinforce the mutual spiritual support through prayer. In this way, the Tipi Loschi Society is transformed into a society of prayer, a mutual organization of assistance that can bind the young members together. In Pier Giorgio's grand vision, the society would include all the "Tipi Loschi" of goodwill on this earth.

To Aunt Elena Ametis

Forte dei Marmi, August 16, 1924

Dearest aunt,

My studying is going quite well and I have now completed my second review but I will come to Pollone a few days before the exam so I can concentrate better because here I am very distracted.

I have only been on the sailboat a few times; first of all because there was not enough wind until now and then almost always during the free time from studying there was no wind but the other day we went sailing for a long time and I thought that you would have enjoyed it a lot.

Perhaps next week I will go for a quick visit to Carrara with the Engineer Micheli to visit the mines and then on Friday I will go visit the airplane factory in Pisa and that night I will leave to go to Turin; therefore I plan to be in Pollone either on Saturday night or Sunday morning.

For your feastday I will not be able to give you my best wishes in person so I will pray a lot for you and I will receive Holy Communion for you and Luciana.[1]

Farewell, dear aunt, I send you a thousand wishes and a thousand kisses also kisses to grandmother from

Pier Giorgio

[1] August 18th was Luciana's birthday.

To Antonio Villani

Forte dei Marmi, August 17, 1924

Dearest friend,

You have good reason to protest now, a little later I'll tell you about the comic drama surrounding my exam.

I should have taken the exam on the 28th and I was well-enough prepared so that on Sunday July 27th I invited Citizen Perrault, Comm. Bonini and Delpiano and Severi to the house for lunch; I acted as cook and for the occasion I wore a white apron and on my head I wore a paper hat I made with the "Becco Giallo."[1] On Monday afternoon I calmly went to take the exam when they told me the not very happy news that the professor had suspended the exam for the regular students. In the evening I made a telephone call to Pollone and you can imagine the lectures I received, but on Tuesday my father asked Grassi[2] if I could take the exam and Grassi said that the exams for the regular students would be taken after those taken by the others on Friday August 2nd and I was really fed up: after having spoken to Rossetti I spoke to Grassi explaining my situation and Grassi said that he would allow me to take the exam as long as my classmates weren't opposed and having obtained their permission I was thus freed from a heavy burden. I certainly could have known the material better, but I was so fed up of walking up and down for a few days that I had already forgotten some of it: just think, I didn't know Grassi's own diagram for the transformer and so instead of getting a good mark I got 70/100: not too bad, it's always one less exam.

Now I'm intensely studying Metallurgy, I have to take the exam on Thursday August 28th; I entrust myself to your prayers but studying here isn't coming along as I would like. Too many distractions: it takes enormous strength of will for me to be able to concentrate therefore on Friday I'll leave this pleasant town to

Turin, July 27, 1924. With the rest of the family away, Pier Giorgio invited friends to a lunch that he prepared himself. In this photo, Pier Giorgio is wearing a hat made of his favorite satirical paper that poked fun at the fascists. Pictured left to right: Isidore Bonini, Checchi Bonini, Marco Beltramo, Antonio Severi.

return to Turin and continue on to Pollone where I'll be on Saturday evening or Sunday morning.

Thank you for Veuillot's testament which is magnificent; I'll memorize it.

Prepare yourself well because you probably have more time than me to confront the problems that will be discussed in Turin; let's hope that this week brings the benefit of freeing Catholic Action from the ambiguity into which it unfortunately has fallen due to certain attitudes of men. Have you seen how disgusting the Catholic Center[3] is? How can a party call itself Catholic, when it supports a government that has no morals namely when it has made the morals of assassins and robbers its own? "Il Popolo" gave a good response to the ex-People's Party members. "We are anti-Fascists." Cordial greetings in J.C.

Pier Giorgio

[1] *Il Becco Giallo* (The Yellow Beak) was a satirical newspaper Pier Giorgio enjoyed reading that often poked fun at the Fascists.
[2] Grassi was professor of Electrotechnology.
[3] The Catholic Center was a hybrid political organization which grew to support Fascism. Pier Giorgio could not but be against it.

To Marco Beltramo

Pisa, August 18, 1924

Dearest friend,

Up until now I was with Commander Rizzoli who took me to San Giusto airfield and arranged a visit to the metal seaplanes factory in Pisa for me, but I received from my mother a prohibition absolutely forbidding me to fly; too bad. I recommended you to him; most likely he'll be your examiner in Livorno;[1] take heart and best wishes.

Robespierre

[1] Marco was in the airforce academy in Livorno.

To Margherita and Maria Polomba

Turin, August 29, 1924

Our common Faith in Christ and our friendship permits me to share in your great sorrow.

My prayers take the place of my useless words.

Pier Giorgio Frassati

To Marco Beltramo

Cogne, September 13, 1924

From the Hotel Grivola in Cogne,
famous for the deeds of our wonderful
Director of Excursions
the 13th day of September '24,
the fifteenth day of the fifth month,
the first year of the new era (non-Fascist).
"Tipi Loschi Society"
Department of "The Restless Ones"
"Terror" Section
"Alpinistic" Sub-section[1]
A Proclamation: "Forbidden Fruit" or Grivola[2]

A formidable Grivolan cannon blast to the wing of the Terror[3] our esteemed companion from other wonderful outings!

And now, O citizen Perrault, we with our spirit taken over by great emotion through the view of the superb spectacles offered by nature send you, besides the already-mentioned cannon blast, this promised proclamation that takes its name from the grandiose majesty of Mt. Grivola.

We set off yesterday evening at 8:30 for the Vittorio Sella shelter with our excellent guide Cavagnet and the porter Marcello Cavagnet; we tore along the path, and our thoughts went to the outing to Mt. Ciamarella and especially to the Swindlers and Swindlerettes alas! forcibly absent. To break the monotony of the path that heads from Cogne to the shelter, we missed the joyful laughter of the Tipi Loschi; to render more beautiful the landscape, illuminated by the moon, we missed the elegant style that adorns the speech of our President; to make our going more comfortable, we missed the exquisite kindness of our Secretary; and especially, to give heart to the climbers, we missed the organizing spirit of our D.d.g., namely Englesina.

We arrived at the Shelter and after drinking a hot tea with jam we rested our bones on a comfortable bed. In the morning of Saturday 13th we began the second day, the day in which we conquered the "Forbidden Fruit."

We set off at 4:30 and around 6 Mt. Grivola presented herself to us in her majesty. In that sublime moment it's hard to say if in our hearts what prevailed was the joy of finding ourselves within a few steps of the foot of the Grivola or the fear of approaching a mountain of such forbidding notoriety.

We raced up the glacier and then attacked the rock face, passing quickly through the central ravine to avoid any eventual unpleasant greeting that the beautiful peak often sends to those who want to climb it; then up the East Ridge (with excellent handholds) and in 2 hours we were at the summit.

Not having a pen, we wrote on a Giovane Montagna Aosta section postcard we found there with a match which we dipped in some rouge left there by an English climber: "P.G. Frassati, C.A.I. and G.M., with the guide Cavagnet and the porter Marcello Cavagnet on 9-13-24." — Undoubtedly few will understand what we wrote. From the summit, our thoughts went to all the Swindlers and all of the Swindlerettes who we would have wanted to have with us on these heights to enjoy the magnificent panorama.

And now that we have climbed Mt. Grivola, believe us that we have the impression that it is not as terrible as it is reputed to be; there are certainly ridges where the rock is rotten and that therefore it would be madness to go up that way; but there are routes, not particularly easy ones, where the rock is very good.

To the D.d.g. and the Secretary who last year were not able to enjoy this wonderful climb, we will bring as a souvenir 2 small stones, picked up on the summit by our terroristic hands.

And now Perrault, I am so happy to have climbed this beautiful and imposing summit, of which I took my leave with a fond farewell: for this year we can put our climbing shoes away and give them a well-earned rest. Farewell illustrious citizen, receive a handshake from

Robespierre

Terror omnia vincit: Grivola victa est.[4]

On Wednesday I took the exam, but unfortunately it didn't go well: I had a total mental blank and so the professor made me pull out; I'll do it again at the end of the month. I'm going to spend 2 more days in Cogne to visit the mines: I have been given a letter of introduction for Dr. Elter made by the president. After that, I'm heading back to Pollone. Greetings to your brothers, my regards to your parents, to you cordial greetings.

Pier Giorgio

[1] The heading of this proclamation reflects the creativity and imagination of Pier Giorgio. He invented categories of sections, sub-sections, departments, etc., based on where a member lived or a particular activity at the time. For example, when he wrote from the beach (often Forte dei Marmi), the proclamation would be issued by the "Acquatic Section." If he were studying in Pollone, it would be the "Pre-Mountaineering Section." From the mountains, it was the "Mountaineering Section."

[2] Having a reputation for being very difficult to climb, Mt. Grivola was given the nickname, the "Forbidden Fruit."

[3] From this point on, Marco was nicknamed "Wing of the Terror" in honor of his aeronautics profession.

[4] Latin for, "Terror conquers all: Grivola is conquered."

To Tina Bonelli

Cogne, September 13, 1924

For the esteemed D.d.g. as well as Englesina a formidable round from the Grivola's machinegun! Today while ascending the "Forbidden Fruit" I thought of you, poor girl, who last year due to a maternal prohibition could not climb to the unjustly famous summit. We spoke of you with Cavagnet and I found out things to horrify any person: he told me you are very skilled in the mountains, and in fact we never had a moment's doubt: inasmuch as Beltramo and I have conferred on you the title of D.d.g.; and as soon as you have conquered other small rockets like that of the Aiguilles du Midi we will bestow on you the diploma of Guide of the "Tipi Loschi Society."

As soon as I get to Turin I will bring you a small stone I took from the top of the Grivola that will serve to motivate you to conquer the "Forbidden Fruit" that we hope one day or another will no longer be forbidden.

The gentian that you will find enclosed in the letter was picked near the Vittorio Sella shelter: I am sending it to you because according to the abbot Henry "maidens are like flowers" and it will serve as an homage from a Tipo Losco to his D.d.g.

Tomorrow I shall visit the mines and then return to Pollone to continue studying. I have added under the responsibility of my sister the word "disobedient" next to pupil on the registered list of passengers. Do you approve? Keep going, you're on the right road!¹

Alpine greetings from

Pier Giorgio Frassati

---

¹ The follow-up to the saying was: "so long as Mussolini is carrying the load." Pier Giorgio's use of the expression would have been meant to be sarcastic.

To Laura Hidalgo

Cogne, September 13, 1924

To the most kind secretary of the Tipi Loschi as well as cook, a Grivoline bombardment!

And above all, I must thank her for suggesting the guide Cavagnet about whom I am enthusiastic.

I spent the night at the shelter and on a marvellous Saturday morning I climbed to the top regretting the absence of all of you, not only for the pleasure of sharing the great joy of planting one's foot on the much-longed-for summit, but also for the delightful company. I also missed the good lunches and especially the sandwiches that you know how to make so well.

I spoke of you with the guide and he told me things that prudence suggests I not write down.

I enclose a gentian for you that I picked near the Vittorio Sella shelter, the offering of a Tipo Losco to his Secretary and of the bearer to the cook and also because the Abbot Henry says that "maidens are like flowers" and so I think that like things like each other.

What nice things are you up to?

After visiting the mines I will return to Pollone to study.

Thank you for the prayers. My exam did not go well, the professor asked me to withdraw. I was almost certain that it was going to happen because it is impossible to study properly at the seaside. I will take the exam again toward the end of the month.

Cordial alpinist greetings from

Pier Giorgio Frassati

To His Mother

Saturday, September 13, 1924, 2:45 p.m.

I have returned safe and sound from a magnificent climb after having spent an hour of sheer bliss contemplating the magnificent glaciers. Kisses

P.G.

To Gian Maria Bertini

Cogne, September 14, 1924

My dream was finally realized yesterday with a magnificent day: at 10 a.m. I set foot on the summit of the Grivola arriving from the Eastern ridge – a climb without any difficulties.
Cordial greetings in J.C.

Pier Giorgio

To Franca Boschetti

Pollone, October 14, 1924

Dear Miss Boschetti,
Today at last I can give you a response regarding your brothers.

The Rome correspondent of "La Stampa" writes me that their application is getting the right support, so let us hope it will be of some use.

Give your brothers my best wishes and if you need something please write to me in Turin and I will be glad to do what little that I can.

Cordial fucini greetings in J.C.

Pier Giorgio Frassati

To Giuseppe Rizzoli

Turin, October 19, 1924

Dearest Rizzoli,
My friend Marco Beltramo will go to Florence in a few days for a medical check-up and then in early November he will go to

Livorno to take the entrance exams for admission to the airforce academy. I highly recommend him. He has studied mathematics and the other subjects all summer and so is certainly prepared, but unfortunately experience has taught me that exams often require a little luck. My dear friend has a passion for aviation and strongly desires to follow this career.

With many thanks for anything you can do for my friend, I remain cordially

Pier Giorgio Frassati

A letter of yours for Luciana has arrived that my mother will take to Pollone today. Is there still any hope that you can make a short visit to Pollone?

To Marco Beltramo

Pollone, October 23, 1924

Dearest friend,

This is my last letter before you abandon the civilian way of life. I shall not make any wishes on your behalf but trust that Providence will provide everything according to His Plans. On the 27th I will go up to Oropa and pray for you at the feet of the Brown Madonna, even if my prayers have little value. Then, as soon as I get to Turin, I will send you a souvenir that, let's hope, should always bind the "Terror" in a non-material way; it is a rosary made of garden seeds and to which I shall add a medallion of the Madonna of Loreto, so that the Virgin will protect you when you fly through the "vast kingdom of the winds."

The hour has struck for me too this year, and that means goodbye to excursions into the mountains and thus to the company of the T.L.[1] I have made my calculations and if I want to graduate in March, I must study intensely mornings and evenings, including all of the holidays and if I want my diploma in July I can only go away on one or 2 Sundays. And yet I must also work in a hurry because the years race by swiftly and I must still serve my Country, but afterward when one returns home, it will be unpleasant and one will mourn the student life, whereas now one longs for its end. But man has always been a discontented animal so this is not surprising.

If Tina has given an answer and if you have time, you will do me a great favor by letting me know what it is.

Severi will have told you about Clementina. How strange! I don't understand anymore.

Regards to your parents and to you a thousand terroristic cannon blasts: Boom! Boom!

Pier Giorgio

[1] He is referring to the Tipi Loschi Society.

To Gian Maria Bertini

Pollone, October 24, 1924

Dearest Bertini,

I read the sad news in the newspaper about your Poor Aunt, even though I was expecting it, informed as I was of her illness.

Express my condolences to your father and your aunt. As for you, I will not use words since they might sound pragmatic and rhetorical, but I will assure you of my poor prayers. For those such as us who have the precious gift of the Faith, prayers serve more than anything else to implore Peace for the elected soul and the resignation to bear such deep sorrow.

All the best to your family and to you a fraternal embrace in J.C.

Fra Girolamo

To Marco Beltramo

Oropa, October 27, 1924

Thanks for the letter and the good advice that I am not going to put into practice because skiing trips are like eating cherries: once you start you cannot stop. I hope you have received my express letter. I am anxiously awaiting the outcome of the visit[1] and would like to know when you are having your exams. I greet you terroristically

Robespierre

[1] He is referring to Marco's medical exam.

Pollone, October 29, 1924

Dearest Marco,

Thanks for the postcards of Florence and Turin as well as the preceding letter; I am studying steam engines very hard in order to make my debut at the end of November.

Friday on the eve of All Saints I shall go back up to Oropa and on that occasion I shall pray to the Madonna for you, but I shall also remember you in my prayers on the 2nd and 3rd. As soon as you know the results, I beg you to let me know in Turin because by November 4th at the latest I shall make my final entrance into the city of the "Terror" alas! widowed of such a good champion. On November 5th in Turin the trial will begin against the Fascist aggressors who broke into the house last June 22nd. I will write you a report about that.

Regards to your family. And for you not wishes but the assurance of my prayers so that God provides what is best. Affectionate greetings and an embrace in J.C.

Pier Giorgio Robespierre

Terror omnia vincit.

Turin, November 4, 1924

Dearest Marco,

Congratulations on your exam results that I learned about from your mother this evening at your house.

Through your friend Bianchini I sent my greetings and very best wishes, good Perrault, you are a truly worthy T.L.[1]

The news made me happy but it also saddened me; indeed, there can be no joy without sorrow; in fact for me it means alas! your absence and my thoughts strayed back to the happy days spent together on our mountain excursions; the only comfort in these happy and at the same time sad thoughts is the certainty that a unique bond that knows no distance unites us and with the Grace of God I hope will always unite us; it is the Faith, the Common Ideals that you will be able to uphold in your career with the means that a military life will offer you and that I, with God's help, will obtain to defend and sustain my future adult life. I hope that this year will be the year I will get down to studying seriously: by the way thanks for the advice which however I cannot accept because if I were to follow your schedule not even by October would I graduate; I need to make great plans that are unfortunately never wholly completed as my laziness often overpowers my will.

I hope to have your news soon and to know how the exams went especially the math one. I will congratulate Lady Laura Hidalgo on your results and will announce your triumph to Lady Tina Bonelli as soon as she gets back from her hermitage at St. Valentino and I will also inform our president, so that she can always be current on the actions of her subordinates.

Let me remind you that in three years' time when you finish at the academy, one of the first flights you make must have Robespierre aboard and then one can say that the Terror rules even just for an instant "the vast kingdom of the winds."

The Terror artillery fires a salvo to commemorate your magnificent victory and you receive a warm terroristic embrace from
Robespierre

Terror omnia vincit.

P.S. Citizen Petronio gives me the good news that you and he together one day soundly trounced the enemy at billiards bravo, bravo, you have upheld the honor of the "Terror" which is what you've always done anyway.
Robespierre

[1] This is a reference to the Tipi Loschi Society.

To Marco Beltramo

Turin, November 14, 1924

Dearest Marco,

I admired your reply to the Commander of Regina Coeli Father Isidoro de' Bonini (it can't get any better than that) a worthy Terror address,[1] even more so when you think that the postcard was written for citizen Danton, enemy of the Terror. I passed on to Tina that part of the letter regarding her and she assured me that she would add a little something bitter to the semi-sweet letter she was writing to you but that first she would roll up her sleeves and get to work. I haven't yet been able to pass on your praises to either Laura or Clementina but as soon as my studies allow me I shall inform them of the noble words addressed to them by the good citizen Perrault.

Again a thousand congratulations for your truly excellent results; very soon, as Head of the Terror, I shall proclaim you General of the forces of Earth, Sky and Sea subordinate to the Terror; carry on like this and then we can say: Keep going, you're on the right road.[2]

Indeed, as you were given to saying when you still lived in the city, magnificent headquarters of the Terror, I'm delighted to have known during my lifetime young women so good and so virtuous from whom one has much to learn.

This year citizen Cadorna is perhaps running for Presidency of the "Cesare Balbo" Club and so in any time free from my studies I campaign against him because if Cadorna were to win, bureaucracy, militarism in the bad sense of the word, would win and therefore the 2 things that are against the Terror. By the way, I'd like to have your opinion on which candidate the Terror should concentrate its efforts.

All the Terror artillery and the field howitzers in town fire a salvo in honor of the Terror, always steadfast, while I send you my best terrorist greetings.

Robespierre

Terror omnia vincit.

[1] Like many letters to members of the Tipi Loschi, this one is full of inside jokes and private references. Commander was the title often given to successful, important-looking businessmen. As a joke, Isidoro Bonini was called Commander of Regina Coeli because Regina Coeli was Rome's central prison where it was thought most of the commanders would eventually end up. In addition, Pier Giorgio also jokingly used the title Father Isidoro de' Bonini to underline Bonini's sense of his own importance. So, when Marco combined both titles, Pier Giorgio was very amused.

[2] This is the saying that ends "so long as Mussolini is carrying the load." Whenever Pier Giorgio used it, he was always being clever.

To Giovanni Gola

Turin, November 15, 1924

Dear Giovanni,[1]

Through Italo I'm sending you the book from which you can learn the theory of becoming a good driver – I'm also sending the cartridges for your father as well as the sickle and the axe. I urge you to go to Holy Mass every Sunday because it is the primary duty of every Christian but especially of a young man who is a member of a Catholic Club; I make the same plea to Pierino and to Nena.

Greetings to everyone and to you a thousand more from
Pier Giorgio Frassati

[1] Giovanni Gola was the son of the gardener at the family home in Pollone.

To Marco Beltramo

Turin, November 22, 1924

Dearest Marco,

I'm just about to leave for a great mountain excursion and you can imagine the joy that fills my soul right now. Severi had suggested leaving for the Bessanese together with Denina and friends; but it would have meant missing Holy Mass and initially I agreed to go, but then the thought of failing in a Duty and consistency with what I had so often maintained when countering Laura's quite valid theory forced me to give up the idea.[1] However, my sacrifice was repaid, as the trip with Denina didn't come off and we organized the same trip leaving Sunday morning at 6:15. Only a few friends are taking part in this climb at a hardly suitable time of year: our guide is to be the excellent Cerutti and with him one can well say keep going, you're on the right road.[2] No fixed plans as to the route we'll take; prudence will suggest the best thing to do. Conditions permitting, it will be the Sigismondi route, otherwise the normal one. Tina was a bit cross at not being invited, but I told her that the whole thing had been arranged in a hurry, and then what could we have done in that she would have been the only girl who could come since Hidalgo isn't available Monday and Tuesday as is required for an excursion like this due to the poor public services available during the winter.

I think of you spending your day in the cell you so elegantly and terroristically described in your dear letter; I wish you were here with me to share the joy and the anxiety that alternate in my soul on this marvellous eve of my departure and again in Balme on Monday hopefully to celebrate our victory with genuine local wine.

And now I would like to give you a word of advice: be a bit

more prudent because carrying on like this just isn't good enough any more, because you know that military life and civilian life are very different.[3]

Terroristic greetings.

Pier Giorgio

From Balme I'll send you and Clementina a telegram as soon as we've done the Bessanese. This evening I'm going to finish my subject then all I have to do is revise and Monday I hope to be ready. The two Miss Guglielminis arrived a short while ago, they complained of not having heard from you so you would be doing well to write: the address is 6 Corso Stupinigi, Turin.

[1] Pier Giorgio never missed Mass for any reason that depended on him alone. As in this case, he even missed mountain trips to go to Mass. He disagreed with Laura Hidalgo's theory that one was exonerated from Sunday obligations just because one had to leave the preceding evening.

[2] This is the anti-Fascist saying that ended, "so long as Mussolini is carrying the load." In this case, Pier Giorgio means it as a true compliment to the skills of the guide Cerutti.

[3] For some reason, Marco had ended up under military arrest.

Turin, November 1924

Dearest Marco,

Too bad that important commitments are keeping you in Livorno otherwise you would surely have been with us to share the joys and inconveniences of a bivouac at 2500 meters in the month of November.

We left with the intention of attacking the Bessanese by the Sigismondi route; if the conditions of the snow had prevented our at least attempting that, then the normal route. Of course, when we reached Balme and saw the rock covered with snow it struck us as injudicious to go up via the Sigismondi route and so we tried to rent skis and do the Albaron di Savoia instead. We lost two hours at Balme and at around 2 we were on our way to the shelter. Maybe because we were no longer used to carrying such loads, our progress was slow and as I was making my way along the path, I thought of our trip to the Ciamarella; seeing again the places, I remembered the details of that splendid report of yours. I saw once again the spot where the "divorce" took place, the opened tomb from which Tutankhamen or else Diogenes emerged.[1] After the Pian dei Morti, the hardest part of the climb began as the snow was frozen and we had to proceed very slowly because we didn't have hands free to use our ice-axes for support. And so we arrived a few feet from where on July 20th Severi took the first photograph, hence in winter an hour from the shelter. But exhaustion and uncertainty regarding the state of the snow persuaded us to stop and bivouac. The good Cerutti set to work at once and, having found a rock with a sort of roof leaning toward a snowy slope, we began to dig out a small apartment composed of the following rooms: a bedroom for three, a dining-room, a kitchen, a reception room for entertaining, a long corridor with a gallery from which one enjoyed a magnificent view that our apartment shared with n. 100.[2]

Our magnificent apartment measured 1.5 m in length, 0.5 m in width and 0.4 m in height. Heating was in short supply, but on the other hand it was very well ventilated, the dictates of hygiene were faithfully and rigorously observed.

Once our apartment was ready, we decided to inaugurate the kitchen and the dining room right away and we drank some excellent tea alas! this time not sweetened by Clementina's words. Afterward we began to look for ways of occupying the time as sleep would have been imprudent. We thought of absent tipi loschi, pleased on one hand that the girls were at Pian Pacias resting after a trip to the hills worthy of the D.d.g. because otherwise the poor things would have frozen to death, but on the other hand it would have been fun if the whole group had to bivouac together. The time would have seemed shorter because Clementina could have enthralled us with 14th-century-style dissertations. Tina with her famous flair for organization could have raised our already high morale, Laura not only to prepare delicious meals but also to provide excellent company. And so between meals, songs, recitations of Dante, astronomy and radiotelegraphy lessons, constant decoration of our home, we passed 12 hours, from 7:30 Sunday evening to 8 Monday morning.

The house, where the Terror together with T.L. citizen "Figaro here Figaro there" and the non-T.L. Cerutti spent a magnificent sleepless night, has been named for St. Pece de' Pazzi[3] who, at the time was surely the only protector we could call upon. We took a photograph which, if it comes out, I will send you so that you can see for yourself whether I have adequately described the house whose kind hospitality we enjoyed.

We left without our packs reaching the shelter an hour later and then we went back down to leave by car for Ceres at 6:30 p.m.

Here you have it, O Perrault, my report. Without a doubt, had you been with us you could have written with your characteristic grace a fine proclamation on this bivouac and dedicated it to the D.d.g., but too bad; I'll give her a personal account as best I can of the high points of the trip.

And now dear Perrault I must leave you but not without telling you that when we were drinking a toast at Balme we expressed the hope that the next bivouac will be on the Rosa glacier on the Guglielmina wall.

Terroristic greetings and may St. Pece de' Pazzi give you the strength to serve your hard jail time with resignation and keep the faith with the motto "Terror omnia vincit."

I hope that by now you will have received the telegram sent from Balme.

Terroristic greetings.

Robespierre

Terror omnia vincit.

[1] On another trip, Marco Beltramo and Pier Giorgio together with the members of the Catholic mountaineering club "Young Mountaineers" had successfully climbed the Ciamarella. Members of the Tipi Loschi Society were all there as well as others who were not members. At the Pian dei Morti, about two hours from the Gastaldi shelter, they made a short stop during which a dispute arose over which itinerary to follow to reach the hut: Marco and Pier Giorgio wanted to take the direct route which was harder but shorter; the excursion leaders of "Young Mountaineers" proposed taking a longer, less taxing route. After some arguing, the "divorce" occurred between the two groups. The first group finished the hike toward the shelter on their own and the following day reached the Ciamarella summit. Included in the light-hearted report of the trip compiled by the leaders of the Tipi Loschi Society was the following event: "Suddenly from an open tomb there rose the huge figure of a lost, wandering soul. There were those who maintained that it was Tutankhamen, those who claimed it was Diogenes still in search of a man: in the end it turned out to be professor Casassa." He had, in fact, thrown himself down, panting, between two rocks placed in such a way as to resemble (with some imagination!) an open tomb.

[2] The apartment Pier Giorgio is humorously describing was, of course, a very small snow cave the men made to take shelter for the night.

[3] This is yet another inside joke as there is no St. Pece de' Pazzi.

Turin, end of November, 1924

Dearest Marco,
I have some news, astounding but true. Our D.d.g. upholding the motto "Few but good like macaroni"[1] this year has decided to start the series of excursions with a climb of Cervino by the normal route which, weather permitting, will take place the 6th and 7th of December. As soon as I heard about the plan I rushed to the phone to give her my best wishes and to tell her that I would gladly have gone along if it hadn't put me in the inconvenient position of having to miss Holy Mass on 2 holy days. I beg you with all my heart as a member of the "Terror" to write to her so that the D.d.g. sets off not only accompanied by Robespierre's best wishes, and the company of very few but very accomplished mountaineers, but also with the wishes of Perrault. We men accustomed to bivouac at altitudes below the shelters cannot take part in such difficult excursions and if intentions must be judged by the first excursion of the year we're going to see our D.d.g. at the top of Everest and the Himalayas while we from Pian Pacias will marvel at such prowess and send her our most heartfelt admiration.[2]

In a few days or more precisely on December 3rd I'll take my exam on thermal machines. I recommend myself to your good prayers. Write to me as soon as you can and I hope soon to be able to embrace you in the city of the magnificent seat of the Terror.

Terroristic greetings from

Pier Giorgio Frassati

P.S. I'm sending you the photographs of our famous non-trip; in one you will see Robespierre wearing a Scottish beret in the company of the good Cerutti. We're standing beside the inn where we spent the night from the 23rd to the 24th, inside the inn you can just glimpse the smoky kitchen where coffee is being made.

I'm really sorry that my telegram had such an unpleasant impact but I didn't realize it was first to be read by your superiors – forewarned is forearmed.[3]

---

[1] This was the playful motto of the Tipi Loschi Society.
[2] Pier Giorgio is, of course, being playful when he describes the supposed difficulty of the trip planned by Tina Bonelli after he had just endured the rigorous physical demands of a bivouac in a snow cave at a high altitude. Climbing mountains

was not Tina's strong point. On one occasion, Pier Giorgio observed her nearly dropping with exhaustion but too proud to stop. He then pretended to be tired and called a halt in order to allow her to rest.

3 Pier Giorgio is referring to a telegram he sent to Marco at the airforce academy in which he used the typical Tipi Loschi language. It read, "Bessanese unassailable, bivouacking outdoors. Cannon shots. Robespierre." The authorities at Beltramo's Academy read the cryptic language and, unaware of the terminology used by the Tipi Loschi, saw the strange message and even stranger signature as being sinister. The times were politically turbulent and the authorities surmised that behind the enigmatic nature of the text was an order for some kind of uprising or some mysterious plot in the final stages of preparation. As a result, Marco was summoned to give an explanation which was accepted only some time later and with some lingering doubts. For his part, Pier Giorgio, clearly unaware of Academy regulations, had no idea that any unusual communication had to be examined by the authorities.

Turin, December 9, 1924

Dearest Marco,

On the eve of the feast of the Madonna of Loreto, your Patron, I want to send you my best wishes for a wonderful day, together with the news that I passed my 29th exam with 75/100. Yesterday at Tina's house the Tribunal of the Tipi Loschi Society was held. Clementina had charged citizen Laura with resolving the question of an issue that had arisen between Tina, Severi and me over lunch last summer. First they made off with L. 40 of mine then that evening, obviously overcome with remorse, Tina returned the entire sum along with a note written in her own "Paw" full of a vast amount of good advice which I will cherish. However I referred the whole business to the decision of the "Tipi Loschi" and in the end I left L. 40 and Tina L. 15 in the petty cash fund which was officially established yesterday; so you'll be receiving a letter informing you of this amazing news. Thank you for the letter with the insults which I wholeheartedly accept even more so when they come from the good Perrault; by the way when are you coming back to Turin? I would like to know so as to be able to come to the station to receive you with all the honors Perrault is due. Cordial greetings and terroristic cannon blasts, boom! boom!!!

To Antonio Villani

Turin, December 16, 1924

Dearest Tonino,

Thanks for your letter, however you don't mention whether or not you received the Machine Construction book that I sent you quite some time ago. We are in perfect agreement over ideas; I hope with the Grace of God to continue along the path of Catholic Ideals and to be able one day, in whatever state God wills, to defend and propagate these rare and true things. Meanwhile I must announce the engagement of my sister to Mr. Jan Gawronski, first secretary to the Polish Legation at The Hague.

As every rose has some thorns, so unfortunately at the joy at seeing my sister happy there is the bitterness of separation because, sadly, Italy will never again be her land. Now I will have to fill the void my sister will leave in our home: I will do my best and for this I beg you to remember me in your prayers.[1] A few days ago, I took the exam on Thermal Machines (general course) and got 75/100; now I have only five more exams that I hope to get rid of quickly and then graduate.

Cordial greetings and best wishes to you and your family for a Merry Christmas in J.C.

Pier Giorgio

[1] Pier Giorgio was profoundly affected by his sister's marriage because it would inevitably separate them. The serious responsibility then fell to him to replace her presence in the home during an unpleasant period of pending separation between their parents.

To Father Mario Frassati

Turin, December 17, 1924

Dear Father Mario,

I'm writing to you after such a long delay, above all to offer you my deepest sympathy for the grief with which you have been afflicted; I'm sure that you, as a priest, have accepted this terrible trial at the hands of Providence Who provides everything for our spiritual good.

I must also express all my sorrow at the loss we Pollonesi have suffered at being deprived of your energetic presence and good will. The young people of the "Pollone Youth" will long feel your absence as they will no longer have someone who understood the shortcomings of long years of atheist teaching by the Biellese, and who was able to steer onto the right path a band of intrepid youngsters who had previously experienced the characteristic indifference of the Biellese;[1] and now permit me to congratulate you on your new appointment which will allow you to carry on your misson of apostolate and the good works which you had begun so well in Pollone and that you will now take up again in Portula, soon to achieve "the Peace of Christ in Christ's Kingdom."

I was in Novara the other day to inaugurate the Catholic University Women's Secretariat. After Holy Mass celebrated by Monsignor Gamba, we had lunch with the Bishop and spoke together at length. He is very pleasant to talk to and seems to have a special fondness for the "Young Catholics." Let's hope he'll do an effective job here in Turin and can settle the many issues still pending.[2] On the matter of the Good Press, I urge you to boycott "Il Momento" which was once Catholic and is now a disgusting newspaper because it deceives people. Now that you're wanting to take out subscriptions, tell your parishoners to subscribe to the "Biellese" and to buy the Piedmont edition of the "Popolo" so that they get P.P.I.[3] news. Fortunately, Canon Garelli is no longer the ecclesiastic assistant of the G.C.P.[4] We now have the ex-federal assistant Canon Pittarelli.

Write and tell me something about what you're doing and again all the best for the new year. In J.C.

Pier Giorgio Frassati

Pax Domini sit tecum.

[1] Long contact with the people of Biella helped Pier Giorgio gain a clear insight into their character. The Biellese were by nature indifferent and, therefore, atheist not by conviction but through habit. The people of Biella accepted life and lived it as best they could without concerning themselves with the transcendental, and without facing the painful thought of metaphysical retribution for their actions. It was quite sufficient to be honest, to mind one's own business and to be staunchly loyal to one's family.

[2] From that day on, Cardinal Gamba was spiritually close to Pier Giorgio right up to the last moments of his life. The Cardinal was struck by Pier Giorgio's moral temperament and Catholic enthusiasm and held him up as one of the brightest lights among the religious youth of the times. When with immense grief, he learned that Pier Giorgio was near death, he prayed for him and even asked to see him. Likewise, Pier Giorgio had infinite admiration and respect for the Cardinal.

[3] The Italian People's Party.

[4] The Piedmont Catholic Youth.

To Marco Beltramo

Turin, December 20, 1924

Dearest Marco,

Dead – what does this word mean? If you are giving dead its usual meaning, then I am still alive unless my senses deceive me. But if we're talking about the word in its true essence, then sadly not only am I dead, but already resuscitated a number of times only alas! to die again. I would like to set off along the straight and narrow path but at every step I stumble and fall; for this reason I beg you to pray for me as much as you can so that one day, whenever Divine Providence wills, I will reach the end of that wearisome but straight path.[1] Meanwhile, these days I alternate my arid studies with the most beautiful readings of St. Augustine; my soul has never till now experienced so forcefully such infinite pleasure, because through those powerful Confessions one feels a little of the joy that is reserved for whoever dies in the Sign of the Cross. Today I bitterly regret having wasted my time and to have waited till this advanced age to savor such pure joy.

I heard that you are first in your Course and also in conduct and that the days served in prison were unjustified so we can well say that the Terror has triumphed. Tuesday evening, at the Bonino home, Isidoro's graduation is to be celebrated and when I speak to him I will inform him that I represent not only Robespierre but also Perrault, who will surely be with us in spirit on Tuesday.

I must also tell you that my sister is engaged to Jan Gawronski, first secretary to the Polish Legation at The Hague; while I am glad my sister is happy, you can well imagine how sad my soul is at this first parting.

Once again I recommend myself to your good prayers; I send you a thousand good wishes for a Merry Christmas, disappointed not to be able to embrace you soon.

In J.C.

Pier Giorgio

---

[1] The usual teasing question to ask a friend one hasn't heard from in some time was, "Are you dead?" Marco could not have anticipated getting such a serious response from Pier Giorgio.

To Isidoro Bonini

Modane Turin, December 28, 1924

Dearest Friend,

I am reading Italo Mario Angeloni's romance novel "I Loved That Way" where he describes in the first part his love for an Andalusian woman and believe me I am moved because it seems like my own love story.

I too loved that way, only that in the novel it is the woman who makes the sacrifice whereas in my case I will be sacrificed. But if that is how God wants it, His Holy Will be done. Today I am going to Sauze d'Oulx to try out the course for the Young Mountaineer race. Tomorrow the group leaves for St. Bernard and I am with them there in spirit for two reasons: because St. Bernard was the cradle of my dream, alas! broken, and because that is where she is whom I loved with a pure Love and today in renouncing it I desire her happiness. I urge you to pray that God gives me the Christian strength to bear it serenely and that He gives her all earthly happiness and the strength to reach the Goal for which we were created. On the day of your graduation, I felt the truth of St. Augustine's words when he says: "Lord, our hearts do not have peace until they rest in you"; in fact, foolish is he who pursues the joys of the world because these are always fleeting and cause pain whereas the one true joy is that which Faith gives us, and our beloved companions particularly by this bond will always stay united even if life's contingencies hurl us very far from each other. Thus she will always be for me a good friend who, having known her in the most dangerous years of my life, will have helped me to keep on the right path toward the Goal. Write me something and pray for me a lot. I wish you and yours a good end and a good beginning, kisses from

Pier Giorgio

To Laura Hidalgo

Sauze d'Oulx, December 28, 1924

Dear ladies,[1]

Before abandoning this splendid location, I send my most cordial greetings to you who, most favored among mortals, are enjoying the beauty of the Little St. Bernard. I am on my way to Turin, because duty calls me, but my whole being is up there at St. Bernard inasmuch as there one may well say I spent the happiest days of my past.

Give my greetings to the Mont Blanc, the dogs and the whole magnificent panorama and if I dared, I would ask for a prayer on my behalf in that charming little church. I hope to arrange an excursion with you this year because the mountains are beautiful, but also because it is so very pleasant to return home in such excellent company as that of the Tipi Loschi.

Enjoy also for me the always fresh snow. We will not dare to join you anymore because we will have to disappear in the sight of who knows what perfect skiers.

Cordial greetings and terroristic cannon blasts: boom! boom! boom! from

Pier Giorgio Frassati

My most fervant good wishes. May God give you that Peace the possession of which is certainly the best of all earthly gifts.

[1] Unlike the other letters addressed to Laura Hidalgo, this letter was written by Pier Giorgio for all the Swindlerettes staying at the Hotel Miravalle even though he addressed it personally to Laura.

To Willibald Leitgebel

Turin, December 30, 1924

Dear Willibald,

You must forgive me if I haven't written for so long; but these last months I have had to work a lot. I still have five exams to prepare and then, praise God, I will be free.

How did you spend the Christmas holidays? I always think with joy of the Christmases I spent in Germany.

I have a great favor to ask of you: my friend from Pola who is almost an engineer would like to know the price of the "Kreisel Pumps" by Hermann and "New Theory of the Kreisel Wheels" 1906 by Dr. Hans Lorenz.

I beg you to let me know the price as soon as possible because the gentleman needs the books for his doctoral examination.

I would also like to inform you of my sister's engagement to Mr. Jan Gawronski. The wedding is set for January 23rd, and my sister will go to the capital of Holland because the groom is the secretary of the Polish Legation to The Hague. You can imagine that for me it is both a joy and a sorrow to have a sister so far away.[1]

Best wishes for the Holy Year to you, to your brother, to your parents, to your sister and her husband. To you cordially from

Pier Giorgio

[1] The sorrow was obviously due to his sister's departure; the joy came from the fact that her new residence would certainly give him a good reason to travel and to visit other distant friends who were very dear to him.

To Gian Maria Bertini

Turin, December 1924

Dearest friend,

When you read this letter, I don't know what you will think of me. I too at this moment feel all the stench I exude and yet my weakness, my inconstant and insecure nature drags me astray from the path. I would like to come with you but my spirit is too depressed and I would not be able to enjoy your company. Noisy company suits me better; I who have accomplished nothing, or if I have done anything it was only nonsense. I know what the better path would be, to stay at home and in silence dedicate myself to my studies. But while I see that this is good, I don't do it because I lack the will.

An inconclusive letter together with few and confused ideas that reflect my mental capacity at the moment.

To you, whose ranks I long to belong, except that I am prevented by the continuous doubt that agitates my mind and the battle without victory that torments my conscience, the struggle to suppress all my past with all its iniquities, in order to rise up toward a better life. To you I ask for compassion and prayers so that I too may find the strength to win this hard but necessary battle.

In J.C.

Pier Giorgio

1925

To Marco Bilotti

Turin, January 3, 1925

Dearest friend,

As we had agreed I am sending you the address of 2 families whom I wholeheartedly recommend to you so that you can pass them on to the appropriate Conferences[1] on Wednesday. They are:

Marianna Bernardi
C. Cairoli, 30 0,20
Cassaro, Via Genova, 16

Excuse me for writing in pencil, but I don't have anything better at the moment. Greetings in J.C.

Pier Giorgio

[1] He is referring to the Conference of St. Vincent de Paul.

To Franz Massetti

January 4, "Holy Year"

Dearest friend,

No ill feelings as they are not worthy of the Holy Year; since the Vicar of Christ has indeed opened the Holy Doors I offer you the Olive branch which is the sign of Peace.

Upon your return you will find a changed Robespierre; and in fact during Advent I prepared for the Holy Year by reading St. Augustine, reading which I haven't yet finished, but from which I have received immense happiness, a profound joy, which until now unfortunately had not penetrated my soul. I'm also doing some literary studies; I've been reading "Testimonies" by Papini[1] and then I'll move on to studies in philosophy, if I find a good translation of the works of St. Thomas Aquinas. You see that my plans for the Holy Year are grand. I believe that I have thus found a better way to alternate my boring study of mechanical Technology with delightful readings.

And what are you doing? When will you be coming? Turin is anxious to hear from you. Turin claims the presence of the stylesetter. When will you return, Citizen Petronius?[2]

The year has begun well, after toasting it in with my family I went to Holy Martyrs Church; there in the Church, crowded with people, we prayed that there would be peace in Italy and Peace among us.

And this Peace, which is the burning Desire of us all, we hope will come in this year in which the Graces of the Lord are multiplied.

And now citizen we wish for a strong will for ourselves, so that we will be able to quickly complete the degree. I am delighted to close my student career in such a beautiful year.

And now I should bid you farewell, because study is calling me back to work and meanwhile all the best for a good prosecution, best wishes above all that you will always possess the True Peace which is the best gift that one can possess on this earth.

Cannon blasts!

Pier Giorgio

[1] Giovanni Papini (1881-1956), Italian novelist, poet and critic, who began his career as a critic of the Church and State, but began practicing his Catholic faith in earnest in 1921 and became a staunch defender of Christian thought while continuing to challenge society.

[2] Because of his attention to fashion, Massetti's nickname in the Tipi Loschi Society was based on Gaius Petronius, the Roman satirical novelist considered to be Emperor Nero's arbiter of elegance who was highly critical of bad taste.

To Antonio Severi

Turin, January 6, 1925

Dearest friend,

I began the year well together with my family and also with the D.D.G. who as I had foreseen did not go to St. Bernard; we toasted the new year together with all the T.L. then I went to the Church of the Holy Martyrs, which was packed with people. After Bertini and I served Holy Mass for Father Righini our first adventure of the Holy Year began; you can imagine it was an adventure worthy of the Holy Year; to have to accompany 6 German nuns and 20 young girls also from Germany all the way past the Great Mother of God Church. I've been studying now really hard and I've been repeating to myself the iron and steel class notes trying to sketch all the main diagrams in the best possible way; but the material is very boring. Last night at the Young Mountaineers meeting the Skiers Group discussed the date of the Cup competition of the Bronzeno: it was set for the 1st of March, namely the first Sunday of Lent with a distance of about 15 Km. I was charged with asking you whether you would be willing that day to run the race or otherwise act as judge. This is the request that the president and the group of skiers asked me to pass on to you.

Thanks for the lovely postcard: I didn't understand what the illustration meant. I would like an explanation because I'm forever becoming more of an imbecile. And when are you returning to Turin?

I'm most upset with Grosso because of the too-frequent contacts which the Cesare Balbo Club has with the Gaetana Agnesi; does he think that n°. 26 Via Principe Amedeo is the headquarters of a Club that is little by little becoming co-ed? Grosso won't be president anymore, but the girls of the Club will be.[1] Certainly at first sight you will blame me but when you have understood the reasons, which would take me too long to list here, you should appreciate the fact that I might indeed have a few reasons. I expressed my opinion at the meeting, because I believe that the right way to go will come out of the discussions, and then also because by communicating with one another everyone can correct and modify the proper idea, if they see the evidence of their mistake.

Greetings to your sister and to all your family and to you a hug in J.C.

Pier Giorgio

[1] The Gaetana Agnesi was the women's club for Catholic university students. Clearly, Pier Giorgio did not like the fact that the men's club mixed so frequently with the women's club.

Turin, January 10, 1925

Dearest friend,

I'm letting you know that the regular exams will commence on January 19th and will last until April 30th, then every month there are your exams for the bachelor's degree namely January 24th, February 23rd, March 23rd, April 24th and May 20th. On Wednesday I hope to pass with good results my thirtieth exam, Mechanical Technology from the third year, then I'll commence studying Practical Geometry because I want with all my heart to be able to graduate on May 29th because the 20th is the date for the presentation of my thesis. But I'm afraid that I won't succeed because I must devote one entire month to a practicum; in any case, we'll see.

Citizen Petronius arrives this evening, and I'll take a break from my studies to go to the station and convey to him the greetings of the Terror. Did you know that Tina was supposed to go to Egypt with her sister but it seems that this year she doesn't have the will to organize anything; I don't telephone anymore because you can never find her at home.

I'm sending you the text of the telegram sent by Cardinal Maffi to Federzoni when the Fascists destroyed the Catholic newspaper "Il Messaggero": "Yesterday Pisa was normalized. As bishop I have wept. As an Italian I have blushed with shame." Since it is very outspoken it wasn't possible to publish it in the newspapers.

Cordial greetings in J.C.

Pier Giorgio

To Isidoro Bonini

Turin, January 15, 1925

Dearest friend,

I should have waited for a letter from you before writing to you, but we are in the Holy Year and since the Vicar of Christ has opened the doors of Justice, doors through which all of us ought to fortify ourselves in Grace in order to obtain the Eternal Prize, to hold grudges would be an unworthy thing. I give you the Olive branch, symbol of that Peace, which I insistently go on seeking. Ah, dear Isidoro! Every day that passes by convinces me all the more how ugly the world is, how much misery there is and unfortunately good people are suffering while we who have been given many graces by God have alas! paid Him back so poorly. It's a terrible admission which torments my brain while I am studying. Every now and then I ask myself: shall I go on trying to follow the right path? Will I have the good fortune to persevere to the end? In this tremendous clash of doubts, the Faith given to me in Baptism suggests to me with a sure voice: "By yourself you can do nothing, but if you have God as the center of your every action then, yes, you will reach the goal." And I would like to be able to do precisely that and to take as a maxim the saying of St. Augustine: "Lord, our heart is restless until it rests in you."

Unfortunately earthly friendships produce sorrow in our hearts because of the departure of those we love, but I would like for us to pledge a pact which knows no earthly boundaries nor temporal limits: union in prayer. Yesterday I took Galassini's exam but the prof. made me pull out because I didn't know how to sketch; your brother had 95/100.

The photographs I took turned out very well and I'll send them to you right away, please send me the ones you took with your camera. And how is your life going? Mine as you can judge by the start of this letter is going through perhaps the most acute period of a grave crisis and right at this moment my sister is going far away and so it's left to me to be cheerful at home and to suppress the somber mood caused by all the various setbacks that are piling up against me.

When will you come to the city where we have spent so many wonderful and happy times (which perhaps will never return) in those days when we were free from every care and we laughed in such a happy-go-lucky way; alas similar times won't ever return for me. I'll always be cheerful on the outside to demonstrate to our companions who don't share our idea that to be Catholic means to be joyful young people; but on the inside when I'm alone I give vent to my sadness.

Write to me if you have a bit of time; I don't need to tell you that your letters always give me great pleasure.

Regards to your family which I haven't yet had the pleasure of meeting, to you a thousand greetings in J.C.

Pier Giorgio

To Marco Beltramo

Turin, January 15, 1925

Dearest friend,

May peace be in your soul, this is the wish which Robespierre offers to Perrault for the Holy Year, every other gift which one possesses in this life is vanity just as all other things of the world are vanity.

It is wonderful to be alive inasmuch as our true life is the life beyond; otherwise who could bear the burden of this life if there weren't a prize for suffering, an eternal joy; how could one explain the admirable resignation of so many poor creatures who struggle with life and often die in the breach if it weren't for the certainty of God's Justice.

In the world which has distanced itself from God, there is a lack of Peace, but there is also a lack of Charity that is true and perfect Love. Maybe if all of us listened more to St. Paul, human miseries would be slightly diminished.

I began the series of exams in this Holy Year poorly enough because yesterday after an hour of tough questioning, the prof. made me withdraw because I didn't know how to sketch well. I telephoned Tina telling her about your postcard and she told me to tell you that she has written to you and that you are a big mouth, then she added that she is known all over Turin especially after the exhibit on Via Roma of the photographs of the 2 excursions that she so ably organized and then she burst out laughing. I found Laura; she has already written to you; she is very upset because Casati made the State exam in the faculty of mathematics and physics a retroactive requirement. Poor Laura, think about how she has studied so much, worn herself out, competing and getting top marks, and all for nothing. In May this year she will take the competitive exam that will serve as the State exam; the poor girl is thoroughly unlucky: pray, O Citizen Perrault, that God will grant her that Peace, which might compensate her for all the crosses which life provides.

No news from Clementina, it's been a long time since I've seen her because I've had a lot of studying and so I can't visit anymore and communicating by telephone is a problem, Clementina's number not yet being automatic.

The other day I went to visit your brother and I learned all about your goings-on and also that little story of keep going, you're on the right road which in your case one could say keep going, you're on the wrong road.[1] I'm doing everything possible to take a day off during those days when you'll be in Turin so that we can spend a few hours together recalling those good times we had which perhaps unfortunately will not ever return.

The dues of the Young Mountaineers increased from L. 15 to 18. Under the presidency of His Exc. Knight Officer Grosso, the Turin Club is turning into a co-ed club; I have decidedly crossed over to the opposition because I am truly outraged at the presidency. The opposition seems to have gained many followers and if this is the case then in the next assembly I will give a very forceful speech on behalf of the opposition.

My sister is getting married in city hall on the 23rd and in the church of the Archbishop's residence on the 24th. His Exc. Msgr. Gamba will bless the marriage.[2]

Terroristic greetings.

In J.C.

Pier Giorgio

[1] Marco was attending the Aeronautics Academy in Livorno. Among the training exercises of a practical nature which crowned the major courses of study, there was a course in transmitting Morse code. One day, at the end of a transmission, Marco jokingly added: "Keep going, you're on the right road, so long as Mussolini is carrying the load." This was the sarcastic anti-Fascist statement that Pier Giorgio sometimes referenced in his letters. Marco thought that the usual sergeant would be at the receiving end of the transmission. However, that day it was the colonel commandant who took the message; as a punishment, Marco received five days in solitary confinement.

[2] It was the law in Italy at that time that a separate civil marriage ceremony had to be conducted in addition to a church wedding.

To Franz Massetti

Turin, January 17, 1925

Dearest Petronius,

I found out that you wanted to act in a play for the Club and so, although it's not up to me, I decided that before I go to the mountains, from where one never knows if one will return, (I'm exaggerating!), I am sending you this epistle so that you can think about whether I have some good reasons.[1]

The pulpit from which I preach is certainly not very suitable, but we ought to help each other as friends and only for this motive do I want to help you hold off from this intention of yours.

Leave it to others who can afford to throw away their precious time, it's not convenient for you to take on commitments this year. I also need a similar sermon because I'm always taking on more than I can do, but I am ready and always will be ready to accept all the admonitions that come to me from my friends.

And where is Petronius' Iron will? That will which becomes Virtue when it results in self-control. And you who were able to stop smoking when you wanted to, you want to give in to the first temptation of some knight officer Grosso, a man without good sense who doesn't realize what he is doing organizing performances for the club which produce the most meager income and on the contrary ruin the studies of young people by making them waste a lot of time. I would address the same words to Araldus if we were closer friends, but think about reading these words of mine to Araldus, if you want, and if you think it's appropriate. I know that I should not have been preaching because I'm unworthy, but believe that I have been compelled by that Love which unites us, which will be for us a bond of enduring friendship.

Pardon me and greetings in J.C.

Pier Giorgio

[1] Pier Giorgio's concern for the moral welfare of his friends compelled him to take on responsibilities of this kind.

To Marco Beltramo

Turin, January 18, 1925

Dear Beltramo,

Today a few of us left by way of Accademia to climb the Denti di Cumiani. We were few but good, it was a magnificent day, although you could say it was too hot. Thanks be to God and St. Bernard that we all returned safely. We weren't able to find the way and were climbing smooth rocks from which we were then unable to climb anymore, and with difficulty and only with great precaution were we able to come down. And then since at 4 we had scarcely arrived at the base of the last peak from which you make it to the top in 2 hours, we made the last stretch on the normal path.

The members of the team were the good Cerutti, a capable guide, who climbs like a deer, but every now and then he found the way blocked by overhanging rocks so it was up to me to climb and help him in the descent, which was more dangerous than the ascent; then Randone, Pasquali, who experienced a freefall for 14 meters of rock and luckily landed on his own backpack which caused him only to completely tear apart his pants; and a Tuscan from Livorno who amused us with his beautiful speech. The outing was marvellous in general, but very difficult; we only regretted the absence of friends of the old guard now scattered to distant places. We also missed the ladies, but in the end we were glad not to have had them along, because otherwise we would have involuntarily exposed them to some very raw emotions.

Arriving home I found the D.d.g. and although I was hardly appropriately dressed I presented the dutiful report; as a T.L. it was my duty to inform her in detail regarding all the particulars which for reasons that you can understand I omitted telling my family. She followed the story very attentively and gave some timely advice about prudence. Tomorrow I will resume my studies with greater earnestness although this week I might have little time to dedicate to study because my sister is getting married on the 24th and therefore you can understand how many things there are to do.

I'm expecting the precise communication about your arrival, the day and the hour of the train's arrival, so that I can hurry to the station and then rehash the old jokes and we'll take some walks again organized by the reunited Terror.

The hours will be brief, but always beautiful, as are unfortunately all things of this world.

Farewell, citizen Perrault, pray for me because I really need some prayers.

Terroristic greetings and hugs from

Pier Giorgio

Turin, January 24, 1925. Pier Giorgio with his sister Luciana on her wedding day.

To Laura Hidalgo

Turin, January 22, 1925

Dear Miss Hidalgo,

High compliments again on Sunday's wonderful excursion; it is unbelievable not to be able to find the Sagra of St. Michael; had it been Tina the D.d.g. I would not have been surprised, but it seems that examples are followed and it would be opportune to confer on you the office of vice-D.d.g. because I see that it is very promising and this year, if you continue in this way, you could become a member of the C.A.A.I.[1]

We have not succeeded by way of the rocks to reach the top of one of the Denti di Cumiana, because the rocks were very slippery; besides last evening I learned that it has never been scaled by anyone. Some Sunday soon we'll attempt it maybe at least armed with some climbing spikes, perhaps the 10th of February if it doesn't snow; if you'd like to plan a trip with your group through the easy way, we could meet on the summit. In any case I shall call on you at the library to plan it. The excursion is economic enough costing L. 10 for the journey plus provisions.

Cordial greetings in J.C.

Pier Giorgio

[1] This is the Italian abbreviation for the Club Alpino Accademico Italiano; that is, the Italian Academic Mountaineers Club.

To Marco Beltramo

Turin, January 25, 1925

Dearest Marco,

Yesterday my sister was married with the Rites of the Catholic Church: the rite is magnificent; the civil marriage is comical in comparison; I would hope that in the near future civil marriage would be abolished completely and only marriage in the Church would be in force and at best, as a temporary solution, both forms would be valid in the eyes of the State.

But while I am happy because my sister is happy, the more so because her husband is good in the sense that you and I understand, on the other hand yesterday the separation was terrible. You can imagine my only sister, the companion of my childhood: to see her leaving for such distant shores was for me a shot in the heart.

I had the great honor of giving my arm to our D.d.g. in the little wedding procession.

Today I was at the Brezzi's house for a tea and dancing no less. I had telephoned Clementina that I wanted to visit her and she graciously invited me to her aunt's house. I met Mrs. Brezzi who is very kind and several other nice people; we spoke at length with Clementina about you. The more I am around Clementina the more I appreciate her rare gifts; truly a good T.L. On every occasion she knows how to find that word which is not so much a compliment as is customary in the world, but which is profoundly spoken by a very good heart. The latest news of Laura is that she directed an outing to the Sagra of St. Michael without succeeding in arriving and finding the Sagra; it doesn't get any better than that. Therefore, I agree with Clementina that she be immediately nominated as explorer of the T.L. so in addition to being secretary she will have the job more suited to her of explorer.

On Wednesday I hope to do a good job on the exam in Elements of Technology: I have studied as much as I could at this time.

January 26, 1925, 10:30 p.m.

Today I received your welcomed letter. Tina was truly moved, because although she has not written you, you have stored up no resentment as a good T.L.

I have been counting the days which still separate us; you tell me that on the 13th you will be at the house to see me and I'm very, very happy and I'm awaiting this visit with great joy. But do you think Robespierre would not hurry to the station to give you the first greeting as soon as you touch the soil of the city of the Terror: this would never happen, no; and so on Thursday the 12th at 9:30 p.m. I want to be among the first to hug you.[1]

Cordial greetings in J.C.

Pier Giorgio

---

[1] In fact, Pier Giorgio went to meet Marco in Asti (at least one hour by train from Turin) in order to make the final part of the trip with him and so as not to impose on the little time Marco had to visit with his family.

To Isidoro Bonini

Turin, January 29, 1925

Dearest friend,

I had wanted so much to reply earlier to your wonderful epistles even more so because I was truly moved by reading them, but things to be done in these times lately have prevented me from responding promptly.

My poor mental capacity doesn't allow me to write a letter worthy of yours, but accept the few words which express to you the gratitude of my heart for your words of comfort which you wanted to send me.

Yes, oh dear friend, this is a grave moment for me, because in these days the sister, who I unfortunately never appreciated as much as in these days when she is far from me, has left home.

The struggle is hard, but it is also necessary to overcome and to find again our little road to Damascus so that we can march along it toward that Goal which we all should attain. A little more effort and then even I will have attained the much longed for diploma, but after all that there is a problem much more difficult to resolve upon which all our responsibility weighs gravely. Will I be able to solve this grave problem? Will I have the strength to succeed? Certainly the Faith is still the sole anchor of salvation to which we must grasp strongly: without it what would our whole life be? Nothing or better it would be spent uselessly; because in the world there is only sorrow, and sorrow without Faith is unbearable, while sorrow nourished by the torch of the Faith becomes a beautiful thing because it fortifies the soul in its struggles. In today's struggle, I cannot but thank God because He has willed in His Infinite Mercy to grant this sorrow to my heart so that by means of these arduous thorns I might return to a life that is more interior, more spiritual. Until this age, I was living too materially and now I need to refortify my soul for future struggles because from now on every day, every hour there will be a new battle to fight and a new victory to conquer. A spiritual upheaval must take place in me and thus this year I will devote myself to reading St. Thomas Aquinas; thus absorbed in those marvellous pages, every thought of the world will die and I will live happy days because only they give to the heart that joy which has no end since it is not human and is true joy.

There is another thing which should unite us and it is Holy Love, holy because it is the everlasting Fire which ought to consume a Christian heart; we should be nourished by it because without Charity every other virtue has no worth.

And now I must leave you; I am enclosing a photograph reprint, please send me the questions to submit to my father and send me the photographs you took with your camera as soon as they are ready.

Cordial greetings in J.C.

Pier Giorgio

To Franz Massetti

February 1925

Hail O Petronius,

Amici te salutant.[1] While I'm writing you are perhaps already on the train and speeding toward the city, the ardent aspiration irrepressible desire of your soul, you come armed with a firm will to be able to attain the diploma in this Holy Year and I in my capacity as citizen of Turin, headquarters of the Terror, give you the welcome.

I had wanted to rush to the station so that I could be the first to greet you, but not knowing the hour of your arrival forced me to write you this proclamation so that when you cross the threshold of your room you will have the terroristic welcome.

I would ask you to telephone Sunday evening around 7 in order to set up an appointment so that we can speak.

Greetings o citizen, cannon blasts.

Robespierre

[1] The Latin expression, "Your friends salute you."

To Marco Beltramo

Turin, February 3, 1925

Dearest friend,

Nine more days and then you will finally be in Turin. Bonelli has the intention of organizing grand festivities to appropriately welcome the returning Tipo Losco, but this year I am inclined toward great skepticism, because I have seen that the events and initiatives that were made by Tina have sunk miserably. We should have gone skiing on Sunday and it was already sort of all planned when Tina invited part of the company to lunch on Sunday morning and so we could not go. Last Friday I went out of my way to look for a third person in order to please Miss Figna who burned with a desire to try out her skis; but in vain, for the third person wasn't found and so I as well as the young lady had to go to the reception in honor of the first year students organized by the 2 clubs. Unfortunately this year 2 Tipi Loschi had to leave us for various reasons, who with their merry spirit were the dynamic force of the company; one of them is you, O Perrault and the other is Clementina who again cherishes a great wish to go to the mountains, but unfortunately her being so far away makes it difficult to be able to plan things.

With the departure of you two, even if the society is not officially broken up, it is broken and only just getting along, but is no longer the society of last year: a sense of indifference and maybe skepticism unfortunately has invaded the Tipi Loschi. Add to the fact that there is no snow, which doesn't seem to want to fall this year, and you will have the complete synthesis of the serious situation or crisis to which our beautiful Society is exposed. I myself wish that when you are in Turin with your good character you can reanimate us all with some sort of outing and thus the Society of the Tipi Loschi can receive from you that breath, that will really make it flourish and not just drag along lifelessly.

I finally took the exam in Technology, the result was not brilliant 60/100 but it's always one exam less; now I've been studying Metallurgy and in a little while I hope to be able to take it. But I have before me still a fairly long way to go in order to reach the so longed for diploma. I am not making plans for the future because I know that unfortunately they would all have unhappy outcomes: the future is in the hands of God and better than that it could not be.

Please keep me informed if you have changed your arrival time, otherwise I dispense you from replying to me because you're so busy; you'll reply better in person than in writing.

See you on Thursday at 9:40 at P.N.[1] and may all the artillery of the Terror fire a blast for your next arrival in this city which is the magnificent seat of the committee of Public Health. Hail, O Perrault the citizen

Robespierre greets you

---

[1] Porta Nuova - Turin's main train station.

To Luciana

Turin, February 4, 1925

Dearest,[1]

Yesterday your very welcome postcard arrived for me. Yesterday afternoon we were at lunch at the Marchisio's. I learned how to play Mahjong. Now I've resumed intense study, so much more that shortly I intend to take a few days of vacation when Beltramo arrives. Sunday I hope I can go skiing since last Sunday I didn't find anyone who was available to go with me.

The weather here is magnificent again. I'm thinking of the disaster it will be this summer; if it continues it will be a very hot summer and we will have poor harvests. Write to me often because at least receiving your letters can fill the enormous void which you have left among us. At first living together every day I wasn't able to sufficiently appreciate all that you mean to me, but unfortunately now that many kilometers separate us, now that we must be separated not for a few days but for life and only to see one another from time to time, I understood what it means to have a sister at home and what a void her distance can leave. Especially write to mama so that she can live happily, you were the one who cheered up Mama in all her sorrows.

Give my greetings to Jan and to you a thousand kisses with the assurance of my poor prayers.

Pier Giorgio

[1] This was the first letter that Pier Giorgio wrote to Luciana after her wedding. He was unable to control his emotions at the time of her departure. At the train station, he broke down sobbing which upset everyone present.

To Marco Beltramo

Turin, February 9, 1925

Dearest friend,

On Sunday we finally succeeded in planning a ski trip: four of us travelled there and six returned. The truly determined ones were Miss Figna, Randone and I and then, and then at the last moment Miss Montafia, a friend of Figna, joined us: Tina as usual was undecided up until the last moment or rather she pretended to be undecided. At 6 p.m. the four of us, gathered with difficulty, met at the station. We bought tickets and then we loaded our skis onto the train as best we could. I went to await the arrival of the train from Genoa to wait for Clementina and to tell her of your coming arrival and to invite her on the Sunday outing. Clementina, good as always, from her beautiful bouquet of violets took out a little bunch and gave it to me and I carried it with me always. Arriving at Oulx we continued on quickly until Sauze where we ordered abundant caffè latte in order to put some coal in the engines so exhausted from the ascent.

We were beginning dinner when a little boy came in and asked me questions and gave me a note on which was written: "If you are brave enough come outside – a fascist from Turin." From the start I thought that it might have been about one of these kids who had followed us and were behind us laughing, exhibiting bad manners and I wanted to go outside willing to see what he was writing about. I made Randone read the note who told me to let it go and not to go outside. If I had gone out, I would have found none other than the D.d.g. dressed like an Apache and with her Miss Maddalena Guglielmini. After waiting around for a while they came into the hotel and then everyone clapped to see Tina in the mountain; it was really great. A bit of caffè latte was shared fraternally then I heard their intention to go on to the Kind shelter; we offered to accompany them for a while. And so making our way along, both because of the company and the enchanting night, without noticing we had arrived as far as halfway between Kind and Sauze. Saying goodbye to the girls and collecting Tina's last wishes, we returned down and went to sleep. On Sunday, after having attended Holy Mass, after breakfast we climbed up to the Kind where the snow was pretty good.

We really had a great time. Tomorrow I'll write to Clementina to find out if she is free on Monday and so if you would like we can leave Sunday morning at 6:30, go to Bardonecchia, from there we could reach Stretta Valley, stay all Sunday until Monday night. Otherwise if Clementina could leave Saturday at 6:25 p.m., we could go to the Kind again; on Thursday we can talk about it to make better plans and by then we'll know Clementina's response.

Affectionate greetings and see you very soon

Pier Giorgio

To Luciana

Turin, February 14, 1925

Dearest,

Thanks first of all for the good letter... You ask me whether I am in good spirits. How could I not be so? As long as Faith gives me strength I will always be joyful; every Catholic cannot but be joyful: sadness ought to be banished from Catholic souls. Sorrow is not sadness, which is a worse illness than any other. This illness is nearly always caused by atheism. But the purpose for which we have been created shows us the path, even if strewn with many thorns, it is not a sad path. It is joyful even in the face of sorrow. Then in these days my soul exults because Marco Beltramo has arrived from Livorno. As you may already know I went to Asti to meet him; the other day I was at his house for a cup of tea: there was Tina, the countess Rossi (she has nothing to do with Rossi vermouth because they are from Parma) with three daughters, other cousins of Beltramo. I was having fun, and I had an invitation to the Rossi home.

Today I am going to the mountains with Beltramo. Tina cannot come because at the last minute she received a letter from her sister announcing her arrival on Sunday. Tutankhamen is truly hoodoo.

Beltramo would want to send you a thousand cannon blasts, but he is afraid that they might not be up to your standards anymore and therefore he sends you respectful regards.

For carnivale we will go to the mountains and we were thinking of the Great St. Bernard, but since Beltramo has only a few days available then probably we will end up at Bardonecchia, all the more because I would like to participate in the 15 km. competition which takes place on Sunday.

The weather is certainly not very favorable because here in Turin it continues to rain; I don't know if it will snow on the mountains but one hopes because otherwise we would be in a fix.

Greetings to Jan and to you a thousand kisses from

Pier Giorgio

You will receive letters of thanks from the Club and from the Conference of St. Vincent de Paul; to each of those I gave 500 lire in your name.[1]

Papa left for Rome for a few days; he'll stay there until the end of the discussion about the army plan.

I am enclosing for you a note given to me by aunt, she can't remember whether or not she already sent it to you.

[1] Grandmother Frassati had given Luciana 3,000 lire on the occasion of her wedding. Luciana gave 1,000 lire to Pier Giorgio and said to him, "This is for you, not for your poor." It was the first time in his life that he possessed such a huge sum of money. Immediately, he divided it between the Cesaro Balbo Club and the Conference of St. Vincent de Paul and sent the donations in Luciana's name so that she would receive the credit.

Bardonecchia, February 22, 1925. Pier Giorgio was an avid skier and belonged to several ski clubs. Here he is pictured at the start of a 15km race. He is not wearing the club's uniform sweater because he had given it to a friend who had forgotten to bring one.

Bardonecchia, February 22, 1925

Just got back from a 15 km skiing competition which was very tiring for me because I haven't trained at all this year and then having the skis so badly waxed was a disaster. At 2 p.m. I leave for Oulx to meet up with the others at Cesana where I'll stay until Wednesday. I took another exam because they forced me to take it and I got 60/100; now I have only three more exams.

Greetings to Jan and a thousand kisses to you from

P. Giorgio

To Marco Beltramo

Turin, February 27, 1925

Dearest Marco,

Today I resumed my studies which had been interrupted by Carnevale. On Wednesday those of our company who were still around left Cesana to return to Turin because the weather had suddenly changed; if it had stayed nice we had wanted to move the tents to Clavières and stay there until Saturday and then go to Sauze d'Oulx and participate in the competitions. Tina, Laura and Begey left by your train on Tuesday and I accompanied them to Oulx. On Sunday I'm going to Sauze for the "Young Mountaineers" competitions and then I'll say goodbye to the mountains for a little while and I'll study very hard so that I can have fairly decent marks on the exams for which I'm preparing, especially as they are in my major. I collected all the things you forgot: a pair of socks, a tin flask with alcohol which I believe belongs to you, and also a cooking burner which I have already delivered to your parents, I also delivered a pair of ski poles; the other pair will be delivered to Miss Musso this evening.

As soon as they're ready I'll send you the photographs which serve as a remembrance of this wonderful Carnevale. Write to me if I should send you the rest of the 110 lire or if I should give it to your brother, in any case I enclose the bill prepared by good Randone. I found out later the result of the race, I came in 26th out of 49 competitors: I didn't believe I was among the first 30 given the total lack of training and the course being rather difficult. This evening

I'll receive the prize at the Giovane.[1] On Sunday I may try to make Clementina come to Sauze so I can teach her the Telemark,[2] although I hardly know it, given the great condition of the snow.

The lawyer Farinet sent me some magnificent photographs taken these days at the Great St. Bernard; I ran into him yesterday and he said that he is always available if we want to make a run and regarding the snow he said it is abundant without danger of avalanches. Maybe after I've taken this exam I can make an excursion for a few days.

The weather here in Turin is unsettled, it rains a bit, it's sunny a while, but the cold has returned this year; the winter will last longer than usual.

On Tuesday all of us were at Clavières and we watched, beyond the border, the international jump competition; what a great spectacle: you should have seen the Swedes jump! Italy also did very honorably, because it took second place, then we had the race between the ladies of our group: Tina, Laura, Figna and your cousin took part. The course was part uphill and part downhill and the winner was Laura, Tina second because Tina took a phenomenal tumble. Then there were races for men only won by the undersigned, then Begey was second, your cousin third and then the others.

Terroristic greetings and write to me when you can.

Kisses from

Pier Giorgio

[1] Short for "Giovane Montagna" or "Young Mountaineers" – the Catholic Mountainclimbing association.
[2] A turning movement in skiing.

To Isidoro Bonini

Turin, February 27, 1925

Dearest friend,

I believe that you may be angry with me because of the long silence, but you ought to excuse me first of all because I had to prepare for my 31st exam, and then these days Marco Beltramo arrived on leave and all of my time has been taken up by the aviator. I went to various teas in honor of the aviator then I went away to the mountains for Carnevale. On Sunday I took part in the races held at

Bardonecchia by the newspaper "La Montagna" – a 15 km. course. Without having trained I came in 26th out of 49 competitors.

Now I've gotten back to my study which was interrupted for Carnevale and I'm preparing for the 32nd exam which will be "Mechanical Preparation of Minerals." The exam won't be difficult, but it will be long. On Sunday, however, I'm going back to the mountains to take part in the "Young Mountaineers" competition and perhaps I'll return the 8th of March and then cease for a bit of time until I have passed the exam. As soon as I've finished the exam I'll go to spend a few days at Great St. Bernard and then I'll begin another: Practical Geometry, and then I'll start the thesis and the last exam and in between I'll make a two-week excursion in the mines. Maybe I might go to Trentino in which case I might take a short trip from Verona to Treviso to see the commander.

Your films are horrible things which I believe aren't good for anything except to be thrown away, in any case I'll ask my photographer his opinion.

I saw that those of the engineer Pantanelli are fairly good and now I'll make him give me a copy.

What are you thinking to do for your career? Write something to me; if I can be of help to you in someway I'll be glad to do so.

Other than that, I have nothing else to tell you except that my life is monotonous, but every day I understand better what a Grace it is to be Catholics. Poor unlucky those who don't have a Faith: to live without a Faith, without a patrimony to defend, without a steady struggle for the Truth, is not living but existing. We must never exist but live, because even through every disappointment we should remember that we are the only ones who possess the Truth, we have a Faith to sustain, a Hope to attain: our Homeland. And therefore let us banish all melancholy which can only exist when the Faith is lost. Human sorrows touch us, but if they are viewed in the light of Religion, and thus of self-surrender, they are not harmful but helpful, because they purify the Soul of the little and inevitable stains by which we men, due to our wicked nature, dirty ourselves many times.

In this Holy Lent, let us lift up our hearts and always go forward for the triumph of the reign of Christ in Society.

Cordial greetings in J.C.

Fra Girolamo

To Isidoro Bonini

Turin, March 6, 1925

Dearest friend,

Truly I have avoided talking to you about such a bitter subject, but I haven't done this out of a lack of confidence, but only because the matter is now over and it's better not to talk about it anymore but to close this episode in my life forever. Yes, this letter's language will amaze you, but you must consider that something has changed in me: it's not my doing, because I did not carry out any of the firm measures I told you about before you left Turin. I have often been in the mountains with Her,[1] often with others; but then I have convinced myself that not being able to attain the Goal, it is necessary to kill the germ which if well looked after produces huge benefits, but otherwise, sorrows. In my internal struggles I have many times asked myself why should I be sad? Why should I suffer, endure this sacrifice unwillingly? Have I perhaps lost the Faith? No, thank God, my Faith is still firm enough and so let us strengthen, let us reaffirm what is the only Joy with which one can be satisfied in this world. Every sacrifice is worthwhile if only for that; then as Catholics, we have a Love which surpasses every other love and which after that owed to God is immensely beautiful, just as our religion is beautiful. Love, which had as its advocate that Apostle who preached it daily in all his letters to the various Faithful. Charity, without which, says St. Paul, every other virtue is worthless. It is indeed that which can be a guide and direction for our whole life, for a whole program. This, with the Grace of God, can be the goal toward which my soul can strive. And so at first we are dismayed, because it is a beautiful plan, but a hard one, full of thorns and not many roses, but we trust in Divine Providence and in His Mercy. Pope Pius X of blessed memory recommended to Youth the practice of Holy Communion, and I cannot but give thanks to God at every moment for having given me parents, teachers, all friends, all of whom have guided me through the main path of the Faith. Imagine if in this moment in which my soul is going through this crisis, I had the misfortune of not believing; life would not be worth living for one more instant and only death would perhaps soothe every human suffering.

But instead, for the one who believes, the controversies of life are not an object of depression, but serve to correct us and to energetically call us back to follow the way perhaps momentarily abandoned.

Well, my plan in this is to transform that special liking that I have had for Her, which wasn't willed, to the end to which we ought to arrive, in the light of Charity, in the respectful bond of friendship understood in the Christian sense, in the respect for her virtue, in the imitation of her illustrious gifts, as I have for the others. Perhaps you might tell me that it's madness to hope this; but I believe, if you pray for me a bit, that in a short time I can achieve this state in prayer.

So this is my plan which I hope to achieve with the Grace of God, even if it will cost me the sacrifice of earthly life, but it matters little.

As for your future, I give you my compliments and praise. You do well to focus on agriculture; I'll submit your plan to my father, but surely you'll be praised, because when one is talking about agriculture he is happiest and he is always saying that Italy's future and fortune lie in agriculture.[2]

---

[1] He is talking about his secret love for Laura Hidalgo and his decision not to act on it.

[2] Bonini wanted to be an agricultural pioneer in America and, with Pier Giorgio as his intermediary, sought advice and help from Senator Frassati.

To Luciana

Turin, March 13, 1925

Dearest

After a long time I'm finally taking the pen in hand again to write to you. Above all a recommendation – don't send any more requests to Mama because she's very tired and not having the automobile available since Italo is ill she tires a lot; rather I recommend that you distract her a lot and make her rest a lot because she's not well at all. On Sunday after the middle-distance races coming down from Sauze to Oulx I injured my left knee a little: it's nothing serious just a pinched nerve in the area of the goose's foot: the best remedy is to ski a little higher. This Sunday of course if I go, maybe not, I'm still not quite sure, it will be at least for a while the last time because I want to successfully conclude the exam I've begun. Then maybe I'll join the Guglielmini to go to the Great St. Bernard if it will still be possible.

I'm sending you as soon as I'm newly supplied a photograph of the Monginevro taken at Carnevale which truly has turned out to be such a masterpiece that I have made an enlargement and framed it in the English fashion and now I will hang it in my study.

I hope that now you will have received letters from Tina who has always written to you at the Embassy and only very recently after having gotten your address wrote you in Turin; it's always quite striking her indecisions and the little desire to organize outings: she should have gone to Madesimo with the Guglielmini girls and it seems that instead she beats a retreat to Mondovi to study zoology and comparative anatomy; I don't understand much anymore, but miraculously she succeeded in planning a perfect Carnevale in Cesana.

This afternoon at the Y.M., I'll get my second medal and then if later there will be races and if my leg permits I'll continue to exercise it.

I heard from Mama that you are becoming a housewife and so you get all the praises from your distant brother. I'd like to give you a piece of advice specially suited to these times of Lent and it's this: that you in these times of mourning for the Church you would prepare yourself with some little sacrifice and self-denial in order to better celebrate a Holy Easter; then if this year unfortunately we cannot be physically together, then spiritually yes, because I in my prayers will remember you and you in yours will remember me and so that day as always our spirits will be firmly united in God.

I think Mama will be arriving on Monday; I advise you to keep her spirits up and make her rest because she needs it.

Give a big greeting to Jan for me and to you a thousand kisses from

Pier Giorgio

You will receive a thank you note from the Conference of St. Vincent at Madonna della Pace Church, for the offering of L. 500. The club hasn't yet sent a thank you note to me so you haven't yet received their note.

I'm enclosing a note from the sister.

Many greetings from the blonde and stupid ass.[1] Very good.[2]

217

¹ This was a note written by the maid Mariscia. It was actually a term of endearment.
² These words were written in German by Pier Giorgio after what Mariscia wrote.

To Marco Beltramo

March 16, 1925

  Yesterday was the last Sunday, at least for a little while, of skiing. I was in Sauze with Hidalgo and Boccalatte because Goria wasn't able to come because he had nothing less than a sinus headache. We left at 6:25 p.m. in a group of three (the minimum possible number) since this year the company is very divided. Arriving in Sauze we didn't find a place to sleep, it was very annoying especially for the ladies who I didn't want to sleep poorly or in a place with little security. And as I saw that there were 2 bunks free in the Y.M. shelter, I thought it was the only safe place to take them to sleep along with us. Now I'm really mortified because it wasn't possible to sleep almost the whole night: first we had the spectacle of a drunk who threw up his wine, then there was noise until 2 in the morning. In short, today I am still living with a guilty conscience having made them spend such a horrible night: I'm sorry, also, because the Y.M. made such a poor showing; luckily Hidalgo and the other girl understood that what happened was an exception, but if it would have been Giuffredi, the situation would have been more serious. In the morning after Holy Mass we went up to the Kind and then we skied down to Clotes. Hidalgo made the whole descent without poles and hardly fell down at all, truly not to praise her but ever since Carnevale she has made wonderful progress. Tina has told me to tell you that all the thanks for the photographs should go to Her and not to Begey. These days she has shown signs of great uncertainty, now she's away from Turin, then she's going up to Madesimo again with the Guglielminis or to Mondovi to study.
  Severi, Randone, Cerutti and Unterichter have gone to Breithorn (4165 m.) I've accompanied them there in my thoughts as it wasn't prudent to climb such a height with my knee. I'll be sending you the photograph of the village a little later because for now I don't have any.

Terroristic greetings

> Robespierre

Sauze d'Oulx, March 23, 1925

I didn't want to came back here anymore, but how can one resist the temptation of the snow?
Terroristic greetings

> Pier Giorgio

To His Mother

Turin, March 25, 1925

Dearest mama,

I'm writing just a few lines because I should go to make my visits.[1] I would have wanted to write to you before, but my laziness prevented me. I'm glad that you are able to rest a little and I'm also glad that Luciana can enjoy you a bit, but alas! I already miss you very much. Sometimes when you are here one doesn't appreciate your company enough, but when you go far away even only for a short time one immediately feels the enormous void that your absence leaves. This evening we are having dinner at Alda's. Everything is going along well enough at home: the cook makes food that is good enough to eat, I would say that every day she improves a little; Gianni on the contrary is always worse, one must watch him otherwise he does nothing and wants no reproof; he is as slow as a snail. I must study and after having told him what he should be doing I can't be at his heels otherwise my studies will go badly.

The snow continues to fall in the mountains but on Sunday I ceased the ski outings, perhaps for good, because otherwise study will go by the wayside. Spring has begun with grayish days and a light but continuous rain is falling.

I'm enclosing a photograph of the Monginevro which I ask you to please give to Luciana, because it will be for her a remembrance of the place where we first skied together.

Ask Luciana if she has received the letters from Grandmother Frassati addressed to the Embassy. Regarding Tina I'm astonished

because she now has the correct address; tell Luciana to write to complain to her because I don't dare anymore.
Greetings and kisses to you and to Luciana and greetings to Jan.

P. Giorgio

[1] He is speaking of his visits to the poor whose cases were assigned to him by the Conference of St. Vincent de Paul.

To Marco Beltramo

Turin, March 30, 1925

Dearest friend,
You can imagine with what joy I received your letter along with the postcard. Indeed, I had a feeling it would come that day. Along with the great joy of getting news from you I also received a letter and a postcard from Clementina; always so good, rather I'd say that if one can find a defect in Clementina, it's that she is too good. I've abandoned sports to get back to the studies, but yesterday believe me to have to study was very hard; my mind wasn't used to it and I asked myself if I was really myself or someone else because I couldn't conceive of myself being in the city on a holiday. In fact I had to drink huge doses of coffee so that I could study. On Sunday I might go to Villa S. Croce[1] and in those places where our Spirit ought to be strengthened for future and present battles, you'll be present to me and I'll try to remember you in my poor prayers. I don't yet have plans for Easter; everything depends on my leg, if the left knee continues to do poorly, then mediocre plans, but if on the other hand I'll be able to take off freely on some little flight, I'll be awaited by the Monte Rosa Group.
I admired the poetry and I'm really envious of you for the flight; who knows when I can taste such a similar joy? Maybe after graduation, for now my time is very limited and so I can't lose one day more. I'll pay the S.A.R.I. quota and if you want to send the C.A.I. card to be stamped, I'll gladly get it done for you. Tina has the poems as an account of the trip to Madesimo, now she's studying or at least she's pretending to, so much so that she's already passed. I think that she will prudently abandon Turin on April 1st: she is afraid of some April fool pranks. I lost a Bonjour Philippine

Rocca Sella, 1925. Pier Giorgio had a great passion for the mountains and would later be referred to as a "tremendous alpinist" by Pope John Paul II in a speech to the Youth of Turin, April 13, 1980.

bet[2] with Laura: since the bet wasn't decided, I would like to give her the Epistles of Saint Paul in Latin with commentary and with a dedication that I will consider in due time; tell me what you think about it.

I have a special affection for the Apostle of Charity.

The weather is now becoming nice again; but unfortunately I ought to content myself with admiring the beautiful mountains through the windows of my study.

The other afternoon I went to hear Irma Gramatica; the engineer Hidalgo[3] was also there; she performs very well and has a very harmonious voice, identical to Clementina's. Who knows if I will go to the mines in Sardinia soon, we'll see.

I'm sending you a photograph taken at Rocca Sella while coming down a crag by double rope: the photograph doesn't show how I'm suspended over a void.

Terroristic greetings.

Pier Giorgio

[1] This was a religious retreat house operated by the Jesuit Fathers.
[2] A Bonjour Philippine bet was a type of wager where the first person to shout something out in a certain situation would be the winner and could then require the other person to give them a gift.
[3] This is the first time he refers to Laura Hidalgo with the title of engineer. It was a sign of respect in recognition of the successful completion of her degree. Pier Giorgio was always quick to honor his friends with the appropriate distinction.

To Isidoro Bonini

Turin, April 3, 1925

Dearest friend,

I think that this letter of mine won't reach you in enough time to convey to you very fervent wishes for your feastday, in any case better late than never. I've now left the mountains behind and I'm concentrating on the books; I hope to be ready to take the exam right after Easter. I would plan to go to Villa Santa Croce on Saturday to do the spiritual exercises, but I am afraid I may have to miss it, because my mother may arrive from The Hague precisely this Saturday evening. In any case, I'll go on Sunday if possible; believe me I need a bit of silent time to review spiritual matters and to do a bit of spiritual housekeeping.

I read your last letter with pleasure because it told me of your coming arrival – I only hope that it doesn't coincide with the Easter vacation in which case you could first come to Pollone and then we could go to Turin together. I reported your dry words to the Landlady, but I ask you to be a bit less crude next time. The weather here is magnificent and it does little to invite one to study. Bruno has already taken all of his exams and has presented his graduation thesis; he's leaving Turin in a few days. Confidentially your brother is loafing a bit. You know that I made Asquini a member of the Club, because Father Cojazzi[1] asked me, but he doesn't attend as he has to study a lot. On May 1st I plan to begin the thesis so that I'll be free of that in July with the help of God, and thus I'll spend my last summer free, completely free. As far as your plans for the future we shall speak with my father in person, given that you'll be in Turin very soon and so you can explain things better than I can. Do you know that Dr. Baggio is engaged to Miss Loretz, rather they will marry after Easter, I've let you know so that you can send them congratulations. Have you heard from Collo?

A few days ago Beltramo made his first flight as a member of the Academy, if you knew how I envied him.

The Sunday after Easter if my studies permit I plan to make a short trip to Savona, where there's a Regional convention of FUCI for the blessing of the banners by the Secretariat of Savona. It's not a bad idea especially if one considers that my cousins are 2 steps from Savona in Albissola and so I can kill two birds with one stone.

Cordial greetings in J.C.

Pier Giorgio

---

[1] Father Cojazzi was a Salesian Father. Pier Giorgio's father had publicly defended the Salesian Fathers in the pages of *La Stampa* during a period when they were under much criticism. After they had been vindicated, the Father General of the Salesians visited Senator Frassati to thank him for his support. Upon asking if there was anything he could do in return, Mr. Frassati mentioned that his son could use help in Latin – a subject he had failed and was struggling with. Father Cojazzi was sent to tutor Pier Giorgio in Latin. He later became the first biographer of Pier Giorgio and was a very good friend of Mrs. Frassati for many years. His books on Pier Giorgio were widely published at that time.

To Marco Beltramo

Turin, April 10, 1925

Dearest friend,

It's already two days since I left Villa S. Croce where I thought about you a lot; your spirit was present within those walls where we've spent so many good days together. I've wanted to reply to your letter earlier but the Spiritual Retreat and the feasts of these days have prevented me from doing so. Yesterday Severi and I paid the Easter visit to the President.[1] What a delightful family. Believe me I left their house enthusiastic. I met her brother Stefano, what a gem of a boy! And I saw the love that reigns in the family where Clementina is the queen of the house. Paolo Luotto delighted us with his wireless telephone, we listened to the news from Rome, concerts from London and Paris. I spent 2 very delightful hours there. We remembered you and if some inconvenience doesn't occur, Clementina wants to come on the trip to Monviso which will be as soon as you have returned to the soil of Piedmont; we ought to give to this outing a certain grandeur worthy of such a person. In this earthly life after the affection for parents and sisters, one of the most beautiful affections is that of friendship; and every day I ought to thank God because he has given me men and lady friends of such goodness who form for me a precious guide for my whole life. Every time I visit Clementina I'm edified by her great kindness and I think of the immense Good that such a beautiful Soul has certainly done and will do. Surely Divine Providence in His Marvelous Plans sometimes uses us miserable little twigs to do Good and we sometimes not only don't want to know God but instead dare to deny His existence; but we who, by the Grace of God, have the Faith, when we find ourselves in the presence of such beautiful souls, surely nourished by Faith, we cannot but discover in them an obvious sign of the Existence of God, because one cannot have such a Goodness without the Grace of God. And what can one then say about Laura and Tina, also such generous souls before whom so many times I think of the ingratitude which I've shown toward God, having responded so little to the great Graces which the Lord in His Great Mercy has always given me overlooking my sins. The example of these three believe me has been so powerful in certain moments of life when the flesh prevails over the spirit.

Your brother gave me L. 15 to deliver to Reviglio for Baggio's slide rule, I hope that you haven't sent the money directly, otherwise let me know what to do. I got your membership card stamped which I'm sending to you.

Tina has taken 2 exams 27 and 30 and now she's gone to San Valentino and afterwards she shall go to Rome, she says to prepare food for her father, poor Father! But the tongues of Turin are spreading the rumors that Eng. Bonelli drinks caffè latte, tea and similar things, so I think that Tina will succeed at something.

Laura however is staying in Turin I think and then on the Monday after Easter she leaves for Genoa with Clementina. I'll leave for Pollone maybe tomorrow or the day after tomorrow, but it completely depends on the weather.

Tomorrow I'll get back to study and this time eagerly I hope, it's time that I get to work with some energy: idleness is the father of vices while study indeed serves to strengthen the spiritual life.

I hope that this letter reaches you for Easter and so I send you my best wishes, rather just one, but I believe it to be the only wish that a true friend can make to a dear friend and it is this: the Peace of the Lord be with you always because when you possess peace every day you will be truly rich.

Cordial greetings in J.C.

Pier Giorgio

P.S. I strongly urge you to pray that I will know how to strengthen my will which is very weak.

[1] He is referring to Clementina Luotto, the president of the Tipi Loschi Society.

To Antonio Severi

Pollone, April 13, 1925

Dearest friend,

Here's my negative decision regarding Savona. I'd wanted to go with you to find Clementina in that despised Genoa, but duty forces me to stay in Turin and postpone our visit until perhaps a bit later.

I carefully looked at the calendar, and I saw with alarm that we were almost in the middle of the month and there are only two weeks left for me to take the exam. Now I need to make an effort because if I am to succeed then I must not have any distractions. I'm going to Turin with a firm decision not to see anyone anymore and to study intensely in these last days so that finally I can take this exam. I only fear that I don't know how to maintain this decision and so I'm asking you to pray for me a little so that God will give me an iron will, that does not bend and does not fail in His projects.

I will write to Clementina telling her of my sorrow in not being able to enjoy a bit of her precious company in that infernal Genoa, but I ask you to also tell her in person all about my sorrow.

While I'm writing to you the sun is shining, but every now and then it rains so I am forced to study a little outside and a little inside. However the house is very cold so I study poorly indoors.

Greetings to your family and especially to your sister and to you a thousand kisses in J.C.

Pier Giorgio

P.S. If you see Villani tell him hello for me and ask him if he's still alive.

To Isidoro Bonini

Pollone, April 15, 1925

Dearest friend,

Surely you've heard from your brother that on Holy Wednesday the Eng. Bruno left for Pola. If I am not mistaken he is the third blackmark on the famous house at Via S. Massimo 21.[1]

Tomorrow I'm leaving this pleasant countryside to return to the city, but I'm leaving this quiet place with a plan which I hope to keep.

The other day paging through the calendar, I made a terrible discovery: we've arrived at the middle of the month and so I told myself that this is the time to intensify the studies and so I've decided that as soon as I've arrived in Turin I'll be dead to everyone except the Conference of St. Vincent and I'll study from morning until evening. I know this will require a lot of energy but I'm trusting in the Providence of God and also in the prayers of friends. I'm happy to see you again and I'd like to devote not just a few days to you, but all the time, provided such arrival of yours doesn't conflict with the exam and then I'd be forced to do violence to my feelings and take away from my exam study time a few hours to be able to enjoy your beloved company.

As soon as I am in Turin I'll ask your brother the name of Pollicina's bride and then I'll ask him if we should send flowers or if they've already thought of it.

I plan to begin the thesis at the beginning of May and in the meantime prepare the Mining Technology exam for the first of June leaving me only that disagreeable subject which is Practical Geometry. I'll finish my exams with a boring subject, too bad; besides it's not possible to do it differently now, it's no longer possible to change the order of the exams.

Tomorrow as is my custom every time I leave Pollone, I'll go up to Oropa[2] to pray in the Pious Sanctuary. I'll remember you at the feet of the Brown Madonna.[3]

When you're back in Turin, I'll tell you in person about the vicissitude of my first rejection. The backstage maneuvering is completely unedifying.

I hope that you've had a good Easter.

Cordial greetings in J.C.

Pier Giorgio

[1] This was the address of Isidoro Bonini's house.
[2] Oropa is the site of a popular Marian sanctuary in the mountains above Pollone.
[3] The Brown Madonna is a wooden statue of Our Lady, representing the Presentation of the Child in the Temple. Local tradition says that it was brought over from the Far East by St. Eusebius, the first bishop of Vercelli and the Piedmont region, in about the middle of the fourth century.

To Luciana

Oropa, April 16, 1925

I remembered you here in beautiful Oropa. Today we are leaving for Turin. The weather is magnificent; greetings to Jan and to you a thousand kisses from

Pier Giorgio

To Clementina Luotto

Oropa, April 16, 1925

Remembering you at the feet of the Virgin; a thousand greetings are sent to you.

Pier Giorgio Frassati

To Franz Massetti

Turin, April 17, 1925

Dearest Franz,
I'm writing with a pencil because I have 2 fountain pens before me which alas are both empty. I returned from the countryside yesterday and found your nice postcard for which I warmly thank you.

As soon as I saw Bertini, I asked him right away whether you had already written him some letter of recrimination, but up to now nothing. I came to Turin with strong plans to stiffen up and to get down to serious study because otherwise this exam won't get taken and by dragging it out, it's becoming annoying. But for sure to put certain plans into action one needs an iron will, which I unfortunately don't have, but instead alas I unfortunately have a will that is used to giving in; so I need prayers because only with them and through them will I be able to obtain from God the Grace to strengthen my will and thus to bring into a safe harbor the ship which is sinking in the last stormy waves of my student career. Time is pressing and therefore I need to study. Ah, if I were able to take the exam within the month I would be happy.

And when will you put an end to your lazy days in Capua? Remember the lesson given by history, how they were fatal to Hannibal. Return right away to stiffen up and take one exam after another in a hurry so that I soon can greet you with the title of engineer.

Today the others are leaving for Savona, but we're staying because first comes the duty of study and then the pleasure.

Cordial greetings in J.C.

Pier Giorgio

To Isidoro Bonini

Turin, April 19, 1925

Both of us are here in the house because your brother is kindly writing for me the title of a design that I must present for the next exam. I'll write to you a little later.
Affectionate greetings in J.C.

Pier Giorgio

To Clementina Luotto

Turin, April 23, 1925

Dear Miss President,
Infinite thanks for the beautiful letter to which I would have wanted to reply earlier, but only now do I have a free moment and I'm taking advantage of it to attend to my back correspondence.

I assume fully and consciously the entire responsibility and therefore I free you from that little which you reserved for yourself, because it would be unjust.

I got the story from Severi about the stay in Genoa; he was enthusiastic and didn't find Genoa so hellish, on the contrary he found it very beautiful and better than Bologna. I explained to him that for you to be forced to live in a city far from your family could seem more ugly than what it really is,[1] but then how can one judge justly when one visits the city having as a guide none other than the President of the T.L. (It doesn't get any better than that.)

I've gotten back to studying but not as tenaciously as I planned, but I hope soon to be ready for the debut. Special thanks go to you for the good advice and for the encouragement that have given me a bit more strength to face the last storms of my student life.

As far as your exam goes I'm certain that you'll have a splendid outcome, we know how you prepare and how you perform, certainly not like us T.L.

Thanks again for the prayers, which truly are the best proof of friendship, because it is exquisite Christian Charity to pray for those in need.

There's nothing more beautiful than Charity, for as St. Paul says in the First Epistle to the Corinthians Chap. XIII: "If I speak with the tongues of men and of angels, but don't have love, I am but a resounding gong, or a tinkling cymbal," and further on, "Now there are only these three things that endure, faith, hope and love, but the greatest of all is love." Indeed faith and hope cease with our death. Love or Charity endures forever or rather I believe it will be even more alive in the next life. As far as I'm concerned I'll pray for you although my prayers are worth little, but God in His Omnipotence does not look at my lack of merits but he will hear my prayers all the same for the sake of your merits.

On Sunday, after the day of the exam, maybe I'll come to pay a visit to you in Turin, I plan to and so I hope to also be able to visit your aunt toward whom I always experience remorse.

Cordial greetings in J.C.

Pier Giorgio Frassati

[1] Clementina Luotto was transferred to Genoa to teach and found that city unlivable and unfriendly.

To Isidoro Bonini

Turin, April 29, 1925

Dearest friend,

You're a bit too pretentious with your waiting game; I ought to say I am waiting too and disregard as worthless the responses you sent me by postcard. In any case I don't want to create a diplomatic incident and so I'm writing to you.

I'm spending my life dedicated to study, I'm like a shipwrecked person who is desperately struggling in the billowing waves always hoping for an anchor of safety, and I am so plunged into the books that one could almost say they are surrounding me trying to drown me in this struggle to make it to port, that is to say the exam. Saturated with this dry science, the mind every now and then finds peace and relief and spiritual enjoyment in reading St. Paul. I would like you to try to read St. Paul: he is marvellous and the soul is exalted by this reading and we are prodded to follow the right path and to return to it as soon as we leave it through sin. Wednesday, if not before, I hope will be the grand debut, the third-last debut of my life as a student at the polytechnic and then I'll begin the thesis. The plan as you see is grandiose; it is however necessary to find the good will to put this into action but I hope to achieve this little by

little with the grace of God.
And what good things are you doing? Write to me at length about your life and also write more often than I do because I have the extenuating circumstances of my studies while you good commander are leisurely awaiting the next retirement at the Regina Coeli.[1]
Cordial greetings in J.C.

Pier Giorgio

[1] Pier Giorgio was teasing Isidoro about his "easy life." He jokingly called Isidoro the commander of Regina Coeli - a well-known prison in Rome where it was thought most commanders would eventually end up.

TO LAURA HIDALGO

Turin, April 30, 1925

Dear Miss Hidalgo,
Here is the translation of the Letters of St. Paul, with this you can better enjoy the beauty of the Latin and better understand the philosophical nexus of the epistles of St. Paul.[1] I'm also attaching a program of the outings of the "Young Mountaineers" which I should really have sent you earlier, but better late than never. You will find underlined an outing to the Picchi del Pagliaio, which could be appropriate, as it is an easy classic, nice and long without being exaggerated. The 24th is the fourth Sunday of May and maybe we could also organize an outing to the Rocca Sella for the third Sunday. What do you think? I'm almost sick and tired of studying this subject and I hope to be able to take the exam on Wednesday. I'm not asking for your prayers, because I know you don't have to be asked — but in any case I very much need them.
Cordial greetings in J.C.

Pier Giorgio Frassati

I heard from my friend Curio Chiaraviglio who was passing through that Tina is arriving on the first of May.

[1] Pier Giorgio lost a bet to Laura Hidalgo and was then required to give her a gift. He chose the letters of St. Paul and gave them to her first in Latin and then in their Italian translation. But the significance of such a gift went beyond the occasion; it reflected his desire to contribute to his friend's spiritual growth. The dedication written in the front of the Latin book was as follows: *"Easter, Holy Year. To Miss Laura Hidalgo, in the hope that St. Paul will be her guide and master in this earthly pilgrimage, offered in Christian spirit in J. C. by Pier Giorgio Frassati."*

To Marco Beltramo

Turin, Tuesday, May 5, 1925, 1:15 a.m.

Dearest Marco,

As you see I've finished studying this evening at a late hour because now I am close to harvesting what I have sown.

I'm writing to you although I have little time to give you some not-so-good news, so that as soon as you have a bit of time you can dash off a note to Clementina who is here because her mother is not very well at all. I don't really know what the illness is but it is some form of fatigue that makes her unable to care for the home and requires a lot of rest; Clementina being at Genoa hasn't been able to help her, so Clementina has left Genoa and her school for a little while to devote herself to caring for her mother.

As soon as I heard these details from the good Severi I hurried to write to her because I didn't dare to go to her house fearing to cause some disturbance; later, after the exams, I'll go to make a visit to give her a bit of consolation; I'm sure you know my feelings about Clementina so you can imagine how very sorry I was to hear such news.[1]

Tina has returned from her leisures at Capua and has no plans for now, Laura is acting as D.d.g. for the trip to the Sagra of St. Michael, let's hope that this time she succeeds in bringing the few members of the group up the so perilous peak.

On Friday May 8th I'll take the exam and so please remember me in your prayers as I also ask you to please pray for Clementina's mother, because only prayers can obtain from God the desired improvement.

And what good things are you doing? I think that you'll be tired of your heavy work as you get near your exams. When will you get your leave? In June or July?

Write me something, but don't worry about it because I know that if you don't write it's a sign that you are too busy and therefore you are excused.

Affectionate greetings in J.C.

Pier Giorgio Frassati

---

[1] He loved Clementina Luotto like an older sister whose good advice and example were helpful in life.

Turin, May 13, 1925

Dearest Marco,

Thanks for your postcard, I had thought that your silence was due to study. On Friday May 8th I took the exam in Mineral Preparation. It wasn't a success, but I got 70/100 and now I've already begun another which I hope to take at the end of the month.

The Magna Carta that is the law of our society[1] assigns the 18th of May as a feastday and I thought, given that this year the 18th falls on a weekday, that we should transfer this solemn day to the 17th celebrating it with an outing to Rocca Sella. I'm sending you a sample printed program so that you can kindly tell me if it has your approval and support because being a social outing of the T.L. it should turn out as best as possible. No one should miss it, at least in spirit, and so I would like your support which I would communicate to the high council along with that of Clementina who is also unable to participate in person.

This evening before going to the theater I stopped by Tina's so that I could get her signature on the programs. Tina offered to make lunch for us at Rocca Sella, who knows how much hunger we will endure; I put in an order for myself (macaroni, roast veal with vegetables, wild game, buttered asparagus, fruits - dessert and wines in abundance). I advised her to bring a small donkey to carry the provisions, but she politely replied that I would fill the bill nicely.

Affectionate greetings in J.C.

Pier Giorgio

[1] He is referring to the Tipi Loschi Society.

Turin, May 26, 1925

Dearest friend,

Above all a heartfelt thank you in the name of the T.L. for your magnificent letter of support; when I'm in Turin I'll read to you the presidential letter of support because it is worth reading.

I haven't gotten any more news from you, but I know that the silence is only due to studies just as I've also delayed in writing to you because I'm under a huge load of work; the day of harvest is approaching and so at this time I need to give greater care to the little plant so that it can bear abundant fruit. Today I went to your house and your brother Paolo filled me in on good news and bad news: the good news is regarding the brilliant outcome of your exams, and for this I send you my best wishes, the bad news alas tells me that you unfortunately are not coming very soon. For now goodbye to outings in the mountains; my plan is to study, but to do that I see that I need injections of good will which I don't have anymore so I'm recommending myself to my friends and especially to prayers. Again I ask you to pray for my Grandmother, who unfortunately is not at all well, luckily it's nothing serious right now but at 86 years of age her condition can change from one moment to the next.[1]

For the Bonjour Philippine[2] Laura rewarded me with a lovely silver medallion depicting on one side a skier descending the vertiginous slopes in the style of the valley dwellers while the other side bears the presidential motto "Percussus elevor contusus gaudeo."[3] It doesn't get any better than that and I am proud and content because it reminds me of 2 very good people.

Affectionate greetings and much good luck for your exams from

Pier Giorgio

[1] The condition of his Grandmother Ametis became much worse. She died on July 1, 1925, preceding Pier Giorgio in death by only three days.

[2] The Bonjour Philippine was a friendly wager that Pier Giorgio and Laura had engaged in at least once before. On that occasion, he lost and gave her the epistles of St. Paul for her prize.

[3] A Latin expression, "Pierced, I am exalted; bruised, I rejoice."

To Tina Bonelli

Turin, May 29, 1925

Dear Miss D.d.g.,

There are still people in the world who have not learned to mistrust; one of these is Beltramo.

Like a good T.L. he writes asking me to arrange an outing with Tina for when he returns. Poor deluded person! I know that ever since Carnevale one ought not to question your attitude toward organizing things, but we, taking to heart your wise advice, are diffident. Beltramo, who is a better sort, has faith in his fellow man.

And now let's get down to brass tacks. In this letter you will find 3 programs for the benefit concert for the poor of the

Madonna della Pace Parish that our conference is aiding. I am sending them to you with faith in what is written in the Gospel: "Knock and it will be opened to you."

A thousand good wishes for your quick recovery and a fraternal paw-shake from the T.L.

Pier Giorgio Frassati

TO FATHER ANTONIO

Turin, May 1925

Very Rev. Father Cojazzi,

Quite some time ago you asked me to write something informative on what the Conference of St. Vincent learns.

Our Conferences – unlike those of other philanthropic organizations who distribute help to the poor who are brought to their headquarters and many times hardly know them – following the principles of our founder, the confreres, go and knock on the doors of the poor, approach those who suffer and bring them words of comfort as well as material help. The Conference of the Madonna della Pace is an offshoot of the Catholic "Cesare Balbo" University Club; I would hope that one day soon all members of the fucini of Turin would enroll in it, because the Conferences have 2 highly admirable goals: first a more intense formation of ourselves, and second relief for the poor.

TO MARCO BELTRAMO

Turin, June 5, 1925

Dearest Marco,

Yesterday I took my next to last exam: I made 70/100, but believe me I feel much lighter today, and then the idea of graduating soon cheers me. On Sunday I may go to the mountains for a little to store up a little physical strength for the last flight.

I have written to Tina that there are still good people in the world who have not learned to mistrust (because of what you wrote me about arranging an outing with Tina). I think it would be better to arrange things when you have arrived because otherwise everyone may have other commitments from now until the outing takes place.

I have no further news of Clementina – but let's hope she is well. Two weeks ago Mrs. Luotto was doing well, she had made a very good recovery.

Today I am going to talk to my professor about my graduation thesis because I intend to begin writing it at once so as to get most of it down before leaving for the country. Then, when I return around the middle of September I can finish it and hand it in.

We are all waiting for you so as to arrange something, God-willing. The heat is dreadful but one must only get used to it and it becomes more bearable.

Here is some news that you may not have heard: Mrs. Brèzzi's father has died. I have not yet sent my condolences but now I shall do so because otherwise it will really look bad.

Write me exactly when you are arriving.

Terroristic greetings from

Pier Giorgio

Please pray for my grandmother who is still not well.

Turin, June 15, 1925

Dearest friend,

Day after day, I am waiting to find the willpower that will give me the strength to finish my last labor since I am about to harvest what I have sown.[1] Alas the days pass and rather than noting a sign of improvement I see the persistence of the Beast in me that wins the battle with the Spirit. Only in the prayers of friends do I see any strong help for me to regain the vigor to win out over my animal nature and so I put particular faith in your prayers.

For some time Tina and Laura have been making mysterious excursions into the mountains, with whom is not known. Later one comes to learn of a very adventurous story. These adventures are the latest news of the season. In the last one, Laura hurt her leg, apparently in the vicinity of the Pian della Mussa, but no one knows the truth.

We wanted to arrange a nice excursion for the 28th but the very bad conditions in the mountains do not permit it. Please write me the exact date of your arrival so that I can organize a worthy of you.

Clementina will leave Genoa for Rome on the 18th where on 20th she has her oral exam in the competition. As you can imagine, the written part went very well: a Latin composition without even the chance to re-read it. (It doesn't get any better than that.) (Please remember that she doesn't want anyone to know about the exam.)

The heat in Turin is quite disturbing, but if one stays shut up inside the house, one cannot still complain.

Your brother gave me your news and the brilliant success of your exams. My heartiest congratulations.

Wednesday evening we may all go to the Liceo Musicale to hear a vocal recital by the Gum.[2]

Greetings and best wishes in J.C.

Pier Giorgio

---

[1] Truer words than these Pier Giorgio could not have written, although he could not possibly known of his imminent death just 19 days away. In his lifetime, he was not able to harvest the fruit of his academic labors. He died before he could complete his exam requirements. However, on what would have been his 100th birthday, April 6, 2001, the Polytechnic of Turin passed a special resolution posthumously granting Pier Giorgio his much-desired degree in mining engineering.

[2] The University Musical Group, in Italian the Gruppo Universitario Musicale.

To Prof. Gamna

Turin, June 19, 1925

Dear Prof.,[1]

Carlo tells me that Pregliasco is kindly seeking to enter St. John's hospital. Allow me to introduce him and to heartily recommend him because he needs a lot of looking after.

Thanking you in advance for everything that you will do for the bearer of this note, my regards

Pier Giorgio Frassati

---

[1] This was a medical doctor and friend whom Pier Giorgio was writing to on behalf of another friend. Ironically, within two weeks from the time of this note, this same doctor, who lived near the Frassati's home in Turin, was called to Pier Giorgio's bedside after he had been stricken with a terrible case of polio.

Turin, June 22, 1925

...ting had been completed it would have been ...would have baptized a new route: in fact past ... no one has ever been up that way, only down. ...day we will return armed with some mountain-climbing pegs and then, if we have the honor of reporting a victory, we could name it Via Tipi Loschi or something similar.

Thank you for your postcard and for the promise of prayers, I am most grateful for these because they are better than anything else especially for someone who is taking a serious step.

There will be a general assembly this evening which unfortunately I can't attend. I would have wanted to take the floor in opposition, but there will be another time.

I'm dispensing you from writing because I know you're very busy; I'll try to write you in free moments but I don't want you to worry about answering. You can tell me everything in person and then there won't be the worries of study or the set time to enter the barracks. I'll pray to God to enlighten you so that you'll obtain a good average.

Terroristic greetings.

Pier Giorgio

For Grimaldi

Turin, July 3, 1925

Here are the injections for Converso.[1] The pawn ticket is Sappa's.[2] I had forgotten it, renew it on my behalf.

[1] Pier Giorgio wrote this note on the day before his death, his hand already paralyzed. It was a Friday, the usual day on which, together with his colleagues in the Conference of St. Vincent de Paul, he went to make visits to the poor. Pier Giorgio asked his sister to take from his jacket pocket the injections to give to his colleague Grimaldi, so that he could give them to Converso, a poor man assisted by the Conference of St. Vincent de Paul.

[2] Pier Giorgio frequently renewed pawn tickets on behalf of the poor to prevent them from losing their belongings. This ticket of Sappa's would have been one of many over the years.

NOTES FOR A SPEECH ABOUT CHARITY[1]

Friends, it is not with you that I should talk about one of the most interesting problems of our daily life. You who belong to the FUCI do not need to listen to things re-hashed in poor words which you have already heard so many times. However, given the gravity of the subject I do not believe it is useless to repeat what has already been said.

Every one of you knows that the foundation of our religion is Charity. Without it all our religion would crumble, because we would not truly be Catholics as long as we did not fulfill, or rather conform our whole life to, the two commandments in which the essence of the Catholic Faith lies: to love God with all our strength and to love our neighbour as ourselves. And here is the explicit proof that the Catholic Faith is based on real Love and not, as so many would like, in order to quiet their conscience, to base the religion of Christ on violence.

With violence hatred is sown and then its evil fruits are harvested. With charity Peace is sown among men, but not the peace of the world, True Peace which only faith in Jesus Christ can give binding us together in brotherly love.

I know this way is steep and difficult and full of thorns, whereas the other at first sight would seem more beautiful and easier and more satisfying, but if we could plunge the depths of those who unfortunately follow the perverse ways of the world, we would see that there is never in them the serenity had by those who have faced thousands of difficulties and have renounced material pleasures in order to follow the laws of God.

Today, after a terrible war that has deluged the whole world bringing material and moral ruin, we have a strict duty to cooperate generously in the moral regeneration of society worldwide so that a radiant dawn may break in which all nations recognize Jesus Christ as King not only in words but in all their people's lives, as the Florentine Republic did in the Middle Ages. But to bring this great plan to fulfillment, this most beautiful plan, we need to work generously and one of the most appropriate tasks is that offered by the Conferences of St. Vincent.

I don't know if you are all aware what these institutions are that were so marvelously conceived by St. Vincent de Paul.

It is a simple institution suitable for students because it does not involve commitment apart from being in a particular place one day a week and then visiting two or three families every week. You will see, in just a little time, how much good we can do to those we visit and how much good we can do to ourselves.

The members who visit these families are, I would say, unworthy instruments of Divine Providence. As we grow closer to the poor little by little we gain their confidence and can advise them in the most terrible moments of this earthly pilgrimage. We can give them the comforting words of faith and we often succeed, not by our own merit, in putting on the right path people who have strayed not out of malice.

I think I can say that the Conference of St. Vincent with its visits to the poor serves to curb our passions, it gives us increasing incentives to get on the right road by which we are all trying to reach the great harbor.

Seeing daily the faith with which families often bear the most atrocious sufferings, the constant sacrifices that they make and that they do all this for the love of God often makes us ask this question: I, who have had so many things from God, have always been so neglectful, so bad, while they, who have not been privileged like me, are infinitely better than me. Then we resolve in our conscience to follow the way of the Cross from then onward, the only way that leads us to Eternal Salvation.

Now there are many conferences in the city of Turin and among those there is one for university students, which however is composed primarily of people who are on the verge of ending their student careers and beginning the life of adults.

Now we direct to you a warm appeal that you might want to swell the ranks of our members which are now very meager and so that each of you can contribute in your own way to relieve those who suffer.

Come with enthusiasm to this conference, come and every sacrifice of yours will certainly be compensated in Heaven because Jesus Christ has promised that all we do for the poor for Love of Him He will consider it as having been done to Himself. You don't want to refuse this Love to Jesus Who, because of infinite love for Humanity, wanted to be in the Sacrament of the Eucharist, as our Consoler and as Bread of the Soul.

To be members one is not required to pay membership dues, it is enough to have good will and nothing else. It is true that at the end of the meeting there is a collection, but everybody is free to put whatever he wants.

Pier Giorgio Frassati

[1] These were Pier Giorgio's notes for a speech made to the FUCI students.

APPENDIX

Since his Beatification in 1990, Blessed Pier Giorgio Frassati has become a significant patron of World Youth Days. He was one of the patrons of the World Youth Day in Rome in the Jubilee Year 2000. For Toronto's World Youth Day in 2002, Pope John Paul II gave Pier Giorgio to young people in Canada and around the world as a powerful role model and mentor. Blessed Pier Giorgio's memory stirred up an intense interest throughout the vast Canadian country, resulting in the establishment of at least four Frassati Houses for young men in Vancouver, Saskatoon, Ottawa and Halifax, and two Religious and Priestly Formation Houses in Toronto for the Congregation of St. Basil (Basilian Fathers) and the Companions of the Cross.

For World Youth Day 2008 in Sydney, the Australian Church brought the mortal remains of Blessed Pier Giorgio Frassati to Sydney for the world celebration of faith and hope. Frassati's simple, wooden casket was placed in the chapel of Sydney's majestic St. Mary's Cathedral for veneration by tens of thousands of young people during July 2008.

On Monday evening, July 14, 2008, a prayer vigil was held in the cathedral, with over 900 young people in attendance from every corner of the globe. The presider and homilist of the evening vigil was Fr. Thomas Rosica, C.S.B., former National Director and Chief Executive Officer of World Youth Day 2002 in Toronto. Fr. Rosica is currently the Chief Executive Officer of the Salt and Light Catholic Television Network in Canada. Blessed Pier Giorgio is one of the patrons of this network, along with St. Gianna Beretta Molla.

In February 2009, Fr. Rosica was appointed a Consultor to the Pontifical Council for Social Communications. His homily is found below.

World Youth Day 2008
St. Mary's Cathedral – Sydney, Australia – July 14, 2008

Dear Friends,
Dear Wanda, niece of Pier Giorgio,

What an honour and privilege it is to be here with you this evening in St. Mary's Cathedral in Sydney, Australia! Led by the young adults of Canada's Catholic Christian Outreach [CCO], one of Canada's outstanding movements for Catholic university students, we have gathered together to adore Jesus, gift of God for the life of the world.

And young people of the entire world have also come here, to pray around the mortal remains of Blessed Pier Giorgio Frassati during World Youth Day 2008.

We have just listened to the blueprint for Christianity in that magnificent text of the Beatitudes from Matthew's Gospel [5:1-12]. The Beatitudes in Christ's Sermon on the Mount are a recipe for extreme holiness. Every crisis that the Church faces, every crisis that the world faces, is a crisis of holiness and a crisis of saints.

If there was ever an age when young men and women needed authentic heroes, it is our age. The Church understands that the saints and blesseds, their prayers, their lives, are for people on earth, that sainthood, as an earthly honor, is not coveted by the saints or blesseds themselves.

What was so unique and special about Blessed Pier Giorgio Frassati? He was born in 1901, at the turn of the last century in Turin, Italy. July 4, 2008 marked the 83rd anniversary of Pier Giorgio Frassati's entry into eternal life. Athletic, full of life, always surrounded by friends, whom he inspired with his life, Pier Giorgio chose not to become a priest or religious, preferring to give witness to the Gospel as a lay person. He never founded a religious order or started a new ecclesial movement. He led no armies, nor was he elected to public office. Death came even before he could complete his university degree (the degree was awarded to him posthumously in 2001). He never had a chance to begin a career; in fact, he hadn't even worked out for sure what his vocation in life would be. He was simply a young man who was in love with his family and friends, in love with the mountains and the sea, but especially in love with God.

Through World Youth Days, Pier Giorgio Frassati has become a special patron to millions of young people around the world, and most especially to the movement "Catholic Christian Outreach" in Canada.

Let us consider three highlights of this young Blessed's life that combined in a remarkable way political activism, solidarity, work for social justice, piety and devotion, humanity and goodness, holiness and ordinariness, faith and life.

Pier Giorgio's Devotional Life and Love of the Eucharist

Pier Giorgio Frassati developed a deep spiritual life which he never hesitated to share with his friends. His friends remember him saying: "To live without faith, without a heritage to defend, without battling constantly for truth, is not to live, but to 'plod along'; we must never just 'plod along.'"

The Eucharist and the Blessed Mother were the two poles of his world of prayer. He felt a strong mysterious urge to be near the Blessed Sacrament. He followed the Eucharistic Jesus in processions, took part enthusiastically in the Eucharistic Congresses, but above everything he loved to spend long hours in nocturnal adoration. And his joy was so much greater when he managed to bring in front of the Blessed Sacrament, his friends, young people he knew, and the poor he looked after. During some Eucharistic vigils, the face of Pier Giorgio would be transfigured with joy and consolation at seeing hundreds of young men and women who were coming to communion.

His spiritual life, like ours, was based on the sacraments. But he went beyond simply doing what is "required": Sunday Mass, the perfunctory confession before Christmas and/or Easter, and perhaps a small Lenten penance like giving up candy.

The Rosary, the Liturgy of the Hours, lectio divina and annual retreats were as much a part of his life as skiing, mountain-climbing or cycling. His life of prayer was his "daily bread," as it should be for anyone who desires to become a saint. He was an athlete, and he knew well that in order to "reach the goal," as he was fond of saying, he had to push himself beyond the ordinary if he wanted to be a champion.

In a letter he wrote [July 29, 1923] to the Members of "Catholic Youth" of Pollone, the mountain town north of Turin, Pier Giorgio said:

> ...I urge you with all the strength of my soul to approach the Eucharistic Table as often as possible. Feed on this Bread of the Angels from which you will draw the strength to fight inner struggles, the struggles against passions and against all adversities, because Jesus Christ has promised to those who feed themselves with the most Holy Eucharist, eternal life and the necessary graces to obtain it.
>
> And when you become totally consumed by this Eucharistic Fire, then you will be able to thank with greater awareness the Lord God who has called you to be part of his flock and you will enjoy that peace which those who are happy according to the world have never tasted. Because true happiness, young people, does not consist in the pleasures of the world and in earthly things, but in peace of conscience which we can have only if we are pure in heart and in mind.

These words demonstrate a remarkable spiritual maturity and love for the Eucharist, especially considering the fact that they were coming from a young man who was only twenty-two years old.

Pier Giorgio's respect for life and sense of social justice

In his own life and times, Pier Giorgio dealt with some of our own contemporary problems and struggles. His love of God and his tremendous sense of human solidarity bonded him with the poor, the needy, the sick, the hungry and the homeless. Frassati had a tremendous respect for human life: all life, from the earliest moments to the final moments. He was constantly defending life wherever it was diminished and under siege.

At the age of 17, in 1918, he joined the St. Vincent de Paul Society and dedicated much of his spare time to serving the sick and the needy, caring for orphans, and assisting the demobilized servicemen returning from World War I. What little he did have, Pier Giorgio gave to help the poor, even using his bus fare for charity and then running home to be on time for meals. The poor and the suffering were his masters, and he was literally their servant, which he considered a privilege. He often sacrificed vacations at the Frassati summer home in Pollone because, as he said, "If everybody leaves Turin, who will take care of the poor?"

Pier Giorgio loved the poor. It was not simply a matter of giving something to the lonely, the poor, the sick - but rather, giving his whole self. He saw Jesus in them and to a friend who asked him how he could bear to enter the dirty and smelly places where the poor lived, he answered: *"Remember always that it is to Jesus that you go: I see a special light that we do not have around the sick, the poor, the unfortunate."*

A German news reporter who observed Frassati at the Italian Embassy wrote, "One night in Berlin, with the temperature at twelve degrees below zero, he gave his overcoat to a poor old man shivering in the cold. His father, the Ambassador scolded him, and he replied simply and matter-of-factly, 'But you see, Papa, it was cold.'"

In that same letter written to the Members of "Catholic Youth" of Pollone, Pier Giorgio urged his peers with these words:

The Apostle St. Paul says, "The charity of Christ needs us," and without this fire, which little by little must destroy our personality so that our heart beats only for the sorrows of others, we would not be Christians, much less Catholics.

Finally there is the apostolate of persuasion. This is one of the most beautiful and necessary. Young people, approach your colleagues at work who live their lives away from the Church and spend their free time not in healthy pastimes, but in vices. Persuade those unfortunate people to follow the ways of God, strewn with many thorns, but also many roses.

But if every one of you were to possess these gifts to the highest degree, and did not have the spirit of sacrifice in abundance, you would not be a good Catholic. We must sacrifice everything for everything: our ambitions, indeed our entire selves, for the cause of the Faith.

Beneath the smiling exterior of the restless young man was concealed the amazing life of a mystic. Love for Jesus motivated his actions.

Pier Giorgio's suffering and death

Just before receiving his university degree in mining engineering, he contracted poliomyelitis, which doctors later speculated he caught from the sick for whom he cared.

His sickness was not understood. His parents, totally taken up by the agony, death and burial of his grandmother, had not even suspected the paralysis. Two days before the end, his mother kept on scolding him for not helping her in difficult moments.

Not even in those desperate final days could he ever forget his closest friends, the poor. While lying on his deathbed he wanted the usual material assistance to be brought to them. It was Friday, the day he visited them. On July 3, 1925, a day before his death, his hand already paralyzed from polio, Pier Giorgio asked his sister Luciana to take a small packet from his jacket and with a semi-paralyzed hand he wrote the following note to Grimaldi: "Here are the injections for Converso. The pawn ticket is Sappa's. I had forgotten it; renew it on my behalf."

We know that Pier Giorgio wanted to see Jesus so much that he used to say: "The day of my death will be the most beautiful day of my life." Pier Giorgio's sacrifice was fulfilled at seven o'clock in the evening of July 4, 1925. His funeral was a triumph. The streets of Turin were lined with a multitude of mourners who were unknown to his family: clergy and students, and the poor and the needy whom he had served so unselfishly for seven years.

God gave Pier Giorgio all the external attributes that could have led him to make the wrong choices: a wealthy family, very good looks, manhood, health, being the only heir of a powerful family. But Pier Giorgio listened to the invitation of Christ: "Come and follow me." He anticipated by at least 50 years the Church's understanding and new direction on the role of the laity.

In beatifying Frassati alone in St. Peter's Square on May 20, 1990, Pope John Paul II described Pier Giorgio as the "man of the eight Beatitudes" and said in his homily:

> *By his example he proclaims that a life lived in Christ's Spirit, the Spirit of the Beatitudes, is "blessed," and that only the person who becomes a "man or woman of the Beatitudes" can succeed in communicating love and peace to others. He repeats that it is really worth giving up everything to serve the Lord. He testifies that holiness is possible for everyone, and that only the revolution of charity can enkindle the hope of a better future in the hearts of people.... He left this world rather young, but he made a mark upon our entire century, and not only on our century.*

Conclusion

Tonight, together with the Servant of God, John Paul II, the young mountain climber of Pollone stands at the window of the Father's house and smiles upon us, as he intercedes for us and for the young people of the world who have come to Sydney to discover the Lord and his holy ones in the vast Communion of Saints and community of the Church. Let me conclude by speaking for a few moments directly to Pier Giorgio on your behalf.

Carissimo Pier Giorgio,

I never had the privilege of meeting you in life. Whoever has met you knows that in your eyes, in your gestures and in your actions, you always carried a little piece of heaven. You shared that with those who knew you in your lifetime, and now with those of us who have known you for the past century.

Since 1925 when you left this earth to return to the house of your Father, you have continued your work on our behalf "dall'alto", from above! In your lifetime you never had the privilege of coming to a World Youth Day. You have watched them from afar, and blessed them with countless graces.

For many years your mortal body remained hidden in the family tomb in Pollone, and then placed in a dark corner of Turin's Cathedral. Many who visited didn't even know you were there! I was one of those visitors several years ago. I simply couldn't find where they had laid you to rest! Such a powerful witness and light must never be hidden, but held up for imitation and inspiration.

We Catholic Christians believe that the body is the temple of the Holy Spirit, the instrument of God's work, the frame of God's house in our midst. And we know, with St. Paul, that "if the earthly tent we live in is destroyed, we have a building from God, a house not made with hands, eternal in the heavens. For in this tent we groan, longing to be clothed with our heavenly dwelling — if indeed, when we have taken it off we will not be found naked. For while we are still in this tent, we groan under our burden, because we wish not to be unclothed but to be further clothed, so that what is mortal may be swallowed up by life." [II Corinthians 5:2-4]

Your presence among us this evening, both from your vantage point at the window of the Father's home in heaven and through your mortal remains in this Cathedral, witnesses to your mortality that has been swallowed up by new life. Pier Giorgio, you almost didn't make it to Sydney! Thank God that the Church in Australia, with the help of the Holy Spirit, prevailed over all those forces which tried to prevent you from attending your first World Youth Day down under!

As we venerate your mortal remains, we give thanks to the Lord Jesus who gave you life, inspiration, strength, hope and the crown of glory. As we reflect on your youthfulness, your simplicity, your beauty, goodness and humanity, we recognize the call given to each of us: to be men and women of the Beatitudes.

Thank you, Pier Giorgio, for listening to Jesus' words and making them your own. Your example has moved me and hundreds of thousands of others to translate the Beatitudes into Good News with our very lives. Be with us on this great expedition to heaven!

Pier Giorgio, help us to strive for simple hearts, attentive to the needs of others, and friendships based on that pact which knows no earthly boundaries or limits of time: union in prayer. If we do not know the road, and if we often abandon the path, **show us the way "verso l'alto," upward to heaven!**

If by being superficial we have not put in our knapsack all that we need for the climb, and if we never lift up our gaze because we do not want to take the first demanding steps to set ourselves on the way, **show us the way "verso l'alto," upward to heaven!**

If we lack the strength to overcome the most difficult passes, and if we have the strength, but prefer to use it to turn back, **show us the way "verso l'alto," upward to heaven!**

If we never pause to be nourished by the bread of eternal life, and if we do not quench our thirst from the fountain of prayer, **show us the way "verso l'alto," upward to heaven!**

When we do not know how to contemplate the beauty of the gifts we have received, and when we do not know how to offer ourselves for others, **show us the way "verso l'alto," upward to heaven!**

If we have committed many sins, **show us the way "verso l'alto," upward to heaven!**

If we lost hope, **show us the way "verso l'alto," upward to heaven!**

Three years ago, at the opening ceremonies for World Youth Day 2005 in Cologne, Germany, Pope Benedict XVI addressed the throng of young people from the entire world:

> *Dear young people, the Church needs genuine witnesses for the new evangelization: men and women whose lives have been transformed by meeting with Jesus, men and women who are capable of communicating this experience to others. The Church needs saints. All are called to holiness, and holy people alone can renew humanity. Many have gone before us along this path of Gospel heroism, and I urge you to turn often to them to pray for their intercession.*

That is why we have gathered together tonight in this great Cathedral down under! May all the young people who have journeyed to Sydney, and those of us who have been young for a while, find in Blessed Pier Giorgio Frassati what Jesus' Sermon on a Galilean hillside really meant.

Pray for us, Pier Giorgio Frassati. **Show us the way "verso l'alto," upward to heaven and deep into the heart of God.** Teach us how to be Saints for the Church and for the world. Amen.

Pier Giorgio's casket in Sydney's St. Mary's Cathedral, World Youth Day 2008.

INDEX OF NAMES AND ABBREVIATIONS

AIMONE CAT, TINA. One of the members of "Gaetana Agnesi," the FUCI Club for women.

AMETIS, ELENA (1874-1944). Sister of Pier Giorgio's mother Adelaide. Aunt Elena always lived with the family.

AMETIS, LINDA COPPELLO (1839-1925). Pier Giorgio's maternal grandmother. She died on July 1, 1925, in Turin in the same house where Pier Giorgio died three days later. She had a particular love for Pier Giorgio and instilled in him the habit of praying for the dead.

BECK, FRITZ. An important member of the Christian social movement in Bavaria whom Pier Giorgio met during his time in Berlin. He died in a massacre by the Nazis.

BELLINGERI, CARLO. A friend who lived in Pier Giorgio's neighborhood. He was a classmate at the state school, Massimo D'Azeglio, and then at the Polytechnic of Turin. He was also a member of the FUCI Club "Cesare Balbo."

BELTRAMO, MARCO. Pier Giorgio's very close friend. He and Pier Giorgio comprised "The Terror" (a subsection of the Tipi Loschi Society) and were frequent collaborators in jokes and pranks played on other members of the Society. Pier Giorgio nicknamed Marco "Perrault" after the two of them had attended a play. In return, Marco said, "Then you are Robespierre" and the names stuck.

BERGONZI, MARIO. He was studying medicine in Parma and was a member of Catholic Action there.

BERTINI, GIAN MARIA. A companion of Pier Giorgio's in the FUCI Club "Cesare Balbo" who became president of the club in 1921. After Pier Giorgio's death, Bertini became a priest.

BILOTTI, MARCO. A friend from the university.

BONELLI, ERNESTINA (Tina). An esteemed member of the Tipi Loschi Society, she was a lively character who often became the target of various jokes and pranks. She was nominated to be the Director of Excursions ("D.d.g.") for the Tipi Loschi Society to jokingly underline her incurable organizational deficiency concerning excursions and trips to the mountains. She was also nicknamed "Englesina" after her trip to London.

BONINI, ISIDORO. The older brother of Francesco Bonini who often studied with Pier Giorgio. Isidoro was a member of the FUCI Club "Cesare Balbo." With the help of Pier Giorgio's father, Isidoro had a very successful career.

BOSCHETTI, FRANCA. A friend who was a member of FUCI.

CESARE BALBO CLUB. The FUCI Club for men in Turin. Pier Giorgio was very active in the Club and it became like a second family to him.

COJAZZI, FR. ANTONIO. A Salesian priest who tutored Pier Giorgio in Latin. He later became the first biographer of Pier Giorgio, working in close contact with Mrs. Frassati for many years.

D.D.G. This was the abbreviation for the title assigned to Tina Bonelli in the Tipi Loschi Society as Director of Excursions. In Italian, the title was Direttrice di gita.

DE NICOLA, PILADE. A friend from the FUCI Club "Cesare Balbo."

FALCHETTI, ALBERTO (Bertino, Berti). A painter who was the artistic pedagogue of Pier Giorgio's mother. He was a very good-natured character and dear friend of the Frassati children who sometimes posed for his paintings.

FISCHER, MARIA. An Austrian student residing in Vienna whom Pier Giorgio met in Ravenna on the occasion of a Pax Romana conference. Maria Fischer did not like St. Peter's Square in Rome and Pier Giorgio often teased her about this.

FRASSATI, ADELAIDE AMETIS (1877-1949). Pier Giorgio's mother.

FRASSATI, ALFREDO (1868-1961). Pier Giorgio's father.

FRASSATI, FATHER MARIO. The assistant pastor in Pollone. He was very much loved by Pier Giorgio, although he was not a relative of the Frassati family.

FRASSATI, GIUSEPPINA (1844-1933). Pier Giorgio's paternal grandmother. She gave all of her savings to her son Alfredo (Pier Giorgio's father) so that he could get financial control of the newspaper, *La Gazetta Piedmontese,* which he later renamed *La Stampa.*

FRASSATI, LUCIANA (1902-2007). Pier Giorgio's younger sister.

FIGNA, NORA. A companion on excursions and in studies at the Polytechnic of Turin. An engineer who later worked very closely with Padre Pio during the building of the hospital in San Giovanni Rotondo. Alfredo Frassati, many years after Pier Giorgio's death, expressed a desire to meet Padre Pio.

FUCI. Abbreviation for the Federation of Italian Catholic University students. Male members were "fucini" and female members were "fucine." The "Cesare Balbo Club" which Pier Giorgio belonged to while he was at the Polytechnic in Turin was a FUCI organization.

GAMNA, PROFESSOR. A well-known physician in Turin who lived near the Frassati home. He was called to Pier Giorgio's bedside after he had been stricken with a terrible case of polio.

GOLA, GIOVANNI. Son of Giuseppe Gola, the longstanding gardener at the family villa in Pollone. Pier Giorgio was particularly close to this family. Giovanni was a childhood playmate of his. Later, Pier Giorgio convinced him to sign up as a member of Catholic Action.

GRESLIG, DR. MAX. He was the leader of the Pax Romana movement which originated in Switzerland.

GRIMALDI, GIUSEPPE. He joined the FUCI Club "Cesare Balbo" and was a member of the Conference of St. Vincent de Paul.

GUARDIA RIVA, COSTANTINO. At a certain point, he was president of the FUCI Club "Cesare Balbo." He and Pier Giorgio had a strong clash on the occasion of Mussolini's visit to Turin. Guardia Riva decided to display the club's banner, much to the disbelief and disapproval of Pier Giorgio.

HIDALGO, LAURA. A member of the FUCI Club for women "Gaetana Agnesi." She became the secretary of the Tipi Loschi Society and the object of Pier Giorgio's very pure love which he never expressed to her. She was three years older than Pier Giorgio and, as an orphan, raised her younger brother. Pier Giorgio admired her for this. She completed her university studies with a degree in mathematics, became a professor of math and the director of a library.

KOHLSTEDT, CHARLOTTE. A German teacher for Pier Giorgio and his sister in Berlin.

LEITGEBEL, WILLIBALD. Pier Giorgio met him in Berlin through the German priest Fr. Karl Sonnenschein. He maintained a friendship with him, his sister Nisse and his family.

LUOTTO, CLEMENTINA. She was a few years older than Pier Giorgio and became the president of the Tipi Loschi Society. She had a literary flair and was often teased for her conversational style. As time went on, Pier Giorgio discovered her spiritual qualities and moral strength and was moved by her example.

MASSETTI, FRANZ. A member of the Tipi Loschi Society who was given the nickname Petronio by Pier Giorgio because of the care he took in dressing stylishly. (The name was based on Gaius Petronius, Emperor Nero's adviser in matters of luxury and extravagance.)

MILITES MARIAE. ("The Soldiers of Mary.") This was the name of a Catholic Youth club that Pier Giorgio started at his parish church, La Crocetta, in Turin – not to be confused with the Legion of Mary.

PALOMBA, MARGHERITA and MARIA. Friends who were members of the FUCI club for women.

PERRAULT. See entry for Marco Beltramo.

PETRONIO. See entry for Franz Massetti.

RAITERI, LEA. A leader of the FUCI Club for women "Gaetana Agnesi" in Turin.

RIZZOLI, GIUSEPPE. He was a young officer of the airforce.

ROBESPIERRE. The nickname given to Pier Giorgio by Marco Beltramo. The name was based on the French Revolutionary leader Maximilien Robespierre who was noted for his role in the Reign of Terror. In keeping with this, Pier Giorgio closed letters with cannon blasts and terroristic greetings. However, in Pier Giorgio's way of thinking, his nickname was certainly a joke; as leader of the group, he had no other intentions than to portray the character of the incorruptible Robespierre in a light-hearted way. He and Marco Beltramo (Perrault) formed a subsection of the Tipi Loschi Society called "The Terror." The Terror, rather than having any sinister intentions, was dedicated to playing pranks and jokes on the other members.

ROBOTTI, FATHER FILIPPO, O.P. A Dominican who often encountered Pier Giorgio in the church of San Domenico in Turin. For a period of time, he served as spiritual director for the Cesare Balbo club. Because of his very outspoken antifascist position, he had to leave Italy for America in 1923. He returned in 1936. Pier Giorgio often accompanied Fr. Filippo as a bodyguard during his propaganda activities for the Italian People's Party.

SCHWAN, MARIA. Pier Giorgio met her in Ravenna during a Pax Romana Conference and visited her later in Bonn. She later married his friend Domanig.

SEVERI, ANTONIO. A friend of Pier Giorgio's from the FUCI Club "Cesare Balbo."

SPATARO, GIUSEPPE. President of the FUCI Club from 1920 to 1922. He later became a noted Italian politician.

TIPI LOSCHI SOCIETY (pronounced tippy lowski). The name of a group of eight formed by Pier Giorgio on May 18, 1924, at a time when their new careers were starting to take them in different directions. (Note: This name has been translated into English for other books as "The Sinister Ones" or "The Shady Characters." Because neither translation fully captures the meaning, the original Italian title is used throughout this book.)

All of the members of the Tipi Loschi Society had been members of various Catholic clubs and they all loved the mountains. Both men and women were members, titled respectively "swindlers" and "swindlerettes." All of the Society's rules and directives were written in the form of French Revolution proclamations. Correspondence often concluded with "terroristic cannon blasts" and/or "Boom!" Playful pranks embellished their excursions in the mountains and the city life of the various "fellow citizens," "swindlers" and "swindlerettes."

All practical joking aside, Pier Giorgio had a more substantial goal for the Society: to keep the group of friends united as much as possible, most importantly in prayer. It was to be a group founded on Faith, the solid rock upon which they would always maintain an indissoluble bond. Pier Giorgio wanted the Society to be a source of mutual spiritual support in order to solidify their friendships and give more substance to the human relations. Through prayer, each member of the Society would help the others to overcome obstacles and reach the ultimate goal: heaven.

VILLANI, ANTONIO. He graduated from the Polytechnic of Turin with a degree in Electronic Engineering. He was three years older than Pier Giorgio and Pier Giorgio thought of him as an older brother. He respected him for the seriousness and thoughtfulness of his opinions. In 1920, he was regional president of the organization Catholic Youth. After World War II, he held a position in the Christian Democratic party.

TO LEARN MORE ABOUT PIER GIORGIO FRASSATI:

FrassatiUSA, Inc.
P.O. Box 50571
Nashville, TN 37205
615.844.3777
www.FrassatiUSA.org
info@frassatiusa.org

Associazione Pier Giorgio Frassati
Via Anicia 12, 00153 Roma
Tel: 39/065895954 -
www.piergiorgiofrassati.org
info@piergiorgiofrassati.org

This book was produced by ST PAULS/Alba House, the Society of St. Paul, an international religious congregation of priests and brothers dedicated to serving the Church through the communications media.

For information regarding this and associated ministries of the Pauline Family of Congregations, write to the Vocation Director, Society of St. Paul, 2187 Victory Blvd., Staten Island, New York 10314-6603. Phone (718) 982-5709; or E-mail: vocation@stpauls.us or check our internet site, www.vocationoffice.org